Cooking

Healthy with

a Microwave

Also by JoAnna M. Lund

The Healthy Exchanges Cookbook
HELP: The Healthy Exchanges Lifetime Plan
Cooking Healthy with a Man in Mind
Cooking Healthy with the Kids in Mind
Diabetic Desserts
Make a Joyful Table
Cooking Healthy Across America
A Potful of Recipes
Another Potful of Recipes
The Open Road Cookbook
Sensational Smoothies
Hot Off the Grill: The Healthy Exchanges Electric Grilling Cookbook
The Healthy Exchanges Splenda Cookbook
The Diabetic's Healthy Exchanges Cookbook
The Strong Bones Healthy Exchanges Cookbook
The Arthritis Healthy Exchanges Cookbook
The Heart Smart Healthy Exchanges Cookbook
The Cancer Recovery Healthy Exchanges Cookbook
The Best of Healthy Exchanges Food Newsletter '92 Cookbook
String of Pearls
Family and Friends Cookbook
JoAnna's Kitchen Miracles

Cooking

Healthy with

a Microwave

A HEALTHY EXCHANGES® COOKBOOK

JoAnna M. Lund

with
Barbara Alpert

A Perigee Book

THE BERKLEY PUBLISHING GROUP
Published by the Penguin Group
Penguin Group (USA) Inc.
375 Hudson Street, New York, New York 10014, USA
Penguin Group (Canada), 10 Alcorn Avenue, Toronto, Ontario M4V 3B2, Canada
(a division of Pearson Penguin Canada Inc.)
Penguin Books Ltd., 80 Strand, London WC2R 0RL, England
Penguin Group Ireland, 25 St. Stephen's Green, Dublin 2, Ireland (a division of Penguin Books Ltd.)
Penguin Group (Australia), 250 Camberwell Road, Camberwell, Victoria 3124, Australia
(a division of Pearson Australia Group Pty. Ltd.)
Penguin Books India Pvt. Ltd., 11 Community Centre, Panchsheel Park, New Delhi—110 017, India
Penguin Group (NZ), Cnr. Airborne and Rosedale Roads, Albany, Auckland 1310, New Zealand
(a division of Pearson New Zealand Ltd.)
Penguin Books (South Africa) (Pty.) Ltd., 24 Sturdee Avenue, Rosebank, Johannesburg 2196, South Africa
Penguin Books Ltd., Registered Offices: 80 Strand, London WC2R 0RL, England

Copyright © 2005 by Healthy Exchanges, Inc.
Diabetic Exchanges calculated by Rose Hoenig
Cover design by Ben Gibson
Cover art by Superstock

Before using the recipes and advice in this book. Consult your physician or healthcare provider to be sure they are appropriate for you. The information in this book is not intended to take the place of any medical advice. It reflects the author's experiences, studies, research, and opinions regarding a healthy lifestyle. All material included in this publication is believed to be accurate. The publisher assumes no responsibility for any health, welfare, or subsequent damage that might be incurred from use of these materials.

For more information about Healthy Exchanges products, contact:
Healthy Exchanges, Inc.
P.O. Box 80
DeWitt, Iowa 52742-0080
(563) 659-8234
www.HealthyExchanges.com

PRINTING HISTORY
Perigee trade paperback edition / June 2005

PERIGEE is a registered trademark of Penguin Group (USA) Inc.
The "P" design is a trademark belonging to Penguin Group (USA) Inc.

Library of Congress Cataloging-in-Publication Data

Lund, JoAnna M.
    Cooking healthy with a microwave / JoAnna M. Lund with Barbara Alpert.
        p. cm.
    Includes index.
    ISBN 0-399-53155-6
    1. Microwave cookery. I. Alpert, Barbara. II. Title.

TX832.L86 2005
641.5'882—dc22

                                                            2004060131

PRINTED IN THE UNITED STATES OF AMERICA

10 9 8 7 6 5 4 3 2 1

Dedication

This book is dedicated in loving memory to my parents, Jerome and Agnes McAndrews. Microwaves were just starting to catch on here in rural Iowa when Daddy passed away back in 1979. And Mom's cooking days were well behind her when Cliff gave me my first microwave as a Christmas gift in 1981. But I know they would have been intrigued by all that this "magic box" could do—from cooking a complete meal to heating up leftovers and everything in between.

Just as microwaves changed the cooking techniques from hours to minutes in kitchens all over America, the magnificent days we experience here in the Midwest for just a few short weeks in September change our season from summer to fall in the "blinking of an eye." So, I'm choosing to share a poem my mother wrote about Iowa around the time I received that first microwave. Her words paint a beautiful picture. May her poem and my recipes help you paint beautiful memories of family meals in the years to come!

Indian Summer in Iowa

When dancing autumn leaves begin to turn to
crimson, gold and brown,
And the wealth of another bountiful harvest can
be seen all around,
When the silhouettes of dried cornshocks look like
teepees built with care,
As tall columns of smoke signals from flaming
bonfires fill the air,
When the heavens are filled with honking geese
and gold finch soaring by,
And the full moon resembles a giant pumpkin
smiling from the sky—
Then, it is Indian Summer in Iowa, the state with
the beautiful land,
Where the great Mississippi and Missouri Rivers
meet and clasp hands,
Making the rolling plains of this prairie state
a garden spot to behold,
With natural beauty and fertile soil, she
reaps her weight in gold.

—Agnes Carrington McAndrews

Acknowledgments

Even though the recipes in this collection are so quick to make, they literally take just minutes—it's not that way when writing a cookbook. From inception to completion of any of my cookbooks, there could be several months dedicated to that special project. After all, there's the quiet time I need for the creation of both the concept and the recipes for the project. Then, each recipe must be typed, tested, tasted, critiqued, calculated, and finally put in some kind of cohesive order so that when you get this book, it's as easy as possible for you to use. After the recipes can be "put on the back burner" so to speak, there is still much writing to be completed before I can turn the manuscript over to my editor so that he can turn it into a book. For helping me make the most of my time so I could finish yet another cookbook by deadline, I want to thank:

Cliff Lund—my husband. What a guy—when deadlines loom and time is short, he's more than willing to pick up the slack and help me. No, he still doesn't offer to wash the dishes, but he does just about everything else!

Shirley Morrow, Rita Ahlers, Phyllis Bickford, Gina Griep, and Jean Martens—my assistants in all Healthy Exchanges endeavors. A better group of helpers can't be found anywhere. Each does whatever it takes—be it typing and retyping recipes, testing and retesting recipes, tasting and retasting recipes—and of course, help with those dishes!

Barbara Alpert—my writing partner. By now she knows what I mean even if that's not what I've written. She helped bring me into the twenty-first century—computer-wise, that is. So now, when I'm finished with a chapter, I simply e-mail it to her so that she can make a good book even better. I don't think there's a better writing partner in all of "Recipe Land"!

Coleen O'Shea—my agent. She continues to support me in all that I have done and want yet to do. When I get an idea for another book, she gladly adds it to my growing list and when the time is right, she helps make my dream a reality!

John Duff—my editor. We've been working together now for ten years and he never ceases to amaze me by how talented and gifted he is when it comes to books in general and my cookbooks in particular. With his enthusiastic support, this makes the thirty-second book I've written for my publisher in the past decade. Who would have ever guessed!

God—my creator and savior. With His blessings I continue to create my "common folk" healthy recipes. And I enjoy it as much today as the day back in 1991 when I changed my prayer from what I wanted to what I needed. To God all the glory and honor belong!

Contents

A Fresh Look at an Old Friend— and at Your Life

Do you remember the first microwave oven you ever saw? It was probably back in the 1970s, when manufacturers first began making them for home kitchens. Mine wasn't fancy or space-age sleek, just a basic rectangular metal box with a glass window in front. It had few of the features available today—no automatic turntable to rotate foods (I had to buy a wind-up turntable to use in it!) and minimal temperature controls (no "thaw" or "popcorn" buttons, just "start" and a timer you set by spinning a dial!).

But I was still excited by the idea of "microwaving"—delighted to know I could bake a potato in ten minutes instead of an hour, pleased to be able to reheat a cup of coffee or soup in no time at all. It was great for heating up TV dinners, too. At the time, I don't think I viewed it as a "real" oven, more as a wacky new kitchen appliance—like a waffle iron or a new kind of blender.

Of course, it turned out that my little "nuker" was a forerunner of today's multitalented machines. I would discover with fascination and pleasure that those mysterious microwaves had the power to produce wonderful homemade meals in a fraction of the time that a traditional range required.

Speaking of mysterious microwaves—did you ever wonder just how these ovens make their culinary magic? I remember years ago chatting with one lady who feared that her microwave would explode, filling her house with nuclear radiation; another confessed that she didn't stay in the room when it was on. "I don't understand how it works, JoAnna, and it scares me a little."

When I was working recently on *JoAnna's Kitchen Miracles,* a cookbook celebrating seven kitchen "marvels," I did a little research into the origins of this unique machine. It turns out that its invention was one of those "happy accidents," way back in 1946, when a scientist working on a radar experiment with a magnetron vacuum tube noticed that a candy bar in his pocket had melted. He was so intrigued, he decided to put some popcorn kernels near the tube and then watched with excitement as popping popcorn exploded all over his lab! Of course he couldn't resist experimenting with an egg next, and I'm sure you can guess what happened. In moments the egg was shaking and getting all superheated up inside. As the man moved closer to study it, the egg exploded, leaving hot egg yolk everywhere!

Out of that mess came a revolutionary kitchen appliance that came to be used all over the world. Yet thirty years later, for many cooks, it had become almost invisible in their renovated kitchens. Perhaps they used it for reheating leftovers or occasionally warming a cup of tea, but it seemed that microwaves had lost their appeal— until recently!

Just as today's children are able to watch old 1960s television series on Nick at Nite, microwaves are "hot" again. Families are rediscovering how easy they are to use and how versatile they can be for making good-tasting food *fast*!

A Fresh Look Means New Possibilities

As I was digging through my stockpile of old microwave dishes to begin testing recipes for this cookbook, I began to think about what it means to take a fresh look at something we've had or done for years.

So often, we get stuck in ruts—eating the same foods, pursuing the same leisure activities, even taking friends and jobs for granted. It's way too easy to start going through the motions in life, but it's an awful trap to fall into, one that allows us to live unaware of all those precious moments passing by at warp speed!

Did you ever notice how fashion designers draw on the styles of the past to get ideas for new clothing pieces? They've just brought back ponchos as I am working on this book, but if you were to unearth one of your old ones to wear over some bell-bottom slacks from thirty years ago, you'd probably look silly and dated, not hip and young.

Times *do* change, times *have* changed, and even if it appears that something old is new again, you want to revisit the past, not relive it. By taking a fresh look at what you loved long ago, you can discover new insights about yourself—and what changes you might want to consider to make the next part of your life even more satisfying.

A Fresh Look for Old Friends

Have you lost touch with people you saw every day during high school, friends who gave you courage and dried your tears, buddies who stuck with you through thick and thin? Most of us do, especially if our families move away from our childhood hometowns.

Maybe it's time to look them up and reconnect. Maybe it's even time to find out if an old love may still have feelings for you. The Sunday wedding sections across the country often feature couples who reunite after spouses have departed or died—could you be one of them?

Even if romance isn't part of your journey back in time, you may find extraordinary comfort from the people who "knew you when" and still care about you. I learned just how strong those old school ties really are when I was diagnosed with breast cancer. Friends from high school days organized a campaign of prayers and healing postcards from everyone in my graduating class, and I know how much their efforts got me through rough times!

Get out those dusty old yearbook photos and think about the people you haven't seen in a decade or two. The Internet can help you find them in many cases, or a few phone calls. You may be surprised at how much joy you find by revisiting old friends—and your old self!

A Fresh Look at Old Dreams

It's often said that life is a series of compromises—that we start out with big dreams and outsized hopes for our lives, but reality has a way of narrowing our sights and placing limits on how many of those goals and wishes we actually make come true.

Well, maybe what they say is true, but that doesn't mean you can't reignite those old fires—and give new life to what once burned in your soul! Were you a wonderful artist in college but put down the paintbrush when you began to raise a family? Why not sign up for an adult ed class and refresh your skills, or if it's hard for you to get out of the house, pick up an art set on QVC that comes with an instructional video? Start small, but start!

Did you promise yourself when you were young that someday you'd see the Eiffel Tower or the Taj Mahal? I can speak from personal experience when I say that fulfilling old travel dreams is one of the best gifts you can give yourself—and the people who love you. Watch for airfare sales, find out about cheap last-minute travel, make sure your passport is up to date (or get one, if you've never had one before!)—and go.

A Fresh Look at Forgotten Goals

Sometimes, we don't see ourselves as clearly as other people do, especially as the years pass and we spend little time in self-examination. You may find that a chance remark by a grandchild reminds you that you really mind not knowing how to tango, or you may discover that a book you hear about on *Oprah* reawakens your desire to get your master's degree in social work or work with animals.

You may also need a nudge to decide it's past time to get back into good physical condition—not for a marathon, necessarily, but just to be healthy and fit enough to do all the things in life that you love . . . some of which you may have forgotten!

As a very smart writer put it in the title of her book, *It's Only Too Late If You Don't Start Now.* Barbara Sher may inspire you to take a fresh look at old goals and figuring out if you still want to reach for them. And even though the years keep racing by, it's important to remember that we get a great gift with each sunrise: a chance to live life fully for one more day.

I hope you'll take a few minutes to reflect on what people, dreams, and goals you may have lost touch with on your journey through life. I'm giving you lots of time with this collection of microwave recipes that are designed to get you out of the kitchen quickly—and on the fast track to your best possible life!

Jo Anna

Please note—in many of my cookbooks I've included my Healthy Exchanges eating plan, which explains how to use my version of the "exchange" system for planning what to eat and how much to eat for optimum health and weight loss (or maintenance). Because this is a "special interest" cookbook featuring microwave and convection oven recipes, if this is your first Healthy Exchanges cookbook, please check one of my other cookbooks for an explanation of the exchange system—and an abundance of healthy cooking tips! Good recent choices include The Open Road Cookbook *or* Cooking Healthy With a Man in Mind.

My "Electrifying Eleven" Best Microwave Cooking Tips

Even if you've been using a microwave for years, there may be some little tricks or "tweaks" that can improve your results. Here are the most important things I've learned while cooking and baking with the microwave:

1. Never turn the microwave on until AFTER you've put your food inside the oven. If you turn it on while it's empty, you can cause damage to the microwave. Something needs to be inside to absorb the microwave energy.

2. Did you know that food cooked in the microwave continues to "cook" after you've removed it from the oven? I like to take advantage of this by placing the baking dish directly on my kitchen counter and letting it set for a few minutes. Remember how I always suggest you let baked goods cool on a wire rack? When you bake with a traditional or convection oven, the goal of using a wire rack is to let the heat radiate away from the cooking pan. The microwave works *differently*: What you want is for the heat

to rise up through the center of whatever you've been baking. Setting the pan on your kitchen counter helps to do just that! (One important exception: Remove muffins from their baking containers immediately after cooking or your muffins will become soggy.)

3. Most people believe that the dishes we use to cook in the microwave don't get hot the way metal or glass dishes do in a traditional oven. But microwave dishes can still become extremely hot—because they contain super-hot food that's just been cooked! I recommend using potholders or mitts to keep from being burned when you're handling dishes that have just been microwaved. The same is true when you're removing plastic wrap or a cover from the heated dish. A "whoosh" of very hot steam can "cook" you along with your food! This is why it's a good idea to "vent" the wrap over your food, to prevent the buildup of that steam.

4. Cover the food that you are cooking in the microwave. Why? There are a couple of very good reasons for this. First, you'll keep your microwave oven cleaner, because food won't splatter on its walls while cooking. Another: Keeping your dish covered also keeps the heat and moisture in, which contributes to a good tasting, fully cooked dish. Just remember to "vent" the cover, per the previous tip.

5. If you're baking something "dry," such as a cake, you'll want to cover it with waxed paper, as that will keep the heat in but allow all the steam to escape. Some people like to use paper towels to wrap baked goods such as bread and rolls when reheating. They work well because they absorb the extra moisture created in the microwave. Plastic wrap keeps both moisture and heat in, so it's best for egg dishes and for other entrée foods such as roasts and burgers. I also like plastic wrap for cooking vegetables.

6. If your microwave has a turntable built into it, you don't have to worry about rotating your dish while cooking. But if you are still using an older model without one (as many

people are—these ovens were built to *last*!), my recipes include instructions about when to rotate your dish manually so that it doesn't overcook in some areas and undercook in others. Turntable or no, you still must remember to stir the food when I suggest it. They haven't yet invented a microwave with a "stirring spoon" built in!

7. Some rules are true for all kinds of cooking, but it's worth reminding you about this one: For even cooking, be sure to chop your vegetables, fruit, or meat pieces into what is called a "uniform size." It makes good sense. Otherwise, some bigger pieces may not cook through—and some smaller pieces may turn into mush!

8. I'm lucky enough to have not one but two microwaves. (Yes, it's true—one is part of my stove fan, and the other is a built-in microwave/convection oven.) Both of mine operate at around 650 watts of power. If you are cooking with a 500-watt oven, you will probably need to increase the cooking time by 10 to 15 seconds *for every minute of cooking time.* If you happen to have a more powerful 700-800 watt machine, then I suggest that reduce your cooking time by 5 to 10 seconds for every minute of cooking time. It's always a good idea to check frequently to make certain you're not overcooking your dish. Remember, you can always add more time if you need it, but you can't get it back to "just right" if you've let it cook it too long in the first place.

9. I've prepared hundreds of dishes in the microwave, and I've learned through experience that most foods cook in 25 to 33 percent of the time they would otherwise take if made using conventional cooking methods such as the stovetop and oven. I've also seen that porous foods (such as puddings) cook more quickly than dense foods (like beef stew). So when you're preparing a recipe for the first time, start with the minimum time suggested. Read directions carefully to see how a finished dish should appear, as your dish will continue to heat through as it rests.

10. I kept most of my original microwave cooking equipment—did you? I always believed that microwave cooking would experience a "renaissance"—and I was right! If you gave yours away or threw it out, check out garage sales or treat yourself to a few new pieces when department and discount stores announce clearance sales. There are great new choices for microwave cooking besides the usual muffin and Bundt cake pans, so look around and find what you think you will use often.

11. I'm a great believer in "clean as you go"—and that means the microwave, too. Get in the habit of wiping out your microwave with a warm, damp cloth after each use, and you'll soon see that it's much easier to keep clean! Did you know that a dirty oven, covered with dried baking "splatters," may be absorbing microwave energy and slowing down your cooking time? For best results, keep it clean. (A super-easy way to clean your microwave: Place 1 cup of water in a 2-cup microwave-safe measuring cup and microwave on HIGH for 3 to 4 minutes to "steam" the splatters. Then they will wipe off easily!)

My Best "Baker's Dozen" Convection Oven Cooking Tips

Unlike traditional ovens (which are also known as radiant or thermal ovens), convection ovens use a fan to constantly circulate air around the oven. When hot air "blows" onto food instead of just surrounding it, food tends to cook more quickly. Just as a brisk wind makes a cold day feel much colder, the air that blows in your convection oven heats your food more effectively.

Convection oven technology was pioneered in hotels, restaurants, and bakeries, places that needed to produce a large quantity of baked goods in a very short time. Professional chefs love the convection oven because it delivers much more even cooking, which contributes to flaky piecrusts and tastier meats and vegetables, crisp exteriors, and juicy insides. But if you want to take best advantage of the convection oven's special gifts, you'll need to make a few changes in how you cook. Knowing these culinary secrets will help you turn out great-looking, great-tasting food!

1. Remember the 25/25 rule: Set your oven to a temperature that is about 25 degrees less than you'd use in a traditional oven, or reduce your cooking time by about 25 percent for best results. Now, I've made those adjustments for you in *this* book, but if you have family favorites you'd like to prepare in your convection oven, keep the 25/25 rule in mind.

2. Use baking pans with low sides to get the full benefit of convection cooking. This lets all that hot air "reach out and touch" whatever you're baking or cooking, which is vital for a convection oven to do its best. If you're using a high roasting pan or a covered casserole you're better off with a conventional oven.

3. Convection ovens do cook much more evenly, but not every rack in your oven may produce exactly the same results. If you're baking several cookie sheets' worth of cookies at the same time, you may still want to rotate them for even browning.

4. *It's windy in there!* If you've covered your food with aluminum foil or parchment paper, it may blow around, so wrap it snugly around the edges of your metal baking pan or consider weighing it down with a metal utensil.

5. Many combination microwave/convection ovens allow you to turn either feature on and off, so you can use both methods in the same recipe if you wish. Why would you want to do this? If you are cooking a roast, for example, and you wanted it to be browned all over but also cooked through, you might want to use both features. You could start it on the microwave so your dish cooks faster, and then finish it on the convection oven for a beautifully browned exterior.

6. Always preheat your convection oven before placing your food inside (unless you are instructed *not to* in the recipe). Again, this allows the oven to do its task more efficiently.

7. Keep in mind that the more food you have cooking in your convection oven, the longer it will take to cook. For instance if you're baking several items at once, you may not need to reduce cooking time very much. You can fill your oven quite full, but it's important to leave space between the dishes and at least one inch on each side of the oven so that air can circulate freely.

8. If you have a microwave/convection combination oven, you may want to let your oven cool off when microwaving after using the convection feature. The oven will be extremely hot and may melt some of your microwave dishes. Either let it cool for a bit longer or place a potholder under the micro dishes.

9. Keep the oven door *closed*! So much heat escapes when you open the oven door to check on your food, much of the benefit of using a convection oven is lost. Instead, turn on the oven light—and only when you're confident your dish is ready should you open the door. Note: When you *do* open the door, do it slowly, so heat and steam can escape without burning you.

10. While glass baking dishes can be used, you'll get best results by baking in metal pans rather than glass. Why? Because metal is a better conductor of heat. Dark metal pans absorb heat, which means your food will brown well. Shiny metal reflects heat, so you'll get a lighter result. Your food won't brown or crisp as well if you bake it in glass, but putting a cookie sheet underneath a glass pan helps to distribute the heat better. Note: Do not use metal pans or a cookie sheet under glass on the microwave setting.

11. In the microwave tip section, you learned that when you remove a dish that's been baked in the microwave, you

should put the item directly on the counter so it can continue cooking—and so the heat goes up through the center. But in convection cooking, it's best to put the just-baked item on a wire rack so that the heat can dissipate from all directions—just as you would with a traditional gas or electric oven. If you've got a combo micro/convection oven, don't forget this important difference—and use the cooling-off technique appropriate for whichever method you choose!

12. Some manufacturers are now combining tabletop toaster ovens and convection ovens. This is great when counter space is at a premium—when you have time, you may choose to use the toaster oven option, but when every minute counts, the faster convection oven can shine in all its glory. Note: If you decide to invest in this type of oven, be sure that you also invest in baking pans that fit the oven's capacity. An 8-by-8-inch cake pan will usually fit just fine, but often a 9-by-9-inch is a bit too big—so the oven door can't close properly. Be sure to try your pans in the oven *before* you actually bake something, so you don't have to hunt around at the last minute for a pan that will fit.

13. Don't be surprised if you purchase or rent an RV and it doesn't have a regular gas oven at all! (This is one of the major reasons I chose to include convection oven information and cuisine in this book.) Now the space formerly filled by a traditional oven has been redirected for storage; the manufacturers usually install a combo micro/convection oven instead. It's a good deal for you, the consumer: You're getting two appliances that take up the space of only one. (This is also true if you purchase a brand-new microwave these days—you're likely to get a micro-convection combination.) With your combo oven and my cookbook, you can now enjoy the best of both worlds—not only in "oven" choices but in recipes as well!

A Peek Into My Pantry and My Favorite Brands

Everyone asks me what foods I keep on hand and what brands I use. There are lots of good products on the grocery shelves today—many more than we dreamed about even a year or two ago. And I can't wait to see what's out there twelve months from now. The following are my staples and, where appropriate, my favorites *at this time*. I feel these products are healthier, tastier, easy to get—and deliver the most flavor for the least amount of fat, sugar, or calories. If you find others you like as well *or better,* please use them. This is only a guide to make your grocery shopping, and cooking, easier.

Fat-free plain yogurt (*Dannon*)
Nonfat dry milk powder (*Carnation*)
Evaporated fat-free milk (*Carnation*)
Fat-free milk
Fat-free cottage cheese
Fat-free cream cheese (*Philadelphia*)
Fat-free mayonnaise (*Kraft*)
Fat-free salad dressings (*Kraft and Hendrickson's*)
No-fat sour cream (*Land O Lakes*)
Reduced-calorie margarine (*I Can't Believe It's Not Butter! Light*)
Cooking sprays
    Olive oil–flavored (*Pam*)
    Butter-flavored (*Pam*)

Butter-flavored for spritzing *after* cooking (*I Can't Believe It's Not Butter!*)

Cooking oil (*Puritan Canola Oil*)

Reduced-calorie whipped topping (*Cool Whip Lite or Cool Whip Free*)

Sugar substitute

White sugar substitute (*SPLENDA*)

Brown sugar substitute (*Brown Sugar Twin*)

Sugar-free gelatin and pudding mixes (*JELL-O*)

Baking mix (*Bisquick Reduced Fat*)

Pancake mix (*Aunt Jemima Reduced Calorie*)

Sugar-free pancake syrup (*Log Cabin or Cary's*)

Parmesan cheese (*Kraft Reduced Fat Parmesan Style Grated Topping*)

Reduced-fat cheese (shredded and sliced) (*Kraft 2% Reduced Fat*)

Shredded frozen potatoes (*Mr. Dell's or Ore Ida*)

Spreadable fruit spread (*Welch's or Smucker's*)

Peanut butter (*Peter Pan reduced-fat, Jif reduced-fat, or Skippy reduced-fat*)

Chicken and beef broth (*Swanson reduced-sodium*)

Tomato sauce (*Hunt's*)

Canned soups (*Healthy Request*)

Reduced sodium tomato juice

Reduced sodium ketchup

Piecrust

unbaked (*Pillsbury—in dairy case*)

graham cracker, shortbread, and chocolate (*Keebler*)

Crescent rolls (*Pillsbury reduced fat*)

Pastrami and corned beef (*Carl Buddig Lean*)

Luncheon meats (*Healthy Choice or Oscar Mayer*)

Ham (*Dubuque 97% fat-free and reduced-sodium or Healthy Choice*)

Bacon bits (*Oscar Mayer or Hormel*)

Kielbasa sausage and frankfurters (*Oscar Mayer Light or Healthy Choice*)

Canned white chicken, packed in water (*Swanson*)

Canned tuna, packed in water (*Starkist*)

95 to 97 percent ground sirloin beef or turkey breast
Crackers (*Nabisco Soda Fat Free and Ritz Reduced Fat*)
Reduced-calorie bread—40 calories per slice or less
Small hamburger buns—80 calories per bun
Rice—instant, regular, brown, and wild (*Minute Rice*)
Instant potato flakes
Noodles, spaghetti, macaroni, and rotini pasta
Salsa
Pickle relish—dill, sweet, and hot dog
Mustard—Dijon, prepared yellow, and spicy
Unsweetened apple and orange juice
Reduced-calorie cranberry juice cocktail (*Ocean Spray*)
Unsweetened applesauce (*Musselman's*)
Fruit—fresh, frozen (no sugar added), and canned in juice
Pie filling (*Lucky Leaf No Sugar Added Cherry* and *Apple*)
Spices (*JO's Spices or any national brand*)
Vinegar—cider and distilled white
Lemon and lime juice (in small, plastic, fruit-shaped bottles
    found in the produce section)
Instant fruit beverage mixes (*Crystal Light*)
Sugar-free hot chocolate beverage mixes (*Swiss Miss or Nesquik*)
Sugar-free and fat-free ice cream (*Wells' Blue Bunny*)

The items on my shopping list are everyday foods found in just about any grocery store in America. But all are as low in fat, sugar, calories, and sodium as I can find—and still taste good! I can make any recipe in my cookbooks and newsletters as long as I have my cupboards and refrigerator stocked with these items. Whenever I use the last of any one item, I just make sure I pick up another supply the next time I'm at the store.

If your grocer does not stock these items, why not ask if they can be ordered on a trial basis? If the store agrees to do so, be sure to tell your friends to stop by, so that sales are good enough to warrant restocking the new products. Competition for shelf space is fierce, so only products that sell well stay around.

JoAnna's Ten Commandments of Successful Cooking

A very important part of any journey is knowing where you are going and the best way to get there. If you plan and prepare before you start to cook, you should reach mealtime with foods to write home about!

1. **Read the entire recipe from start to finish** and be sure you understand the process involved. Check that you have all the equipment you will need *before* you begin.

2. **Check the ingredient list** and be sure you have *everything* and in the amounts required. Keep cooking sprays handy—while they're not listed as ingredients, I use them all the time (just a quick squirt!).

3. **Set out *all* the ingredients and equipment needed** to prepare the recipe on the counter near you *before* you start. Remember that old saying, *A stitch in time saves nine?* It applies in the kitchen, too.

4. **Do as much advance preparation as possible** before actually cooking. Chop, cut, grate, or do whatever is

needed to prepare the ingredients and have them ready before you start to mix. Turn the oven on at least ten minutes before putting food in to bake, to allow the oven to preheat to the proper temperature.

5. **Use a kitchen timer** to tell you when the cooking or baking time is up. Because stove temperatures vary slightly by manufacturer, you may want to set your timer for five minutes less than the suggested time just to prevent overcooking. Check the progress of your dish at that time, then decide if you need the additional minutes or not.

6. **Measure carefully.** Use glass measures for liquids and metal or plastic cups for dry ingredients. My recipes are based on standard measurements. Unless I tell you it's a scant or full cup, measure the cup level.

7. **For best results, follow the recipe instructions exactly.** Feel free to substitute ingredients that *don't tamper* with the basic chemistry of the recipe, but be sure to leave key ingredients alone. For example, you could substitute sugar-free instant chocolate pudding for sugar-free instant butterscotch pudding, but if you used a six-serving package when a four-serving package was listed in the ingredients, or you used instant when cook-and-serve is required, you won't get the right result.

8. **Clean up as you go.** It is much easier to wash a few items at a time than to face a whole counter of dirty dishes later. The same is true for spills on the counter or floor.

9. **Be careful about doubling or halving a recipe.** Though many recipes can be altered successfully to serve more or fewer people, *many cannot.* This is especially true when it comes to spices and liquids. If you try to double a recipe that calls for 1 teaspoon pumpkin-pie spice, for example, and you double the spice, you may end up with a too-spicy taste. I usually suggest increasing spices or liquid by 1½ times when doubling a recipe. If it tastes a little bland to you, you can increase the spice to 1¾ times the original

amount the next time you prepare the dish. Remember: You can always add more, but you can't take it out after it's stirred in.

The same is true with liquid ingredients. If you wanted to **triple** a main dish recipe because you were planning to serve a crowd, you might think you should use three times as much of every ingredient. Don't, or you could end up with soup instead! If the original recipe calls for 1¾ cups tomato sauce, I'd suggest using 3½ cups when you **triple** the recipe (or 2¾ cups if you **double** it). You'll still have a good-tasting dish that won't run all over the plate.

10. **Write your reactions next to each recipe once you've served it.** Yes, that's right, I'm giving you permission to write in this book. It's yours, after all. Ask yourself: Did everyone like it? Did you have to add another half teaspoon of chili seasoning to please your family, who like to live on the spicier side of the street? You may even want to rate the recipe on a scale of 1☆ to 4☆, depending on what you thought of it. (Four stars would be the top rating—and I hope you'll feel that way about many of my recipes.) Jotting down your comments while they are fresh in your mind will help you personalize the recipe to your own taste the next time you prepare it.

The Recipes

How to Read a Healthy Exchanges Recipe

The Healthy Exchanges Nutritional Analysis

Before using these recipes, you may wish to consult your physician or health-care provider to be sure they are appropriate for you. The information in this book is not intended to take the place of any medical advice. It reflects my experiences, studies, research, and opinions regarding healthy eating.

Each recipe includes nutritional information calculated in three ways:

Healthy Exchanges Weight Loss Choices™ or Exchanges
Calories; Fat, Protein, Carbohydrates, and Fiber in grams;
    Sodium and Calcium in milligrams
Diabetic Exchanges

In every Healthy Exchanges recipe, the Diabetic Exchanges have been calculated by a registered dietitian. All the other calculations were done by computer, using the Food Processor II software. When the ingredient listing gives more than one choice, the first ingredient listed is the one used in the recipe analysis. Due to inevitable variations in the ingredients you choose to use, the nutritional values should be considered approximate.

The annotation "(limited)" following Protein counts in some recipes indicates that consumption of whole eggs should be limited to four per week.

Please note the following symbols:

☆ This star means read the recipe's directions carefully for special instructions about **division** of ingredients.

❋ This symbol indicates **FREEZES WELL.**

Soups and Salads

Soup-making is an art that goes back generations, when thrifty home cooks transformed a few odds and ends into a hearty, soul-satisfying bowl of culinary joy! But times have changed, and many people don't find the time to keep a stockpot bubbling away on top of the stove for hours on end. Does that mean we have to forgo the myriad pleasures of homemade soups, stews, and chilies?

Not at all. Thanks to the miracle of the microwave, we can savor rich, aromatic broths and marvelous, meaty blends served up in mere minutes! What takes long, slow cooking atop a burner can be accomplished in much less time inside the "magic box."

Whether you're dreaming of a truly healthy version of your favorite restaurant soup (Cheesy Broccoli Soup) or longing for a "meal-in-a-bowl" (Country Ham and Corn Stew), whether you prefer a selection of garden greats (Micro Minestrone Soup) or a quick-fix version of a classic (Micro French Onion Soup), you'll find sensational soups in this chapter. You'll also discover delectable salads (including my Pennsylvania Dutch Potato Salad) whose brief encounter with your microwave will produce astonishing results!

Micro French Onion Soup

The microwave is a miracle worker when it comes to preparing classic dishes like French onion soup. Instead of spending hours on the stovetop, this savory soup is ready in no time at all!

● Serves 4

3 cups thinly sliced onion
1 (14-ounce) can Swanson Lower Sodium Fat Free Beef Broth
1½ cups water
⅛ teaspoon black pepper
1 teaspoon dried parsley flakes
4 slices reduced-calorie French or white bread, toasted
4 (¾-ounce) slices Kraft reduced-fat Swiss cheese

In an 8-cup microwave-safe mixing bowl, combine onion, beef broth, water, black pepper, and parsley flakes. Cover and microwave on HIGH (100% power) for 16 to 18 minutes or until onion is tender, stirring after every 5 minutes. Evenly spoon 1 cup soup mixture into 4 microwave-safe soup bowls. Top each with a slice of toast and a slice of Swiss cheese. Arrange soup bowls in a circle in microwave and microwave on HIGH for 2 minutes or until cheese starts to melt. Place soup bowls on counter and let set for 2 minutes before serving.

Each serving equals:

HE: 1½ Vegetable • 1 Protein • ½ Bread • 8 Optional Calories

169 Calories • 5 gm Fat • 11 gm Protein • 20 gm Carbohydrate • 703 mg Sodium • 232 mg Calcium • 2 gm Fiber

DIABETIC EXCHANGES: 1½ Vegetable • 1 Meat • 1 Starch

Blushing Onion Soup

Doesn't the name of this recipe just hint perfectly at its luscious color, the gift of some juicy tomatoes? They mesh beautifully with those fragrant onions. ☻ Serves 4

1 tablespoon + 1 teaspoon I Can't Believe It's Not Butter!
    Light Margarine
3 cups thinly sliced onion
1/2 teaspoon dried minced garlic
1 (14-ounce) can Swanson Lower Sodium Fat Free Beef Broth
1 (15-ounce) can diced tomatoes, undrained
2 cups reduced-sodium tomato juice
2 teaspoons dried parsley flakes
4 slices reduced-calorie Italian or white bread, toasted
4 (3/4-ounce) slices Kraft reduced-fat mozzarella cheese

In an 8-cup microwave-safe mixing bowl, combine margarine, onion, and garlic. Cover and microwave on HIGH (100% power) for 7 to 8 minutes or until onion is tender, stirring after 3 minutes. Stir in beef broth, undrained tomatoes, tomato juice, and parsley flakes. Re-cover and continue to microwave on HIGH for 15 minutes or until mixture starts to boil, stirring every 5 minutes. Evenly spoon a full 1 1/2 cups soup mixture into 4 microwave-safe soup bowls. Top each with a slice of toast and a slice of mozzarella cheese. Arrange soup bowls in a circle in microwave and microwave on HIGH for 2 minutes or until cheese starts to melt. Place soup bowls on counter and let set for 2 minutes before serving.

Each serving equals:

HE: 3 1/2 Vegetable • 1 Protein • 1/2 Bread • 1/2 Fat •
8 Optional Calories

217 Calories • 5 gm Fat • 12 gm Protein •
31 gm Carbohydrate • 980 mg Sodium •
260 mg Calcium • 4 gm Fiber

DIABETIC EXCHANGES: 3 1/2 Vegetable • 1 Meat •
1/2 Starch • 1/2 Fat

Green Pea Soup

Soup is a great way to get all members of the family to eat more vegetables—and this scrumptious version of pea soup is a comfort on a chilly fall evening. ☺ Serves 4 (1 cup)

1 (15-ounce) can peas, rinsed, drained, and ¼ cup liquid reserved
1 (14-ounce) can Swanson Lower Sodium Fat Free Chicken Broth
⅓ cup Carnation Nonfat Dry Milk Powder
1 (2.5-ounce) jar sliced mushrooms, drained
1 cup grated carrots
½ teaspoon lemon pepper

Place peas and reserved liquid in a blender container. Cover and process on HIGH (100% power) for 15 seconds or until smooth. Pour pea mixture into an 8-cup microwave-safe mixing bowl. Add chicken broth and dry milk powder. Mix well to combine. Stir in mushrooms, carrots, and lemon pepper. Cover and microwave on MEDIUM (50% power) for 10 to 12 minutes, or until carrots are tender, stirring after every 5 minutes. Place bowl on counter, remove cover, and let set for 2 minutes. Mix well before serving.

Each serving equals:

HE: 1 Bread • ¾ Vegetable • ¼ Fat Free Milk • 8 Optional Calories

104 Calories • 0 gm Fat • 8 gm Protein • 18 gm Carbohydrate • 506 mg Sodium • 101 mg Calcium • 5 gm Fiber

DIABETIC EXCHANGES: 1 Starch • 1 Vegetable

Hearty Tomato Soup

If you've grown up sipping regular tomato soup, then you'll understand immediately why I call this recipe a "hearty" version. Instead of the pureed, smooth-as-silk style, you'll taste bits of tomato and green onion in every bite. ☻ Serves 4 (1 cup)

1 tablespoon water
½ cup finely chopped green onion
1 (15-ounce) can diced tomatoes, undrained
1 (10¾-ounce) can Healthy Request Tomato Soup
1 cup fat-free milk
1 teaspoon dried parsley flakes

In an 8-cup microwave-safe mixing bowl, combine water and onion. Microwave on HIGH (100% power) for 5 minutes or until onion is tender. Add undrained tomatoes, tomato soup, and milk. Mix well to combine. Stir in parsley flakes. Continue to microwave on HIGH for 7 to 8 minutes or until mixture is hot, stirring after every 3 minutes. Place bowl on counter and let set for 2 minutes. Mix well before serving.

Each serving equals:

HE: 1¼ Vegetable • ¼ Fat Free Milk • ½ Slider • 5 Optional Calories

97 Calories • 1 gm Fat • 4 gm Protein •
18 gm Carbohydrate • 506 mg Sodium •
96 mg Calcium • 2 gm Fiber

DIABETIC EXCHANGES: 1 Vegetable • 1 Starch

Cheesy Broccoli Soup

This all-American favorite in its traditional form is high in fat and calories, so I took on the challenge of finding a delicious way to reinvent it—and with one taste, I hope you'll agree that my Healthy Exchanges microwaved marvel is a winner!

● Serves 4 (1½ cups)

> 2 cups chopped celery
> 1 cup chopped onion
> 1 (10-ounce) package frozen chopped broccoli
> 1 cup fat-free cottage cheese
> 1 cup fat-free milk ☆
> 1 (10¾-ounce) can Healthy Request Cream of
>   Chicken Soup
> 1 cup cubed Velveeta Light processed cheese
> 1 teaspoon dried parsley flakes
> ⅛ teaspoon black pepper

In an 8-cup microwave-safe mixing bowl, combine celery, onion, and broccoli. Cover and microwave on HIGH (100% power) for 6 minutes, stirring after 3 minutes. Meanwhile, in a blender container, combine cottage cheese and ½ cup milk. Cover and process on BLEND for 15 seconds or until mixture is smooth. Add remaining ½ cup milk, chicken soup, and Velveeta cheese. Re-cover and process on BLEND for 15 seconds or until mixture is smooth. Pour milk mixture into vegetable mixture. Add parsley flakes and black pepper. Mix well to combine. Cover and micro-wave on HIGH for 3 minutes or until heated through. Do not allow mixture to boil. Place bowl on counter, uncover, and let set for 2 minutes. Mix well before serving.

Each serving equals:

HE: 2½ Vegetable • 1½ Protein • ¼ Fat Free Milk • ½ Slider • 5 Optional Calories

194 Calories • 2 gm Fat • 19 gm Protein • 25 gm Carbohydrate • 603 mg Sodium • 204 mg Calcium • 4 gm Fiber

DIABETIC EXCHANGES: 2 Vegetable • 1½ Meat • ½ Starch

Red Bean Soup

Kidney beans are wonderfully high in fiber, which makes them very good for you, but that wouldn't matter at all if this soup didn't taste good. Everyone who tasted it agreed that it's as filling as it is fantastic!

☻ Serves 4 (1 full cup)

> 1 (8-ounce) can Hunt's Tomato Sauce
> 1 (8-ounce) can tomatoes, chopped and undrained
> 1 cup chopped onion
> ½ teaspoon dried minced garlic
> 2 (15-ounce) cans Bush's red kidney beans, rinsed and drained ☆
> 2 tablespoons Oscar Mayer or Hormel Real Bacon Bits

In a blender container, combine tomato sauce, undrained tomatoes, onion, garlic, and 1 can rinsed kidney beans. Cover and process on BLEND for 15 seconds or until mixture is smooth. Pour mixture into an 8-cup microwave-safe mixing bowl. Add remaining can of rinsed kidney beans and bacon bits. Cover and microwave on HIGH (100% power) for 6 minutes or until mixture is hot, stirring after 3 minutes. Place bowl on counter, uncover, and let set for 2 minutes. Mix well before serving.

Each serving equals:

HE: 2 Vegetable • 1½ Protein • 1 Bread •
13 Optional Calories

---

181 Calories • 1 gm Fat • 11 gm Protein •
32 gm Carbohydrate • 990 mg Sodium •
61 mg Calcium • 11 gm Fiber

DIABETIC EXCHANGES: 2 Vegetable • 1½ Meat •
1½ Starch

Chili Cheese Soup

Here's a scrumptious homemade soup with all the satisfaction of a bowl of chili topped with ooey, gooey cheese. It's high in fiber and tastes like Fiesta Day in Acapulco!   ☻   Serves 4 (1 cup)

> 1 (15-ounce) can diced tomatoes, undrained
> 1 (10¾-ounce) can Healthy Request Tomato Soup
> 1½ teaspoons chili seasoning
> 1 (15-ounce) can Bush's pinto beans, rinsed and drained
> 1½ cups diced Velveeta Light processed cheese

In an 8-cup microwave-safe mixing bowl, combine undrained tomatoes, tomato soup, and chili seasoning. Add pinto beans and Velveeta cheese. Mix well to combine. Microwave on HIGH (100% power) for 7 to 9 minutes or until mixture is heated through and cheese is melted, stirring after every 3 minutes. Place bowl on counter and let set for 2 minutes. Mix well before serving.

Each serving equals:

HE: 2¼ Protein • 1 Vegetable • ½ Bread • ½ Slider • 5 Optional Calories

221 Calories • 5 gm Fat • 13 gm Protein • 31 gm Carbohydrate • 984 mg Sodium • 283 mg Calcium • 5 gm Fiber

DIABETIC EXCHANGES: 2 Meat • 1 Starch • 1 Vegetable

Micro Minestrone Soup

I like to think of minestrone as an Italian "kitchen sink" soup—it contains an abundance of ingredients that join their flavors in a rich and rewarding thick soup. This dish comes together quickly but tastes like you fussed for hours.   ○   Serves 4 (1½ cups)

> 2 cups water
> 1 (15-ounce) can diced tomatoes, undrained
> ½ cup chopped onion
> ⅓ cup uncooked elbow macaroni
> 1 cup chopped unpeeled zucchini
> 1 cup finely shredded cabbage
> 1 cup frozen cut green beans, thawed
> 1 cup frozen sliced carrots, thawed
> 1 (15-ounce) can Bush's navy beans, rinsed and drained
> 1½ teaspoons Italian seasoning
> 1 tablespoon Splenda Granular
> ⅛ teaspoon black pepper

In an 8-cup microwave-safe mixing bowl, combine water, undrained tomatoes, and onion. Add uncooked macaroni, zucchini, cabbage, green beans, carrots, and navy beans. Mix well to combine. Stir in Italian seasoning, Splenda, and black pepper. Cover and microwave on HIGH (100% power) for 15 to 17 minutes or until vegetables and macaroni are tender, stirring after every 5 minutes. Place bowl on counter, uncover, and let set for 3 minutes. Mix well before serving.

HINT: Thaw vegetables by placing in a colander and rinsing under hot water for 1 minute.

Each serving equals:

HE: 3 Vegetable • ¾ Bread • ¾ Protein •
1 Optional Calorie

---

116 Calories • 0 gm Fat • 6 gm Protein •
23 gm Carbohydrate • 252 mg Sodium •
64 mg Calcium • 4 gm Fiber

DIABETIC EXCHANGES: 2 Vegetable • 1 Starch • 1 Meat

Pronto Veggie Soup

Imagine the scene—you arrive home from work exhausted, but you need something warm and fast for dinner. This speedy recipe couldn't be easier: you just open a can, add a bag of frozen veggies and one of pre-cut cabbage, season—and sit down!

🍲 Serves 4 (¾ cup)

> 1 (14-ounce) can Swanson Lower Sodium Fat Free Beef Broth
> 1 (10-ounce) package frozen mixed vegetables, thawed
> 1 cup purchased cole slaw mix
> 2 teaspoons dried onion flakes
> 1 teaspoon dried parsley flakes
> ⅛ teaspoon black pepper

In an 8-cup microwave-safe mixing bowl, combine beef broth, mixed vegetables, and cole slaw mix. Add onion flakes, parsley flakes, and black pepper. Mix well to combine. Cover and microwave on HIGH (100% power) for 10 to 12 minutes or until vegetables are tender, stirring after every 5 minutes. Place bowl on counter, uncover, and let set for 3 minutes. Mix well before serving.

HINTS: 1. Thaw vegetables by placing in a colander and rinsing under hot water for 1 minute.
2. One cup of shredded cabbage may be used in place of purchased cole slaw mix.

Each serving equals:

HE: 1 Vegetable • ½ Bread • 8 Optional Calories

64 Calories • 0 gm Fat • 4 gm Protein •
12 gm Carbohydrate • 283 mg Sodium •
30 mg Calcium • 3 gm Fiber

DIABETIC EXCHANGES: 1 Vegetable • ½ Starch

Chunky Tuna Chowder

Talk about satisfaction in just one bowl! Almost any chowder comes to the table brimming with goodies, but this one is a real star—cheesy *and* creamy, with chunks of fish and vegetables. It's a tummy-soothing delight in every bite.

Serves 4 (1¼ cups)

> 1 (10¾-ounce) can Healthy Request Cream of Mushroom Soup
> ¾ cup shredded Kraft reduced-fat Cheddar cheese
> 1 (6-ounce) can white tuna, packed in water, drained and flaked
> 1 cup fat-free milk
> 1 teaspoon dried onion flakes
> 2 teaspoons dried parsley flakes
> 1 (8-ounce) can tomatoes, coarsely chopped and undrained
> 1½ cups diced cooked potatoes

In an 8-cup microwave-safe mixing bowl, combine mushroom soup and Cheddar cheese. Stir in tuna, milk, onion flakes, and parsley flakes. Add undrained tomatoes and potatoes. Mix well to combine. Cover and microwave on HIGH (100% power) for 6 to 8 minutes or until mixture is heated through and cheese is melted, stirring after every 3 minutes. Place bowl on counter, uncover, and let set for 2 minutes. Mix well before serving.

Each serving equals:

HE: 2 Protein • ½ Bread • ½ Vegetable •
¼ Fat Free Milk • ½ Slider • 1 Optional Calorie

226 Calories • 6 gm Fat • 20 gm Protein •
23 gm Carbohydrate • 727 mg Sodium •
297 mg Calcium • 2 gm Fiber

DIABETIC EXCHANGES: 2 Meat • 1½ Starch •
½ Vegetable

Cliff's Clam Chowder

My husband, Cliff, the truck drivin' man, has traveled to nearly every corner of this country and developed a taste for many regional specialties, so I decided to create a clam chowder to please him. This is the dish that won his heart, and just a spoonful will tell you why. ☻ Serves 4 (1 cup)

> ¼ cup finely chopped onion
> 1 cup peeled and diced raw potatoes
> ¾ cup finely chopped celery
> 1 cup water
> 1 (12-fluid-ounce) can Carnation Evaporated Fat Free Milk
> 3 tablespoons all-purpose flour
> 1 (6½-ounce drained weight) can minced clams, undrained
> 1 teaspoon lemon pepper
> 1 tablespoon + 1 teaspoon I Can't Believe It's Not Butter! Light
>   Margarine
> 2 tablespoons Oscar Mayer or Hormel Real Bacon Bits

In an 8-cup microwave-safe mixing bowl, combine onion, potatoes, celery, and water. Cover and microwave on HIGH (100% power) for 4 to 6 minutes or until potatoes and celery are tender. In a small bowl, combine evaporated milk and flour. Mix well using a wire whisk. Add to potato mixture. Mix well to combine. Stir in undrained clams, lemon pepper, and margarine. Continue to microwave on HIGH for 6 to 8 minutes or until mixture is heated through, stirring after every 3 minutes. Place bowl on counter and let set for 3 minutes. Just before serving, stir in bacon bits.

Each serving equals:

HE: 1 Protein • ¾ Fat Free Milk • ½ Bread • ½ Fat •
½ Vegetable • 13 Optional Calories

---

166 Calories • 2 gm Fat • 12 gm Protein •
25 gm Carbohydrate • 698 mg Sodium •
255 mg Calcium • 1 gm Fiber

DIABETIC EXCHANGES: 1½ Meat • 1 Fat Free Milk •
½ Starch • ½ Fat

Creamy Chicken Chowder

The microwave makes soup the ultimate convenience food. Because it speeds up the cooking of some ingredients, it makes a luscious meal-in-a-bowl ready in minutes! This recipe even uses uncooked pasta, so you don't have to plan in advance.

❂ Serves 4 (1¼ cups)

> 1 (10¾-ounce) can Healthy Request Cream of Chicken Soup
> 1 (12-fluid-ounce) can Carnation Evaporated Fat Free Milk
> 1 cup water
> 6 tablespoons shredded Kraft reduced-fat Cheddar cheese
> 1 cup frozen cut broccoli, thawed
> 1 cup frozen sliced carrots, thawed
> 1 teaspoon dried parsley flakes
> 1 teaspoon dried onion flakes
> 1 cup diced cooked chicken breast
> ¾ cup uncooked rotini pasta

In an 8-cup microwave-safe mixing bowl, combine chicken soup, evaporated milk, and water. Stir in Cheddar cheese, broccoli, carrots, parsley flakes, and onion flakes. Cover and microwave on HIGH (100% power) for 5 minutes, stirring after 3 minutes. Add chicken and uncooked rotini pasta. Mix well to combine. Re-cover and continue to microwave on HIGH for 6 to 8 minutes or until mixture is heated through and rotini pasta is cooked, stirring after every 3 minutes. Place bowl on counter, uncover, and let set for 3 minutes. Mix well before serving.

HINTS: 1. Thaw broccoli and carrots by placing in a colander and rinsing under hot water for 1 minute.
2. If you don't have leftovers, purchase a chunk of cooked chicken breast from your local deli.

Each serving equals:

HE: 1¾ Protein • 1 Vegetable • ¾ Fat Free Milk • ½ Bread • ½ Slider • 5 Optional Calories

---

264 Calories • 4 gm Fat • 23 gm Protein • 34 gm Carbohydrate • 546 mg Sodium • 350 mg Calcium • 3 gm Fiber

---

DIABETIC EXCHANGES: 1½ Meat • 1 Vegetable • 1 Fat Free Milk • 1 Starch

Cheyanne's Veggie Beef Soup

She's just a little girl, but my granddaughter Cheyanne has always known what she loves to eat! This meaty vegetable soup is one of her favorites, and she likes to sit in the kitchen with me and eat it while I test recipes. ☻ Serves 4 (1 full cup)

8 ounces extra-lean ground sirloin beef or turkey breast
¼ cup finely chopped onion
1 (15-ounce) can cut green beans, rinsed and drained
1 (8-ounce) can Hunt's Tomato Sauce
1 (14½-ounce) can stewed tomatoes, chopped and undrained
¾ cup water
1 tablespoon Splenda Granular

Crumble meat into a plastic colander. Stir in onion. Place colander in a glass pie plate. Microwave on HIGH (100% power) for 4 to 5 minutes or until meat is browned, stirring after 3 minutes. In an 8-cup microwave-safe mixing bowl, combine green beans, tomato sauce, undrained tomatoes, water, and Splenda. Stir in browned meat mixture. Cover and microwave on HIGH for 8 to 10 minutes or until mixture is heated through, stirring after every 3 minutes. Place bowl on counter, uncover, and let set for 2 minutes. Mix well before serving.

Each serving equals:

HE: 3 Vegetable • 1½ Protein • 1 Optional Calorie

147 Calories • 3 gm Fat • 14 gm Protein •
16 gm Carbohydrate • 870 mg Sodium •
64 mg Calcium • 4 gm Fiber

DIABETIC EXCHANGES: 3 Vegetable • 1½ Meat

Zach's Chili Classic

For those of you who love their chili *with* beans, here's a dish inspired by my grandson Zach, who shares a taste for pleasantly spicy food with his Poppa Cliff.   ☻   Serves 6 (1 cup)

> 16 ounces extra-lean ground sirloin beef or turkey breast
> 1 cup chopped onion
> 1 cup chopped green bell pepper
> 1 (15-ounce) can diced tomatoes, undrained
> 1 (8-ounce) can Hunt's Tomato Sauce
> ¼ cup reduced-sodium ketchup
> 2 teaspoons chili seasoning
> 1 (15-ounce) can Bush's kidney beans, rinsed and drained

Crumble meat into a plastic colander. Stir in onion and green pepper. Place colander in a glass pie plate. Microwave on HIGH (100% power) for 4 to 5 minutes or until meat is browned, stirring after 3 minutes. In an 8-cup microwave-safe mixing bowl, combine undrained tomatoes, tomato sauce, ketchup, and chili seasoning. Add kidney beans. Mix well to combine. Stir in browned meat mixture. Cover and microwave on HIGH for 8 to 10 minutes or until mixture is heated through, stirring after every 4 minutes. Place bowl on counter, uncover, and let set for 2 minutes. Mix well before serving.

Each serving equals:

HE: 2½ Protein • 2 Vegetable • ½ Bread •
10 Optional Calories

---

192 Calories • 4 gm Fat • 19 gm Protein •
20 gm Carbohydrate • 337 mg Sodium •
57 mg Calcium • 5 gm Fiber

DIABETIC EXCHANGES: 2½ Meat • 2 Vegetable •
½ Starch

Tex Mex Chili

Do you enjoy watching the annual chili cookoff on the Food Network as much as we do? I'm always intrigued to see what kinds of ingredients find their way into different recipes. Here, I've added some corn to a favorite dish—and made it even better!

● Serves 4 (1 cup)

> 8 ounces extra-lean ground sirloin beef or turkey breast
> ¾ cup chopped onion
> 1 (8-ounce) can Hunt's Tomato Sauce
> 1 (14½-ounce) can stewed tomatoes, undrained
> ¼ teaspoon dried minced garlic
> 2 teaspoons chili seasoning
> 1 tablespoon Splenda Granular
> 1 (15-ounce) can Bush's red kidney beans, rinsed and drained
> 1 cup frozen whole-kernel corn, thawed

Crumble meat into a plastic colander. Stir in onion. Place colander in a glass pie plate. Microwave on HIGH (100% power) for 4 to 5 minutes or until meat is browned, stirring after 3 minutes. In an 8-cup microwave-safe mixing bowl, combine tomato sauce, undrained stewed tomatoes, garlic, chili seasoning, Splenda, and kidney beans. Add browned meat mixture and corn. Mix well to combine. Cover and microwave on HIGH for 8 to 10 minutes or until mixture is heated through, stirring after every 4 minutes. Place bowl on counter, uncover, and let set for 2 minutes. Mix well before serving.

HINT: Thaw corn by placing in a colander and rinsing under hot
      water for 1 minute.

Each serving equals:

HE: 2½ Protein • 2¼ Vegetable • 1 Bread • 1 Optional Calorie

---

227 Calories • 3 gm Fat • 18 gm Protein • 32 gm Carbohydrate • 804 mg Sodium • 67 mg Calcium • 8 gm Fiber

---

DIABETIC EXCHANGES: 2 Meat • 2 Vegetable • 1 Starch

Country Ham and Corn Stew

When do you "cross the line" between a soup and a stew? It's a good question, with no perfect answer, but I tend to feel that when there's more "stuff" than soup in the bowl, it's a stew.

Serves 4 (1¼ cups)

> ¾ cup finely chopped celery
> ¼ cup finely chopped onion
> 2 tablespoons water
> 1 (10¾-ounce) can Healthy Request Cream of Celery Soup
> 1 (12-fluid-ounce) can Carnation Evaporated Fat Free Milk
> 1 full cup diced Dubuque 97% fat-free ham or any extra-lean ham
> 2 cups frozen whole-kernel corn, thawed
> 1 teaspoon dried parsley flakes
> ⅛ teaspoon black pepper

In an 8-cup microwave-safe mixing bowl, combine celery, onion, and water. Cover and microwave on HIGH (100% power) for 5 minutes or until vegetables are tender. Stir in celery soup and evaporated milk. Add ham, corn, parsley flakes, and black pepper. Mix well to combine. Re-cover and microwave on HIGH for 5 minutes or until mixture is heated through, stirring after 3 minutes. Place bowl on counter, uncover, and let set for 2 minutes. Mix well before serving.

HINT: Thaw corn by placing in a colander and rinsing under hot water for 1 minute.

Each serving equals:

HE: 1 Bread • 1 Protein • ¾ Fat Free Milk •
½ Vegetable • ½ Slider • 1 Optional Calorie

231 Calories • 3 gm Fat • 17 gm Protein •
34 gm Carbohydrate • 701 mg Sodium •
315 mg Calcium • 2 gm Fiber

DIABETIC EXCHANGES: 1½ Starch • 1 Meat •
1 Fat Free Milk • ½ Vegetable

Manhattan Ham and Bean Soup

A bean soup all on its own delivers enough healthy protein to deserve to be called a main dish, but when you add ham to the mix, you get a wonderfully substantial entrée. This is a tasty one, too!

● Serves 6 (1 cup)

> 1 (15-ounce) can Bush's great northern beans, rinsed and drained
> ½ cup chopped onion
> 1 cup shredded carrots
> 1 cup finely chopped celery
> 2 tablespoons water
> 1 (15-ounce) can diced tomatoes, undrained
> 1 full cup diced Dubuque 97% fat-free ham or any extra-lean ham
> 1 teaspoon dried parsley flakes
> ⅛ teaspoon black pepper
> 1 (12-fluid-ounce) can Carnation Evaporated Fat Free Milk

In an 8-cup microwave-safe mixing bowl, combine great northern beans, onion, carrots, celery, and water. Cover and microwave on HIGH (100% power) for 10 minutes, stirring after 5 minutes. Add undrained tomatoes, ham, parsley flakes, and black pepper. Mix well to combine. Re-cover and continue to microwave on HIGH for 5 minutes. Stir in evaporated milk. Place uncovered bowl on counter and let set for 2 minutes. Mix well before serving.

Each serving equals:

HE: 1½ Protein • 1½ Vegetable • ½ Fat Free Milk • ½ Bread

---

197 Calories • 1 gm Fat • 15 gm Protein • 32 gm Carbohydrate • 385 mg Sodium • 229 mg Calcium • 5 gm Fiber

---

DIABETIC EXCHANGES: 1½ Meat • 1½ Vegetable • ½ Fat Free Milk • ½ Starch

Cheesy California Sausage Soup

It doesn't take very much sausage to flavor a big pot of soup, but the effect is splendid. There's lots of California sunshine in every spoonful, plus the tangy taste of savory meat.

○ Serves 4 (1½ cups)

8 ounces Healthy Choice lean kielbasa sausage
½ cup chopped onion
1½ cups water ☆
1 (14-ounce) can Swanson Lower Sodium Fat Free Chicken Broth
1½ cups frozen cut broccoli, thawed
1½ cups frozen cauliflower, thawed
1½ cups frozen sliced carrots, thawed
1 teaspoon dried parsley flakes
⅛ teaspoon black pepper
1 cup diced Velveeta Light processed cheese
¼ cup Land O Lakes Fat Free Half & Half

Slice sausage into ½-inch pieces and then chop each slice into 3 pieces. In an 8-cup microwave-safe mixing bowl, combine sausage, onion, and ¼ cup water. Microwave on HIGH (100% power) for 4 minutes. Add chicken broth, remaining 1¼ cups water, broccoli, cauliflower, and carrots. Mix well to combine. Stir in parsley flakes and black pepper. Continue to microwave on HIGH for 15 to 17 minutes or until vegetables are tender, stirring after every 5 minutes. Place bowl on counter. Stir in Velveeta and half & half. Continue stirring until cheese melts. Serve at once.

HINTS: 1. One (16-ounce) package frozen California Blend vegetables may be used in place of broccoli, cauliflower, and carrots.
2. Thaw vegetables by placing in a colander and rinsing under hot water for 1 minute.

Each serving equals:

HE: 3 Protein • 2½ Vegetable • ¼ Slider •
2 Optional Calories

194 Calories • 6 gm Fat • 17 gm Protein •
18 gm Carbohydrate • 914 mg Sodium •
228 mg Calcium • 3 gm Fiber

DIABETIC EXCHANGES: 3 Meat • 2 Vegetable

Hot Dog and Corn Chowder

What a kid-pleaser this inspiration turned out to be! It's just brimming with all those childhood favorites—bits of hot dogs, creamy corn, and good old Velveeta cheese (made just enough lighter to be enjoyed often).   ☾   Serves 4 (1 cup)

> 1 (15-ounce) can cream-style corn
> ¼ cup fat-free milk
> ¼ cup Land O Lakes Fat Free Half & Half
> 1 cup diced Velveeta Light processed cheese
> 8 ounces Oscar Mayer or Healthy Choice reduced-fat
>   frankfurters, cut into ¼-inch pieces
> 2 teaspoons dried onion flakes
> 1 teaspoon dried parsley flakes

In an 8-cup microwave-safe mixing bowl, combine corn, milk, and half & half. Stir in Velveeta cheese, frankfurters, onion flakes, and parsley flakes. Cover and microwave on HIGH (100% power) for 5 to 7 minutes or until mixture is heated through and cheese is melted, stirring after every 3 minutes. Place bowl on counter, uncover, and let set for 2 minutes. Mix well before serving.

Each serving equals:

HE: 2¼ Protein • 1 Bread • 14 Optional Calories

221 Calories • 5 gm Fat • 16 gm Protein •
28 gm Carbohydrate • 989 mg Sodium •
193 mg Calcium • 2 gm Fiber

DIABETIC EXCHANGES: 2 Meat • 1 Starch

Wilted Tossed Salad

Sometimes, you just don't want to munch all that crunch of a traditional salad—but you want your veggies. A wilted salad takes the edge off, by heating the dressing, and when you toss it with your greens, a little magic takes place.   ☻   Serves 4

> 6 cups torn mixed salad greens
> ¼ cup finely chopped onion
> ⅓ cup white distilled vinegar
> 2 tablespoons water
> ¼ cup Splenda Granular
> ½ teaspoon lemon pepper
> ¼ cup Oscar Mayer or Hormel Real Bacon Bits
> 2 hard-boiled eggs, chopped

In a large bowl, combine salad greens and onion. In a small microwave-safe mixing bowl, combine vinegar, water, Splenda, and lemon pepper. Microwave on HIGH (100% power) for 45 seconds. Stir in bacon bits. Drizzle hot mixture over salad greens. Toss lightly to coat. For each salad, place about 1½ cups salad on a salad plate and sprinkle ¼ of the chopped eggs over top. Serve at once.

Each serving equals:

HE: 1½ Vegetable • ½ Protein • ¼ Slider •
11 Optional Calories

---

92 Calories • 4 gm Fat • 7 gm Protein •
7 gm Carbohydrate • 316 mg Sodium •
62 mg Calcium • 2 gm Fiber

DIABETIC EXCHANGES: 1½ Vegetable • 1 Meat

Hot Cabbage Slaw

Serving your slaw warm is a good old European tradition, but it's one I'm happy to take for my own! This is a terrific salad to offer alongside pork tenders. ☻ Serves 6 (⅔ cup)

> ½ cup apple cider vinegar
> ⅓ cup Splenda Granular
> ⅛ teaspoon black pepper
> 4 cups coarsely shredded cabbage
> 1 (15-ounce) can cut green beans, rinsed and drained
> ½ cup finely chopped onion
> 6 tablespoons Oscar Mayer or Hormel Real Bacon Bits

In an 8-cup microwave-safe mixing bowl, combine vinegar, Splenda, and black pepper. Add cabbage, green beans, and onion. Mix well to combine. Cover and microwave on HIGH (100% power) for 6 to 8 minutes or just until cabbage is tender, stirring after every 3 minutes. Place bowl on counter, uncover, and let set for 2 minutes. Just before serving, stir in bacon bits.

Each serving equals:

HE: 1½ Vegetable • ¼ Slider • 10 Optional Calories

---

61 Calories • 1 gm Fat • 4 gm Protein •
9 gm Carbohydrate • 409 mg Sodium •
45 mg Calcium • 1 gm Fiber

DIABETIC EXCHANGES: 1½ Vegetable

Confetti Corn Relish Salad

Isn't the word *confetti* enough to make you smile? I love the image of colors exploding into the air on a sunny day. This colorful dish simply lights up the room! ☻ Serves 6

> 1 tablespoon cornstarch
> ¾ cup Splenda Granular
> ½ teaspoon lemon pepper
> ⅓ cup apple cider vinegar
> ½ teaspoon prepared yellow mustard
> 2 cups frozen whole-kernel corn, thawed
> ½ cup chopped green bell pepper
> ½ cup chopped red bell pepper
> ½ cup chopped onion
> 6 lettuce leaves

In an 8-cup microwave-safe mixing bowl, combine cornstarch, Splenda, and lemon pepper. Add vinegar and mustard. Mix well using a wire whisk. Microwave on HIGH (100% power) for 3 to 5 minutes or until mixture thickens and starts to boil, stirring after every 2 minutes. Stir in corn, green pepper, red pepper, and onion. Continue to microwave on HIGH for 1 minute. Place bowl on counter and let set for 10 minutes. Cover and refrigerate for at least 2 hours. When serving, place a lettuce leaf on each salad plate and spoon about ½ cup corn salad over top.

Each serving equals:

HE: ⅔ Bread • ½ Vegetable • 17 Optional Calories

76 Calories • 0 gm Fat • 2 gm Protein •
17 gm Carbohydrate • 48 mg Sodium •
9 mg Calcium • 2 gm Fiber

DIABETIC EXCHANGES: 1 Starch

Trio Bean Salad

Three-bean salad is a Midwestern tradition, but even experienced cooks are always looking for a fun new way to prepare this classic. There's something about the microwave that brings out deeper, richer flavors here.   ☻   Serves 6 (⅔ cup)

¼ cup water
¼ cup apple cider vinegar
½ cup Splenda Granular
1 tablespoon cornstarch
1 teaspoon dried parsley flakes
⅛ teaspoon black pepper
1 (15-ounce) can French-style green beans, rinsed and drained

1 (15-ounce) can Bush's wax beans, rinsed and drained
1 (15-ounce) can Bush's red kidney beans, rinsed and drained
½ cup finely chopped onion
¼ cup Oscar Mayer or Hormel Real Bacon Bits

In an 8-cup microwave-safe mixing bowl, combine water, vinegar, Splenda, cornstarch, parsley flakes, and black pepper. Microwave on HIGH (100% power) for 3 to 4 minutes or until mixture thickens, stirring after every minute. Add green beans, wax beans, kidney beans, and onion. Mix well to combine. Cover and continue to microwave on HIGH for 5 minutes, stirring after 3 minutes. Place bowl on counter, uncover, and let set for 10 minutes. Stir in bacon bits. Serve warm or cold.

Each serving equals:

HE: 1½ Vegetable • ½ Bread • ½ Protein •
¼ Slider • 9 Optional Calories

125 Calories • 1 gm Fat • 8 gm Protein •
21 gm Carbohydrate • 633 mg Sodium •
72 mg Calcium • 6 gm Fiber

DIABETIC EXCHANGES: 1½ Vegetable • 1 Meat •
½ Starch

Marinated Veggie Salad

You can marinate any veggies in the refrigerator, but nothing brings out the best in them than some speedy heat! I was impressed by how much tastier this was than a traditional version.

● Serves 4 (1 cup)

> 1 (16-ounce) package frozen carrot, broccoli, and cauliflower
>   blend, thawed
> ½ cup Kraft Fat Free Italian Dressing
> ¼ cup chopped green onion
> ¾ cup chopped ripe red tomatoes
> ¼ cup sliced ripe olives

In an 8-cup microwave-safe mixing bowl, combine thawed vegetable blend and Italian dressing. Cover and microwave on HIGH (100% power) for 6 minutes, stirring after 3 minutes. Place bowl on counter, uncover, stir, and let set for 15 minutes. Stir in onion, tomatoes, and olives. Cover and refrigerate for at least 2 hours. Mix well before serving.

HINTS: 1. 1 cup frozen carrots, 1 cup frozen broccoli and 1 cup frozen cauliflower may be used in place of blended vegetables.
2. Thaw vegetables by placing in a colander and rinsing under hot water for 1 minute.

Each serving equals:

HE: 2 Vegetable • ¼ Fat • 8 Optional Calories

---

57 Calories • 1 gm Fat • 2 gm Protein •
10 gm Carbohydrate • 502 mg Sodium •
47 mg Calcium • 4 gm Fiber

DIABETIC EXCHANGES: 2 Vegetable

Pennsylvania Dutch Potato Salad

It just isn't summer without this old-fashioned favorite! It's flavorful and tender, perfect for any Sunday supper.

◒ Serves 4 (1¼ cups)

> 1¾ cup frozen cut green beans
> 3 cups diced raw potatoes
> ½ cup water
> 1 cup diced Dubuque 97% fat-free ham or any extra-lean ham
> ¼ cup finely chopped onion
> ½ cup Kraft fat-free mayonnaise
> 2 teaspoons Grey Poupon mustard
> 2 teaspoons white distilled vinegar
> 1 teaspoon dried parsley flakes

In an 8-cup microwave-safe mixing bowl, combine green beans, potatoes, and water. Cover and microwave on HIGH (100% power) for 6 to 7 minutes or until vegetables are tender, stirring after every 3 minutes. Drain and return vegetables to bowl. Stir in ham and onion. In a small bowl, combine mayonnaise, mustard, vinegar, and parsley flakes. Add mayonnaise mixture to potato mixture. Mix gently to combine. Cover and refrigerate for at least 30 minutes. Mix well before serving.

Each serving equals:

HE: 1 Bread • 1 Protein • 1 Vegetable • ¼ Slider

174 Calories • 2 gm Fat • 11 gm Protein •
28 gm Carbohydrate • 603 mg Sodium •
35 mg Calcium • 4 gm Fiber

DIABETIC EXCHANGES: 1½ Starch • 1 Vegetable •
1 Meat

Hot Potato and Romaine Salad

Do you love red potatoes as much as I do? The skins may just be the tastiest of any potatoes, and I always eat the skin—it's so full of healthy fiber. This salad is pretty *and* tasty!

🕑 Serves 4 (1 cup)

2 cups peeled and cubed
    uncooked red potatoes
10 tablespoons water ☆
3 tablespoons white distilled
    vinegar
1 tablespoon all-purpose flour
1 tablespoon Splenda Granular

1 tablespoon dried onion flakes
1 teaspoon dried parsley flakes
3 tablespoons Oscar Mayer or
    Hormel Real Bacon Bits
2 cups shredded Romaine
    lettuce
2 hard-boiled eggs, chopped

In an 8-cup microwave-safe mixing bowl, combine potatoes and 2 tablespoons water. Cover and microwave on HIGH (100% power) for 4 to 6 minutes or until potatoes are tender, stirring after 3 minutes. Drain and return potatoes to bowl. In a medium microwave-safe mixing bowl, combine remaining ½ cup water, vinegar, flour, Splenda, onion flakes, and parsley flakes. Microwave on HIGH for 2 to 3 minutes or until mixture thickens and starts to boil, stirring after 1 minute. Stir in bacon bits. Drizzle hot mixture evenly over potatoes. Mix well to coat. Stir in Romaine lettuce and eggs. Serve at once.

Each serving equals:

HE: ½ Bread • ½ Protein • ½ Vegetable • ¼ Slider •
8 Optional Calories

120 Calories • 4 gm Fat • 7 gm Protein •
14 gm Carbohydrate • 203 mg Sodium •
29 mg Calcium • 2 gm Fiber

DIABETIC EXCHANGES: 1 Starch • 1 Meat • ½ Vegetable

Tapioca Fruit Salad

Some people say that tapioca is too old-fashioned for today's families, but if there ever was a dish that would convince the hippest young people to give tapioca a try, this is it! Cliff has always loved it, so he's passed his passion on to our grandkids!

☻ Serves 8

> 1 (4-serving) package JELL-O sugar-free vanilla cook-and-serve
>   pudding mix
> 3 tablespoons Quick Cooking Minute Tapioca
> ⅔ cup Carnation Nonfat Dry Milk Powder
> 1 (8-ounce) can pineapple tidbits, packed in fruit juice, drained
>   and ¼ cup liquid reserved
> 1 (8-ounce) can sliced peaches, packed in fruit juice, drained and
>   ¼ cup liquid reserved
> 1¼ cups water
> 1 (11-ounce) can mandarin oranges, rinsed and drained
> 1 cup (1 medium) diced banana
> ½ cup Cool Whip Lite
> 4 maraschino cherries, halved

In an 8-cup microwave-safe mixing bowl, combine dry pudding mix, tapioca, and dry milk powder. Add reserved pineapple and peach liquids and water. Mix well to combine. Let set for 5 minutes. Cover and microwave on HIGH (100% power) for 4 to 6 minutes, or just until mixture thickens and starts to boil, stirring after every 2 minutes. Place bowl on counter, uncover, and let set for 1 minute. Stir in mandarin oranges, pineapple, peaches, and banana. Evenly spoon mixture into 8 dessert dishes. Refrigerate for at least 30 minutes. Just before serving, top each with 1 tablespoon Cool Whip Lite and ½ maraschino cherry.

HINT: To prevent banana from turning brown, mix with 1 teaspoon lemon juice or sprinkle with Fruit Fresh.

Each serving equals:

HE: 1 Fruit • ¼ Fat Free Milk • ¼ Slider •
13 Optional Calories

---

116 Calories • 0 gm Fat • 3 gm Protein •
26 gm Carbohydrate • 92 mg Sodium •
82 mg Calcium • 1 gm Fiber

DIABETIC EXCHANGES: 1 Fruit • ½ Starch/Carbohydrate

Raspberry Yogurt Salad

This is such a luscious pink color, you may be tempted to match your outfit to it if you're serving it at a card party or graduation lunch! If raspberries are in season, you may want to garnish each cup with a couple.   ☕   Serves 6

1¼ cups water
1 (4-serving) package JELL-O sugar-free raspberry gelatin
2¼ cups frozen unsweetened raspberries
1½ cups Dannon plain fat-free yogurt
⅓ cup Carnation Nonfat Dry Milk Powder
¼ cup Splenda Granular

In an 8-cup microwave-safe mixing bowl, combine water and dry gelatin. Microwave on HIGH (100% power) until mixture comes to a boil, about 2 minutes. Mix well to dissolve gelatin. Stir in raspberries. Add yogurt, dry milk powder, and Splenda. Mix gently to combine. Evenly spoon mixture into 6 (6-ounce) custard cups. Refrigerate for at least 2 hours.

Each serving equals:

HE: ½ Fat Free Milk • ½ Fruit • 8 Optional Calories

88 Calories • 0 gm Fat • 8 gm Protein •
14 gm Carbohydrate • 71 mg Sodium •
179 mg Calcium • 3 gm Fiber

DIABETIC EXCHANGES: ½ Fat Free Milk • ½ Fruit

Hot Tuna Salad

Some research suggests that warm or hot food can be more filling and satisfying than cold food. (They could be right!) All I know is, this tuna casserole is downright scrumptious. ☻ Serves 4

2 cups cooked elbow macaroni,
    rinsed and drained
1 (6-ounce) can white tuna,
    packed in water, drained
    and flaked
1 hard-boiled egg, chopped
¾ cup shredded Kraft reduced-
    fat Cheddar cheese

1¾ cups chopped celery
¼ cup chopped onion
½ cup Kraft fat-free
    mayonnaise
2 teaspoons lemon juice
1 teaspoon dried parsley flakes
¼ teaspoon lemon pepper

Spray an 8-by-8-inch microwave-safe baking dish with butter-flavored cooking spray. In a large bowl, combine macaroni, tuna, egg, Cheddar cheese, celery, and onion. In a small bowl, combine mayonnaise, lemon juice, parsley flakes, and lemon pepper. Add dressing mixture to macaroni mixture. Mix gently to combine. Spoon mixture into prepared baking dish. Cover and microwave on HIGH (100% power) for 8 minutes, stirring after 4 minutes. Place baking dish on counter, uncover, and let set for 3 minutes. Evenly divide into 4 servings.

HINTS: 1. Usually 1⅓ cups uncooked elbow macaroni cooks to about 2 cups.
2. If you want the look and feel of egg without the cholesterol, toss out the yolk and dice the whites.

Each serving equals:

HE: 2¼ Protein • 1 Bread • 1 Vegetable • ¼ Slider

268 Calories • 8 gm Fat • 22 gm Protein •
27 gm Carbohydrate • 677 mg Sodium •
178 mg Calcium • 3 gm Fiber

DIABETIC EXCHANGES: 2½ Meat • 1 Starch •
½ Vegetable

Hot Ham Salad

Our taste buds just love to be entertained by a variety of flavors and textures, so they're sure to be pleased by this appetizing salad. There's just enough crunch and variety to awaken all the senses.

● Serves 6

> 2 full cups diced Dubuque 97% fat-free ham or any extra-lean ham
> 1 cup + 2 tablespoons shredded Kraft reduced-fat Cheddar cheese
> 1½ cups chopped celery
> 1½ cups dry unseasoned bread cubes
> ¾ cup Kraft fat-free mayonnaise
> 1 (2-ounce) jar sliced pimiento, undrained
> 1 teaspoon dried parsley flakes
> 1 teaspoon dried onion flakes
> 6 tablespoons slivered almonds, toasted
> 6 lettuce leaves

In an 8-cup microwave-safe mixing bowl, combine ham, Cheddar cheese, celery, and bread cubes. Add mayonnaise, undrained pimiento, parsley flakes, and onion flakes. Mix well to combine. Stir in almonds. Cover and microwave on HIGH (100% power) for 5 to 6 minutes, stirring after 3 minutes. Place bowl on counter, uncover, and let set for 2 minutes. Mix well before serving. For each serving, place a lettuce leaf on each plate and spoon a scant 1 cup of ham mixture over top.

HINT: To toast almonds, spread in a glass pie plate and microwave on HIGH for 6 to 7 minutes or until golden. Stir after 3 minutes; then each minute after until done.

Each serving equals:

HE: 2½ Protein • ½ Bread • ½ Fat • ½ Vegetable • ¼ Slider • 4 Optional Calories

221 Calories • 9 gm Fat • 19 gm Protein • 16 gm Carbohydrate • 725 mg Sodium • 202 mg Calcium • 2 gm Fiber

DIABETIC EXCHANGES: 2 Meat • 1 Starch/Carbohydrate • ½ Fat

Veggies and Sides

You know how it feels when you're trying to get dinner for your family on the table, but juggling pots on more than a couple of burners is just TOO HARD? I like to say that that is why the microwave was invented, to provide you with another cooking "surface"—one that requires less attention than your stovetop most of the time, too!

When you're preparing your entrée in a skillet on your stovetop, consider using your microwave to get your vegetables and side dishes ready. You can often plan to microwave more than one side dish because most of these recipes taste even better when they've had some time to set. Also, cooking continues even once a dish has left the oven.

Fresh vegetables LOVE the microwave because they don't get soggy as they might if boiled in a saucepan. Taste my **Fresh Asparagus and Mushrooms** *and you'll see that I'm right! It's also a great way to mix up a cheesy veggie dish, because cheese melts beautifully (try* **Onions au Gratin**) *but doesn't burn as it might in your traditional oven. It's also wonderful for tasty spuds (**Savory Potatoes**) as well as splendid rice and pasta dishes (**Rising Sun Rice Pilaf**)!*

Vegetable Delight

One of a cook's greatest challenges is finding something fresh and new to do with the vegetables we eat often. In this dish, I took "same old, same old" and performed a bit of culinary magic!

◐ Serves 6 (½ cup)

> 1 cup sliced unpeeled zucchini
> ½ cup chopped celery
> ½ cup chopped onion
> ½ cup chopped green bell pepper
> 1 cup sliced carrots
> ½ cup sliced fresh mushrooms
> 1 (15-ounce) can diced tomatoes, drained and 2 tablespoons juice reserved
> 1 tablespoon Splenda Granular
> 1 teaspoon Italian seasoning

In an 8-cup microwave-safe mixing bowl, combine zucchini, celery, onion, green pepper, carrots, and mushrooms. Stir in reserved tomato juice. Cover and microwave on HIGH (100% power) for 6 to 8 minutes or until vegetables are tender, stirring after every 3 minutes. Add tomatoes, Splenda, and Italian seasoning. Mix well to combine. Re-cover and microwave on MEDIUM-HIGH (70% power) for 6 minutes, stirring after 3 minutes. Place bowl on counter, uncover, and let set for 2 minutes. Mix well before serving.

Each serving equals:

HE: 2 Vegetable • 1 Optional Calorie

40 Calories • 0 gm Fat • 2 gm Protein • 8 gm Carbohydrate • 155 mg Sodium • 29 mg Calcium • 2 gm Fiber

DIABETIC EXCHANGES: 2 Vegetable

Italian Zucchini-Tomato Side Dish

It doesn't take a lot of cheese to get your family's attention, but you'll be delighted to hear their eager approval of this succulent summer treat that celebrates what is fresh and flavorful from the garden. ☺ Serves 4 (¾ cup)

2 cups chopped unpeeled zucchini
2 cups peeled and chopped fresh tomato
½ cup chopped onion
1 teaspoon Italian seasoning
1 tablespoon Splenda Granular
6 tablespoons shredded Kraft reduced-fat mozzarella cheese

In a medium microwave-safe mixing bowl, combine zucchini, tomato, and onion. Stir in Italian seasoning and Splenda. Cover and microwave on HIGH (100% power) for 10 minutes or until vegetables are tender, stirring after 5 minutes. Place bowl on counter, uncover, and let set for 2 minutes. When serving, top each with 1½ tablespoons mozzarella cheese.

Each serving equals:

HE: 2¼ Vegetable • ½ Protein • 1 Optional Calorie

70 Calories • 2 gm Fat • 5 gm Protein •
8 gm Carbohydrate • 83 mg Sodium •
108 mg Calcium • 2 gm Fiber

DIABETIC EXCHANGES: 2 Vegetable

Italian Stewed Tomatoes

It's the little details that make the difference when you invent a dish inspired by a particular nation's regional cuisine. In this case, adding bread to a warm tomato dish is common in Italy, and it certainly makes a pleasing recipe more sumptuous.

⏱ Serves 4 (½ cup)

> 1 (15-ounce) can diced tomatoes, undrained
> ½ cup finely chopped celery
> ¼ cup finely chopped onion
> 1 tablespoon Splenda Granular
> 1½ teaspoons Italian seasoning
> 2 slices reduced-calorie Italian bread, torn into pieces

In an 8-cup microwave-safe mixing bowl, combine undrained tomatoes, celery, and onion. Microwave on HIGH (100% power) for 5 minutes. Stir in Splenda and Italian seasoning. Add bread pieces. Mix gently to combine. Continue to microwave on HIGH for 3 minutes. Place bowl on counter and let set for 2 minutes. Mix gently before serving.

Each serving equals:

HE: 1¼ Vegetable • ¼ Bread • 1 Optional Calorie

48 Calories • 0 gm Fat • 2 gm Protein •
10 gm Carbohydrate • 204 mg Sodium •
33 mg Calcium • 2 gm Fiber

DIABETIC EXCHANGES: 1 Vegetable

Celery and Peas Supreme

Why do we cut veggies on the diagonal or bias? They do look attractive on the plate, but the real reason is to expose more of the vegetable to the sauce it's cooking in! More time soaking in the sauce = more flavor. ☻ Serves 4 (½ cup)

> 1¼ cups bias-cut celery
> 1 (8-ounce) can Hunt's Tomato Sauce
> 1 tablespoon Splenda Granular
> ¼ cup chopped onion
> ½ teaspoon Italian seasoning
> ⅛ teaspoon black pepper
> 2 cups frozen peas

In an 8-cup microwave-safe mixing bowl, combine celery, tomato sauce, Splenda, onion, Italian seasoning, and black pepper. Cover and microwave on HIGH (100% power) for 6 to 8 minutes or until vegetables are tender, stirring after 4 minutes. Add peas. Mix well to combine. Re-cover and continue to microwave for 4 minutes, stirring after 2 minutes. Place bowl on counter, uncover, and let set for 2 minutes. Mix well before serving.

Each serving equals:

HE: 1¾ Vegetable • 1 Bread • 1 Optional Calorie

80 Calories • 0 gm Fat • 5 gm Protein •
15 gm Carbohydrate • 430 mg Sodium •
29 mg Calcium • 4 gm Fiber

DIABETIC EXCHANGES: 1 Vegetable • 1 Starch

Cheesy Bacon Cauliflower

I doubt there's a kid or adult around who wouldn't cheer the arrival of this cheesy veggie dish! Even those who don't necessarily adore cauliflower will find this creamy, tangy version irresistible.

● Serves 6 (½ cup)

3 cups frozen cut cauliflower, thawed
2 tablespoons water
1 (10¾-ounce) can Healthy Request Cream of Mushroom Soup
2 tablespoons Oscar Mayer or Hormel Real Bacon Bits
⅛ cup shredded Kraft reduced-fat Cheddar cheese
1 teaspoon dried parsley flakes

In an 8-cup microwave-safe mixing bowl, combine cauliflower and water. Microwave on HIGH (100% power) for 5 minutes or just until cauliflower is tender. In a small bowl, combine mushroom soup, bacon bits, Cheddar cheese, and parsley flakes. Stir soup mixture into cauliflower. Microwave on HIGH for 3 minutes. Place bowl on counter and let set for 3 minutes. Mix well before serving.

Each serving equals:

HE: 1 Vegetable • ⅓ Protein • ¼ Slider •
16 Optional Calories

75 Calories • 3 gm Fat • 4 gm Protein •
8 gm Carbohydrate • 355 mg Sodium •
103 mg Calcium • 2 gm Fiber

DIABETIC EXCHANGES: 1 Vegetable • ½ Meat

Glazed Beets

You may be astonished by how special just a little glaze can make a vegetable dish taste. A glaze often gives the vegetables a delectable shimmer, making your dinner table glow just that much brighter!

◉ Serves 4 (½ cup)

> 1 (15-ounce) can sliced beets, coarsely chopped, drained and
> ½ cup liquid reserved
> ¼ cup water
> ¼ cup Splenda Granular
> 1 tablespoon cornstarch
> ¼ cup white distilled vinegar
> ⅛ teaspoon lemon pepper

In an 8-cup microwave-safe mixing bowl, combine reserved beet liquid, water, Splenda, cornstarch, vinegar, and lemon pepper. Mix well using a wire whisk. Microwave on HIGH (100% power) for 3 minutes or until mixture thickens and just starts to boil, stirring after 2 minutes. Add beets. Mix gently to combine. Cover and continue to microwave on HIGH for 4 minutes or until beets are hot, stirring after 2 minutes. Place bowl on counter, uncover, and let set for 2 minutes. Good warm or cold.

Each serving equals:

HE: 1 Vegetable • 14 Optional Calories

---

44 Calories • 0 gm Fat • 1 gm Protein •
10 gm Carbohydrate • 244 mg Sodium •
0 mg Calcium • 1 gm Fiber

DIABETIC EXCHANGES: 1 Vegetable

Onions au Gratin

Onions are always such a good value, but many people never think of serving them on their own, as the centerpiece of a dish. Yet when combined with a creamy sauce, bread crumbs, and cheese, they turn into superstars!   ☻   Serves 6

> 3 cups thinly sliced onion
> 1 tablespoon water
> 1 (12-fluid-ounce) can Carnation Evaporated Fat Free Milk
> 3 tablespoons all-purpose flour
> 1 teaspoon prepared yellow mustard
> 1 tablespoon I Can't Believe It's Not Butter! Light Margarine
> ¾ cup diced Velveeta Light processed cheese
> ⅛ teaspoon black pepper
> 15 Ritz Reduced Fat Crackers, made into crumbs

In an 8-by-8-inch microwave-safe baking dish, combine onion and water. Cover and microwave on HIGH (100% power) for 6 minutes, stirring after 3 minutes. Place baking dish on counter, uncover, and let set while preparing sauce. Meanwhile, in a covered jar, combine evaporated milk and flour. Shake well to blend. Pour milk mixture evenly over partially cooled onion. Add mustard, margarine, Velveeta cheese, and black pepper. Mix gently to combine. Microwave on HIGH for 4 minutes. Sprinkle cracker crumbs evenly over top. Lightly spray crumbs with butter-flavored cooking spray. Continue to microwave on HIGH for 3 minutes. Place baking dish on counter and let set for 2 minutes. Divide into 6 servings.

Each serving equals:

HE: 1 Vegetable • ½ Fat Free Milk • ½ Bread • ½ Protein • ¼ Fat

---

172 Calories • 4 gm Fat • 8 gm Protein • 26 gm Carbohydrate • 399 mg Sodium • 268 mg Calcium • 1 gm Fiber

---

DIABETIC EXCHANGES: 1 Vegetable • ½ Fat Free Milk • ½ Starch • ½ Meat

Oriental Pea Pods

My friend Barbara told me that in England, they call pea pods by a French name, "mange-tout"—which means "eat all." Traditional pea pods tend to be much too stringy and bitter to eat, but Asian snow peas are sweet and delicious.   ☻   Serves 6 (¾ cup)

> 6 cups fresh pea pods
> ½ cup finely chopped onion
> 1 tablespoon I Can't Believe It's Not Butter! Light Margarine
> 1 (8-ounce) can sliced water chestnuts, rinsed and drained
> 1 tablespoon reduced-sodium soy sauce
> ⅛ teaspoon black pepper

In an 8-cup microwave-safe mixing bowl, combine pea pods, onion, and margarine. Cover and microwave on HIGH (100% power) for 5 minutes or just until pea pods are tender, stirring after 3 minutes. Add water chestnuts, soy sauce, and black pepper. Mix well to combine. Re-cover and continue to microwave on HIGH for 2 minutes. Place bowl on counter, uncover, and let set for 1 minute. Mix well before serving.

HINT: Only fresh pea pods will work with this recipe. Do not use frozen!

Each serving equals:

HE: 1½ Vegetable • ¼ Fat

---

53 Calories • 1 gm Fat • 2 gm Protein •
9 gm Carbohydrate • 108 mg Sodium •
31 mg Calcium • 2 gm Fiber

DIABETIC EXCHANGES: 1½ Vegetable

Fresh Asparagus and Mushrooms

Are you one of those busy cooks who walk on by the display of fresh asparagus because you're not sure how to prepare it? Well, I hope this recipe will persuade you to stop and buy! When those beautiful stalks appear in late May or early June, go for it.

○ Serves 4 (½ cup)

2 cups chopped fresh asparagus
1 tablespoon water
2 cups sliced fresh mushrooms
2 tablespoons I Can't Believe It's Not Butter! Light Margarine
1 tablespoon lemon juice
1 teaspoon lemon pepper

In an 8-cup microwave-safe mixing bowl, combine asparagus and water. Cover and microwave on HIGH (100% power) for 6 minutes, stirring after 3 minutes. Add mushrooms, margarine, lemon juice, and lemon pepper. Mix well to combine. Re-cover and continue to microwave on HIGH for 3 minutes. Place bowl on counter, uncover, and let set for 1 minute. Mix well before serving.

Each serving equals:

HE: 2 Vegetable • ¾ Fat

51 Calories • 3 gm Fat • 2 gm Protein •
4 gm Carbohydrate • 163 mg Sodium •
18 mg Calcium • 1 gm Fiber

DIABETIC EXCHANGES: 1½ Vegetable • ½ Fat

Sunshine Carrots

Close your eyes and imagine the warmth of the sun caressing your skin. It's a beguiling feeling, isn't it? Now you can enjoy that same sensation in a sweet and succulent side dish. (If you don't have orange spreadable fruit, try apricot.) ☺ Serves 4 (½ cup)

> 3 cups thinly sliced fresh or frozen carrots, thawed
>
> 2 tablespoons Diet Mountain Dew
>
> 1 tablespoon + 1 teaspoon I Can't Believe It's Not Butter! Light Margarine
>
> 3 tablespoons orange marmalade spreadable fruit
>
> 1 tablespoon chopped fresh parsley or 1 teaspoon dried parsley flakes

In a medium microwave-safe mixing bowl, combine carrots and Diet Mountain Dew. Cover and microwave on HIGH (100% power) for 6 to 8 minutes or just until carrots are tender, stirring after every 3 minutes. Add margarine, spreadable fruit, and parsley. Mix well to combine. Re-cover and continue to microwave on HIGH for 2 minutes. Place bowl on counter, uncover, and let set for 2 minutes. Mix well before serving.

HINT: Thaw carrots by placing in a colander and rinsing under hot water for 1 minute.

Each serving equals:

HE: 1½ Vegetable • ½ Fruit • ½ Fat

102 Calories • 2 gm Fat • 1 gm Protein •
20 gm Carbohydrate • 108 mg Sodium •
37 mg Calcium • 3 gm Fiber

DIABETIC EXCHANGES: 1½ Vegetable • ½ Fruit •
½ Fat

Peachy Keen Carrots

My grandkids loved helping me taste-test this dish, and I bet your family will, too. The luscious orange color brings warmth and light to any supper plate.   ☻   Serves 4 (scant ½ cup)

> 1 (15-ounce) can cut carrots, rinsed and drained
> ¼ cup peach or apricot spreadable fruit
> 1 teaspoon dried onion flakes
> 1 teaspoon dried parsley flakes
> 2 teaspoons I Can't Believe It's Not Butter! Light Margarine

In an 8-cup microwave-safe mixing bowl, combine carrots, spreadable fruit, onion flakes, parsley flakes, and margarine. Cover and microwave on HIGH (100% power) for 4 minutes or until mixture is heated through, stirring after 2 minutes. Place bowl on counter, uncover, and let set for 2 minutes. Mix well before serving.

Each serving equals:

HE: 1 Fruit • 1 Vegetable • ¼ Fat

77 Calories • 1 gm Fat • 1 gm Protein •
16 gm Carbohydrate • 276 mg Sodium •
21 mg Calcium • 2 gm Fiber

DIABETIC EXCHANGES: 1 Fruit • 1 Vegetable

Creamy Carrot Casserole

This microwave dish is healthy, easy, and downright delectable—you can even serve it to visiting friends! I love to microwave vegetables because they don't lose their shape during cooking.

Serves 4

3¼ cups sliced carrots
¼ cup water
½ cup Kraft fat-free mayonnaise
¼ cup chopped onion
1 teaspoon prepared horseradish sauce

1 teaspoon dried parsley flakes
14 small fat-free saltine crackers, made into crumbs
6 tablespoons shredded Kraft reduced-fat Cheddar cheese

In an 8-cup microwave-safe mixing bowl, combine carrots and water. Cover and microwave on HIGH (100% power) for 10 to 12 minutes or until carrots are tender, stirring after 5 minutes. Drain if necessary. Return carrots to bowl. Add mayonnaise, onion, horseradish sauce, and parsley flakes. Mix well to combine. Spray an 8-by-8-inch microwave-safe baking dish with butter-flavored cooking spray. Spoon carrot mixture into prepared baking dish. In a small bowl, combine crushed crackers and Cheddar cheese. Sprinkle mixture evenly over carrots. Lightly spray top with butter-flavored cooking spray. Microwave on HIGH for 3 minutes. Place baking dish on counter and let set for 2 minutes. Divide into 4 servings.

HINT: A self-seal sandwich bag works great for crushing crackers.

Each serving equals:

HE: 1¾ Vegetable • ½ Bread • ½ Protein • ¼ Slider • 2 Optional Calories

135 Calories • 3 gm Fat • 5 gm Protein • 22 gm Carbohydrate • 494 mg Sodium • 101 mg Calcium • 4 gm Fiber

DIABETIC EXCHANGES: 2 Vegetable • 1 Starch • ½ Meat

Pineapple Carrot Combo

Of all the vegetables I cook—and I cook plenty of them—I think carrots go best with a sweet tropical fruit like pineapple. Maybe it's because they're sweet vegetables, maybe because they're from the same color family, or maybe just because!

● Serves 4 (1 cup)

> 3 cups frozen cut carrots, thawed
> 1 (8-ounce) can pineapple tidbits, packed in fruit juice, drained
>   and 2 tablespoons liquid reserved
> ½ cup chopped green bell pepper
> 2 tablespoons chopped green onion
> ⅛ teaspoon ground ginger

In an 8-cup microwave-safe mixing bowl, combine carrots and reserved pineapple liquid. Cover and microwave on HIGH (100% power) for 5 minutes. Stir in green pepper and green onion. Re-cover and continue to microwave on HIGH for 5 minutes or just until vegetables are tender, stirring after 3 minutes. Add pineapple tidbits and ginger. Mix well to combine. Re-cover and continue to microwave on HIGH for 1 minute. Place bowl on counter, uncover, and let set for 2 minutes. Mix well before serving.

HINTS: 1. Thaw carrots by placing in a colander and rinsing under hot water for 1 minute.
2. If you can't find tidbits, use chunk pineapple and coarsely chop.

Each serving equals:

HE: 1¾ Vegetable • ½ Fruit

---

64 Calories • 0 gm Fat • 1 gm Protein •
15 gm Carbohydrate • 71 mg Sodium •
36 mg Calcium • 1 gm Fiber

DIABETIC EXCHANGES: 1½ Vegetable • ½ Fruit

Harvest Time
Carrots and Apples

Here's a recipe for my version of a fruit-and-veggie compote, a side dish that offers a pleasing change in flavor and texture from whatever main dish you're serving. I call this "Harvest Time" but it's a great twenty-first century fact that you can get good apples year-round now. ○ Serves 4 (¾ cup)

> 3 cups thinly sliced fresh or frozen carrots, thawed
> 1 cup (2 small) cored, peeled, and coarsely chopped cooking apples
> 1 tablespoon water
> 3 tablespoons peach or apricot spreadable fruit
> 1 tablespoon + 1 teaspoon I Can't Believe It's Not Butter! Light
>   Margarine
> ¼ cup chopped walnuts
> 1 teaspoon dried parsley flakes

In an 8-cup microwave-safe mixing bowl, combine carrots, apples, and water. Add spreadable fruit, margarine, walnuts, and parsley flakes. Mix well to combine. Cover and microwave on HIGH (100% power) for 15 to 17 minutes or until carrots are tender, stirring after every 5 minutes. Place bowl on counter, uncover, and let set for 2 minutes. Mix well before serving.

HINT: Thaw carrots by placing in a colander and rinsing under hot
    water for 1 minute.

Each serving equals:

HE: 1½ Vegetable • 1 Fruit • 1 Fat • ¼ Protein

138 Calories • 6 gm Fat • 2 gm Protein •
19 gm Carbohydrate • 82 mg Sodium •
36 mg Calcium • 4 gm Fiber

DIABETIC EXCHANGES: 1½ Vegetable • 1 Fruit • 1 Fat

Fiesta Green Beans

This is such a great "pantry-pleaser," since the major ingredients come from cans and jars you keep on your shelves. Oh, sure, you'll need a bit of green pepper and onion—both of which you can pick up at a deli salad bar if you can't get to the market. So go ahead, party hearty, and turn up the music! 🌀 Serves 4 (½ cup)

> 1 (15-ounce) can diced tomatoes, drained and liquid reserved
> 1 tablespoon cornstarch
> ¼ cup chopped onion
> ¼ cup chopped green bell pepper
> 1 (15-ounce) can cut green beans, rinsed and drained
> 2 teaspoons Splenda Granular
> ⅛ teaspoon black pepper
> 2 tablespoons Oscar Mayer or Hormel Real Bacon Bits

In an 8-cup microwave-safe mixing bowl, combine reserved tomato juice and cornstarch. Mix well using a wire whisk. Stir in onion and green pepper. Microwave on HIGH (100% power) for 3 minutes, stirring after 2 minutes. Add green beans, tomatoes, Splenda, and black pepper. Mix well to combine. Continue to microwave on HIGH for 5 minutes or until mixture is heated through, stirring after 3 minutes. Stir in bacon bits. Place bowl on counter and let set for 2 minutes. Mix well before serving.

Each serving equals:

HE: 2¼ Vegetable • ¼ Slider

65 Calories • 1 gm Fat • 3 gm Protein •
11 gm Carbohydrate • 428 mg Sodium •
35 mg Calcium • 3 gm Fiber

DIABETIC EXCHANGES: 2 Vegetable

Creamy French Beans

The finished dish is so velvety and luxurious, you may be the only one who knows how fast it came together—and that its main ingredients came from a can! If your family loves rich sauces, here's one that won't wreck anyone's healthy eating plan.

Serves 4 (½ cup)

> ¼ cup Land O Lakes Fat Free Half & Half
> ¼ cup Kraft fat-free mayonnaise
> 2 teaspoons dried onion flakes
> 2 teaspoons Splenda Granular
> ½ teaspoon dried dill weed
> ⅛ teaspoon black pepper
> 2 (15-ounce) can French-style green beans, rinsed and drained

In an 8-cup microwave-safe mixing bowl, combine half & half, mayonnaise, onion flakes, Splenda, dill weed, and black pepper. Add green beans. Mix well to combine. Microwave on HIGH (100% power) for 4 minutes or until mixture is heated through, stirring after 2 minutes. Place bowl on counter and let set for 2 minutes. Mix well before serving.

Each serving equals:

HE: 2 Vegetable • ¼ Slider • 1 Optional Calorie

48 Calories • 0 gm Fat • 2 gm Protein •
10 gm Carbohydrate • 644 mg Sodium •
49 mg Calcium • 3 gm Fiber

DIABETIC EXCHANGES: 2 Vegetable

Swiss Creamed Peas

This dish is luscious with a capital L—so cheesy-creamy and fragrant when you remove it from the oven. You'll see just why I choose reduced-fat cheeses instead of fat-free versions: They melt *and* taste better! ◗ Serves 6 (scant ½ cup)

3 (¾-ounce) slices Kraft reduced-fat Swiss cheese, shredded
¼ cup Kraft fat-free mayonnaise
½ cup Land O Lakes no-fat sour cream
3 cups frozen peas, thawed
½ teaspoon dill weed

In an 8-cup microwave-safe mixing bowl, combine Swiss cheese, mayonnaise, and sour cream. Cover and microwave on HIGH (100% power) for 1 minute. Add peas and dill weed. Mix well to combine. Re-cover and continue to microwave on HIGH for 2 minutes. Place bowl on counter, uncover, and let set for 2 minutes. Mix well before serving.

HINT: Thaw peas by placing in a colander and rinsing under hot water for 1 minute.

Each serving equals:

HE: 1 Bread • ½ Protein • ¼ Slider •
7 Optional Calories

---

119 Calories • 3 gm Fat • 8 gm Protein •
15 gm Carbohydrate • 205 mg Sodium •
170 mg Calcium • 3 gm Fiber

DIABETIC EXCHANGES: 1 Starch • ½ Meat

Corn-Stuffed "Baked" Tomatoes

Whenever I see really ripe, gloriously grand tomatoes, I find myself wanting to STUFF them! This dish is festive in both color and flavor, perfect for a summer patio party. And—you can bake them without heating up the house. ☻ Serves 4

> 4 ripe, large fresh tomatoes
> 1½ cups fresh or frozen whole-kernel corn, thawed
> ¼ cup finely chopped onion
> ¼ cup finely chopped green bell pepper
> 1 tablespoon + 1 teaspoon I Can't Believe It's Not Butter!
>   Light Margarine
> 2 tablespoons Oscar Mayer or Hormel Real Bacon Bits
> 1 tablespoon Splenda Granular
> ⅛ teaspoon black pepper
> ¼ cup Kraft Reduced Fat Parmesan Style
>   Grated Topping

Cut tops off tomatoes. Cut tomatoes into quarters, being careful not to cut all the way through the bottom. Spread wedges slightly apart. Evenly arrange tomatoes in an 8-by-8-inch microwave-safe baking dish. In a medium microwave-safe mixing bowl, combine corn, onion, green pepper, margarine, bacon bits, Splenda, and black pepper. Cover and microwave on HIGH (100% power) for 3 minutes. Evenly spoon corn mixture into center of each tomato. Top each with 1 tablespoon Parmesan cheese. Cover and microwave on HIGH for 5 minutes. Place baking dish on counter, uncover, and let set for 2 minutes before serving.

HINT: Thaw corn by placing in a colander and rinsing under hot
    water for 1 minute.

Each serving equals:

HE: 1¼ Vegetable • ¾ Bread • ½ Fat • ¼ Protein •
14 Optional Calories

---

152 Calories • 4 gm Fat • 5 gm Protein •
24 gm Carbohydrate • 259 mg Sodium •
67 mg Calcium • 4 gm Fiber

DIABETIC EXCHANGES: 1 Vegetable • 1 Starch •
½ Fat • ½ Meat

Continental Corn Combo

Chives are a member in good standing of the onion family, and they bring something unique to a veggie dish like this one. (If you happen to be growing your own, feel free to substitute some fresh-cut chives instead.) A little bit of olives go a long way in flavoring this recipe. ☻ Serves 4 (½ cup)

> 2 cups frozen whole-kernel corn, thawed
> 3 tablespoons Kraft Fat Free French Dressing
> 2 tablespoons freeze-dried chopped chives
> ½ teaspoon Italian seasoning
> ¼ teaspoon dried minced garlic
> ¼ cup sliced ripe olives
> ¼ cup Kraft Reduced Fat Parmesan Style Grated Topping

In an 8-cup microwave-safe mixing bowl, combine corn, French dressing, chives, Italian seasoning, and garlic. Stir in olives. Cover and microwave on HIGH (100% power) for 5 minutes or until corn is tender, stirring after 3 minutes. Add Parmesan cheese. Mix well to combine. Re-cover and microwave on HIGH for 1 minute. Place bowl on counter, uncover, and let set for 2 minutes. Mix well before serving.

HINT: Thaw corn by placing in a colander and rinsing under hot water for 1 minute.

Each serving equals:

HE: 1 Bread • ¼ Protein • ¼ Fat •
17 Optional Calories

139 Calories • 3 gm Fat • 3 gm Protein •
25 gm Carbohydrate • 269 mg Sodium •
46 mg Calcium • 3 gm Fiber

DIABETIC EXCHANGES: 1½ Starch

Scalloped Broccoli and Corn

I've made so many scalloped side dishes in my life, and almost all of them have received applause from my husband. I knew when I created this recipe that Cliff would give it a pass, so this is for all of you broccoli-lovers out there, with my best wishes. ☺ Serves 6

3 cups frozen chopped broccoli, thawed
2 tablespoons finely chopped onion
1 tablespoon I Can't Believe It's Not Butter! Light Margarine
1 (15-ounce) can cream-style corn
2 eggs, beaten, or equivalent in egg substitute
2 tablespoons Land O Lakes Fat Free Half & Half
10 Ritz Reduced Fat Crackers, made into crumbs
½ teaspoon lemon pepper

In an 8-by-8-inch microwave-safe baking dish, combine broccoli, onion, and margarine. Cover and microwave on HIGH (100% power) for 3 minutes. Add corn, eggs, half & half, cracker crumbs, and lemon pepper. Mix well to combine. Re-cover and microwave on HIGH for 8 to 10 minutes or until center is set, turning dish after 5 minutes. Place baking dish on counter, uncover, and let set for 3 minutes. Divide into 6 servings.

HINTS: 1. Thaw broccoli by placing in a colander and rinsing under hot water for 1 minute.
2. A self-seal sandwich bag works great for crushing crackers.

Each serving equals:

HE: 1 Bread • 1 Vegetable • ⅓ Protein • ¼ Fat •
3 Optional Calories

---

148 Calories • 4 gm Fat • 6 gm Protein •
22 gm Carbohydrate • 326 mg Sodium •
47 mg Calcium • 3 gm Fiber

DIABETIC EXCHANGES: 1 Starch • 1 Vegetable • ½ Fat

Savory Potatoes

One of my favorite "magic ingredients" is nonfat dry milk powder, because it makes any dish it touches so smooth and scrumptious. Here, it helps transform some handy instant potatoes into a dreamy casserole that is sure to become a new family favorite!

❂ Serves 4 (1 cup)

⅔ cup Carnation Nonfat Dry Milk Powder
1½ cups water
1⅓ cups instant potato flakes
1 teaspoon dried onion flakes
1 teaspoon dried parsley flakes
¾ cup Dannon plain fat-free yogurt
1 egg, slightly beaten, or equivalent in egg substitute
6 tablespoons shredded Kraft reduced-fat Cheddar cheese

In an 8-cup microwave-safe mixing bowl, combine dry milk powder and water. Cover and microwave on HIGH (100% power) for 5 minutes or until mixture starts to boil. Stir in potato flakes, onion flakes, and parsley flakes. Add yogurt, egg, and Cheddar cheese. Mix well to combine. Re-cover and microwave on HIGH for 1 minute or until cheese melts. Place bowl on counter, uncover, and let set for 2 minutes. Mix well before serving.

Each serving equals:

HE: 1 Bread • ¾ Fat Free Milk • ¾ Protein

187 Calories • 3 gm Fat • 13 gm Protein •
27 gm Carbohydrate • 224 mg Sodium •
329 mg Calcium • 1 gm Fiber

DIABETIC EXCHANGES: 1 Starch • 1 Fat Free Milk •
½ Meat

Buttered Dill Potatoes

Dill is one of my favorite herbs, and I think this recipe demonstrates just why I love to sprinkle it into so many different dishes. With just a teaspoon, these piquant potatoes earn a place on your fanciest menus. ☉ Serves 6 (¾ cup)

4½ cups unpeeled, diced raw red potatoes

3 tablespoons I Can't Believe It's Not Butter! Light Margarine

1 teaspoon dried dill weed

1 tablespoon chopped fresh parsley or 1 teaspoon dried parsley flakes

¼ teaspoon black pepper

In an 8-cup microwave-safe mixing bowl, combine potatoes and margarine. Cover and microwave on HIGH (100% power) for 8 minutes or just until potatoes are tender, stirring after 4 minutes. Stir in dill weed, parsley, and black pepper. Re-cover and microwave on HIGH for 2 minutes, stirring after 1 minute. Place bowl on counter, uncover, and let set for 2 minutes. Mix well before serving.

Each serving equals:

HE: 1 Fat • ¾ Bread

107 Calories • 3 gm Fat • 2 gm Protein •
18 gm Carbohydrate • 49 mg Sodium •
8 mg Calcium • 2 gm Fiber

DIABETIC EXCHANGES: 1 Fat • 1 Starch

Cheesy Broccoli Potatoes

I wish I could tell you that this yummy dish was inspired by a kitchen accident in which a pot of broccoli-cheese soup fell into a bowl of hash browns—but it didn't, at least not in real life. In the kitchen in my mind, I thought "what if . . ." and this was the splendid result!   ☻   Serves 4 (1 cup)

> 3 cups frozen loose-packed shredded hash brown potatoes
> 1½ cups frozen chopped broccoli, thawed
> ½ cup chopped onion
> ¾ cup diced Velveeta Light processed cheese
> 1 (2.5-ounce) jar sliced mushrooms, drained
> 1 (10¾-ounce) can Healthy Request Cream of Mushroom Soup
> ⅛ teaspoon black pepper

In an 8-cup microwave-safe mixing bowl, combine potatoes, broccoli, and onion. Stir in Velveeta cheese and mushrooms. Add mushroom soup and black pepper. Mix well to combine. Cover and microwave on HIGH (100% power) for 10 minutes or just until vegetables are tender, stirring after 5 minutes. Place bowl on counter, uncover, and let set for 2 minutes. Mix well before serving.

HINTS: 1. Mr. Dell's frozen shredded potatoes are a good choice, or raw shredded potatoes, rinsed and patted dry, may be used in place of frozen potatoes.

2. Thaw broccoli by placing in a colander and rinsing under hot water for 1 minute.

Each serving equals:

HE: 1¼ Vegetable • ¾ Protein • ½ Bread •
½ Slider • 1 Optional Calorie

---

160 Calories • 4 gm Fat • 8 gm Protein •
23 gm Carbohydrate • 689 mg Sodium •
229 mg Calcium • 3 gm Fiber

DIABETIC EXCHANGES: 1 Vegetable •
1 Starch/Carbohydrate • 1 Meat

Scalloped Potatoes au Gratin

Another great reason to use your microwave to cook with (instead of just for reheating coffee!) is that sauces don't thin out—they stay thick and rich and luscious. This cheesy potato dish is certain to rise to the top of your list of cozy side dishes perfect for anytime at all. ☻ Serves 4 (¾ cup)

1 (10¾-ounce) can Healthy Request Cream of Mushroom Soup
⅓ cup Carnation Nonfat Dry Milk Powder
¼ cup water
¼ cup Land O Lakes Fat Free Half & Half
3 cups thinly sliced raw potatoes
½ cup chopped onion
1 cup diced Velveeta Light processed cheese
1 teaspoon dried parsley flakes
⅛ teaspoon black pepper

In an 8-cup microwave-safe mixing bowl, combine mushroom soup, dry milk powder, water, and half & half. Stir in potatoes, onion, and Velveeta cheese. Add parsley flakes and black pepper. Mix well to combine. Cover and microwave on HIGH (100% power) for 10 minutes, then on MEDIUM (50% power) for 15 minutes or until potatoes are tender, stirring after every 5 minutes. Place bowl on counter, uncover, and let set for 3 minutes. Mix well before serving.

Each serving equals:

HE: 1 Protein • ¾ Bread • ¼ Fat Free Milk •
¼ Vegetable • ½ Slider • 10 Optional Calories

---

213 Calories • 5 gm Fat • 11 gm Protein •
31 gm Carbohydrate • 802 mg Sodium •
323 mg Calcium • 2 gm Fiber

DIABETIC EXCHANGES: 2 Starch/Carbohydrate • 1 Meat

Potatoes and Veggies Side Dish

Potatoes just "love" this style of cooking. How can I tell? Well, they cook up faster in the microwave than by any other method besides deep-fat frying! If your goal is health and your passion is potatoes, you'll adore this cozy, colorful blend.   ☻   Serves 4 (1 cup)

> 4 cups thinly sliced raw potatoes
> 2 cups thinly sliced carrots
> 1 cup thinly sliced onion
> 1 teaspoon lemon pepper
> 1 teaspoon dried parsley flakes
> 2 tablespoons I Can't Believe It's Not Butter! Light Margarine

In an 8-cup microwave-safe mixing bowl, combine potatoes, carrots, and onion. Stir in lemon pepper and parsley flakes. Drop margarine by teaspoon over top. Cover and microwave on HIGH (100% power) for 8 minutes or until vegetables are tender, stirring after 5 minutes. Place bowl on counter, uncover, and let set for 3 minutes. Mix well before serving.

Each serving equals:

HE: 1½ Vegetable • 1 Bread • ¾ Fat

---

171 Calories • 3 gm Fat • 4 gm Protein •
32 gm Carbohydrate • 371 mg Sodium •
35 mg Calcium • 4 gm Fiber

DIABETIC EXCHANGES: 1½ Vegetable • 1½ Starch

Spinach Noodles

Make every night special when you serve up a noodle dish like this one: it's hearty and substantial but not heavy. Better still, it's just as Popeye promised—good for building strong bones and muscles no matter your age!   ☻   Serves 4 (¾ cup)

> 2 cups chopped fresh spinach leaves, stems removed and discarded
> 1 cup chopped fresh mushrooms
> 2 tablespoons I Can't Believe It's Not Butter! Light Margarine
> 2 cups cooked noodles
> ¼ cup Land O Lakes Fat Free Half & Half
> ⅛ teaspoon ground nutmeg
> ⅛ teaspoon black pepper
> ¼ cup Kraft Reduced Fat Parmesan Style Grated Topping

In an 8-cup microwave-safe mixing bowl, combine spinach, mushrooms, and margarine. Microwave on HIGH (100% power) for 3 minutes. Stir in noodles, half & half, nutmeg, and black pepper. Continue to microwave on HIGH for 2 minutes. Add Parmesan cheese. Mix well to combine. Place bowl on counter and let set for 1 minute. Mix well before serving.

HINT: Usually 1¾ cups uncooked noodles cook to about 2 cups.

Each serving equals:

HE: 1 Bread • 1 Vegetable • ¾ Fat • ¼ Protein • 10 Optional Calories

165 Calories • 5 gm Fat • 6 gm Protein • 24 gm Carbohydrate • 155 mg Sodium • 79 mg Calcium • 1 gm Fiber

DIABETIC EXCHANGES: 1½ Starch • 1 Vegetable • 1 Fat

Roman Holiday Pasta Side Dish

I wish I could promise that someone as wonderful as Gregory Peck, Audrey Hepburn's handsome co-star in the film *Roman Holiday*, would stop by for dinner if you put this pretty pasta platter on the menu. Then again, I can't be sure that you won't capture the heart of someone special after he or she takes a few bites!

☻ Serves 4 (1 cup)

> 1 (15-ounce) can diced tomatoes, undrained
> 2 tablespoons reduced-sodium ketchup
> 1 (2.5-ounce) jar sliced mushrooms, drained
> 1½ teaspoons Italian seasoning
> ⅛ teaspoon black pepper
> 1½ cups cooked rotini pasta, rinsed and drained
> ½ cup frozen peas, thawed
> ¼ cup Kraft Reduced Fat Parmesan Style Grated Topping

In an 8-cup microwave-safe mixing bowl, combine undrained tomatoes, ketchup, mushrooms, Italian seasoning, and black pepper. Cover and microwave on HIGH (100% power) for 2 minutes. Stir in rotini pasta and peas. Re-cover and microwave on HIGH for 3 minutes or until mixture is heated through. Place bowl on counter, uncover, and let set for 2 minutes. Just before serving, stir in Parmesan cheese.

HINTS: 1. Usually 1 cup uncooked rotini pasta cooks to about 1½ cups.
2. Thaw peas by placing in a colander and rinsing under hot water for 1 minute.

Each serving equals:

HE: 1¼ Vegetable • 1 Bread • ¼ Protein •
8 Optional Calories

137 Calories • 1 gm Fat • 5 gm Protein •
27 gm Carbohydrate • 312 mg Sodium •
62 mg Calcium • 3 gm Fiber

DIABETIC EXCHANGES: 1½ Starch • 1 Vegetable

Veggie Fettuccine Alfredo Side Dish

Take this most enchanting pasta dishes off your list of "no-nos" once and for all! True, the restaurant version is super high in fat and not especially heart-friendly, but I'm pleased to present you with my "live long and love it" version. Enjoy the foods you love without a drop of guilt! ◐ Serves 6 (scant 1 cup)

> 1 (16-ounce) package frozen carrot, broccoli, and cauliflower
>   blend, thawed
> ¼ cup water
> 1 (10¾-ounce) can Healthy Request Cream of Mushroom Soup
> 1 (2.5-ounce) jar sliced mushrooms, undrained
> ⅓ cup Land O Lakes Fat Free Half & Half
> ½ cup Kraft Reduced Fat Parmesan Style Grated Topping
> 1½ cups cooked fettuccine noodles
> 1 teaspoon dried parsley flakes

In an 8-cup microwave-safe mixing bowl, combine vegetable blend and water. Cover and microwave on HIGH (100% power) for 8 to 10 minutes or just until vegetables are tender, stirring after 5 minutes. Add mushroom soup, undrained mushrooms, half & half, and Parmesan cheese. Mix well to combine. Stir in fettuccine and parsley flakes. Re-cover and continue to microwave on HIGH for 5 minutes or until mixture is hot and bubbly. Place bowl on counter, uncover, and let set for 3 minutes. Mix gently before serving.

HINTS: 1. Thaw vegetable blend by placing in a colander and rins-
    ing under hot water for 1 minute.
2. Usually a full 1 cup uncooked fettuccine noodles cooks
    to about 1½ cups.

Each serving equals:

HE: 1 Vegetable • ½ Bread • ⅓ Protein • ¼ Slider • 15 Optional Calories

127 Calories • 3 gm Fat • 5 gm Protein • 20 gm Carbohydrate • 359 mg Sodium • 119 mg Calcium • 2 gm Fiber

DIABETIC EXCHANGES: 1 Vegetable • 1 Starch

Rising Sun Rice Pilaf

One-pot cooking in the microwave is a busy cook's best friend, and you'll be relaxed as never before in the kitchen when you prepare this aromatic rice dish! ☻ Serves 4 (1 cup)

> 1 tablespoon + 1 teaspoon I Can't Believe It's Not Butter! Light
>   Margarine
> 1½ cups boiling water
> 2 tablespoons reduced-sodium soy sauce
> 1 cup uncooked Minute Rice
> ¾ cup grated carrots
> ½ cup finely diced celery
> ¼ cup finely chopped green onion
> 1 (2.5-ounce) jar sliced mushrooms, drained

Place margarine in an 8-cup glass microwave-safe mixing bowl. Microwave on HIGH (100% power) for 30 seconds. Stir in water, soy sauce, and uncooked rice. Add carrots, celery, onion, and mushrooms. Mix well to combine. Cover and microwave on HIGH for 5 minutes or until rice and vegetables are tender, stirring after 3 minutes. Place bowl on counter, uncover, and let set for 2 minutes. Mix well before serving.

Each serving equals:

HE: 1 Vegetable • ¾ Bread • ½ Fat

---

122 Calories • 2 gm Fat • 3 gm Protein •
23 gm Carbohydrate • 395 mg Sodium •
23 mg Calcium • 2 gm Fiber

DIABETIC EXCHANGES: 1 Vegetable • 1 Starch • ½ Fat

Mexican Fiesta Rice

One of the tastiest partnerships you'll ever find is the "beautiful friendship" that is highlighted by mixing your favorite salsa with rice. They combine so easily and offer a splendid side dish for any South-of-the-Border supper. ☻ Serves 4 (½ cup)

> ½ cup chunky salsa (mild, medium, or hot)
> 1½ cups reduced-sodium tomato or V8 juice
> 1 tablespoon Splenda Granular
> ½ teaspoon dried minced garlic
> 1 teaspoon dried parsley flakes
> ⅛ teaspoon black pepper
> 1⅓ cups uncooked Minute Rice

In an 8-cup microwave-safe mixing bowl, combine salsa, tomato juice, Splenda, garlic, parsley flakes, and black pepper. Add uncooked rice. Mix well to combine. Cover and microwave on HIGH (100% power) for 5 minutes or until rice is tender, stirring after 3 minutes. Place bowl on counter, uncover, and let set for 2 minutes. Mix well before serving.

Each serving equals:

HE: 1 Bread • 1 Vegetable • 2 Optional Calories

---

140 Calories • 0 gm Fat • 4 gm Protein •
31 gm Carbohydrate • 403 mg Sodium •
17 mg Calcium • 2 gm Fiber

DIABETIC EXCHANGES: 1½ Starch • 1 Vegetable

Main Dishes

The microwave is a terrific choice for preparing "the main event" whenever the temperature rises. The reason is a simple one: The food gets hot but the kitchen doesn't! That's a real consideration if you have the kind of house that stays warm once it gets that way—as many older homes and apartments do. Microwaving an entrée is just smart cooking, and the ease of it can free you up for more pleasurable pursuits, like strolling in your garden while a family favorite bubbles away!

In order to get the best use out of your microwave, especially for real main-dish cooking, I recommend treating yourself to some quality microwave cooking equipment. Glass is a great choice for your 8-inch-by-8-inch baking dish, and you can even purchase handy snap-on plastic lids for your dishes so they can go from microwave to table to refrigerator and back!

If you've mostly used your microwave to reheat frozen dinners, you're in for a real treat! With just a few minutes of preparation and a list of simple ingredients, you'll look like a culinary superstar to your family, especially when you serve such delectable treats as **Grandma's Macaroni and Cheese, Pronto Pizza Steaks,** *and* **Catalina Isle Fish Fillets.** *Whether you're in the mood for* **Stroganoff Supreme** *or* **Broccoli Lasagna,** *you'll discover that your microwave is a busy cook's best friend.*

Grandma's Macaroni and Cheese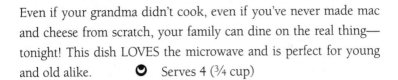

Even if your grandma didn't cook, even if you've never made mac and cheese from scratch, your family can dine on the real thing— tonight! This dish LOVES the microwave and is perfect for young and old alike.   ☻   Serves 4 (¾ cup)

⅓ cup Carnation Nonfat Dry Milk Powder
1 tablespoon all-purpose flour
⅔ cup water
2 cups diced Velveeta Light processed cheese
1½ teaspoons Worcestershire sauce
1½ teaspoons prepared yellow mustard
⅛ teaspoon black pepper
2 cups cooked elbow macaroni

In an 8-cup microwave-safe mixing bowl, combine dry milk powder, flour, and water. Mix well using a wire whisk. Stir in Velveeta cheese, Worcestershire sauce, mustard, and black pepper. Microwave on HIGH (100% power) for 2 minutes, stirring after 1 minute. Add macaroni. Mix well to combine. Continue to microwave on HIGH for 3 minutes or until mixture is heated through and cheese is melted, stirring after 2 minutes. Place bowl on counter and let set for 3 minutes. Mix well before serving.

HINT: Usually 1⅓ cups uncooked elbow macaroni cooks to about 2 cups.

Each serving equals:

HE: 2 Protein • 1 Bread • ¼ Fat Free Milk •
7 Optional Calories

246 Calories • 6 gm Fat • 17 gm Protein •
31 gm Carbohydrate • 903 mg Sodium •
409 mg Calcium • 1 gm Fiber

DIABETIC EXCHANGES: 2 Meat •
1½ Starch/Carbohydrate

Broccoli Italiano Supper

This dish might remind you of a broccoli-topped pizza, without the crust. The cheese and tomatoes definitely "sing that tune" but adding the creamy mushroom soup to the mix sends it out of this world!

● Serves 6

> 3 cups frozen cut broccoli, slightly thawed
> ½ cup chopped onion
> 2 tablespoons water
> 1 (10¾-ounce) can Healthy Request Cream of Mushroom
>   Soup
> 1 (8-ounce) can stewed tomatoes, coarsely chopped
>   and undrained
> 1 teaspoon Italian seasoning
> ½ cup + 1 tablespoon shredded Kraft reduced-fat
>   mozzarella cheese
> 3 cups hot cooked noodles, rinsed and drained
> ¼ cup Kraft Reduced Fat Parmesan Style Grated Topping

In an 8-cup microwave-safe mixing bowl, combine broccoli, onion, and water. Cover and microwave on HIGH (100% power) for 6 minutes. Stir in mushroom soup, undrained stewed tomatoes, and Italian seasoning. Add mozzarella cheese. Mix well to combine. Continue to microwave on HIGH for 5 minutes or until mixture is hot and bubbly and cheese is melted, stirring after 3 minutes. Place bowl on counter and let set for 2 minutes. Mix well before serving. For each serving, place ½ cup noodles on a plate, spoon ½ cup broccoli mixture over noodles, and top with 1 tablespoon Parmesan cheese.

HINT: Usually 2½ cups uncooked noodles cook to about 3 cups.

Each serving equals:

HE: 1½ Vegetable • 1 Bread • ⅔ Protein • ¼ Slider • 8 Optional Calories

205 Calories • 5 gm Fat • 10 gm Protein • 30 gm Carbohydrate • 427 mg Sodium • 198 mg Calcium • 3 gm Fiber

DIABETIC EXCHANGES: 1½ Starch • 1 Vegetable • ½ Meat

Garden Spaghetti

Even when the garden is covered by ten inches of snow, you NEED to keep eating your vegetables! Here's a simple solution to that desire—a cheesy-creamy pasta dishes with the flavors of spring.

Serves 4 (1½ cups)

2 cups frozen cut green beans
2 cups frozen cut carrots
½ cup chopped onion
1 (2.5-ounce) jar sliced mushrooms, undrained
1 (10¾-ounce) can Healthy Request Cream of Mushroom Soup
⅓ cup Carnation Nonfat Dry Milk Powder
½ cup water
¼ cup Kraft Reduced Fat Parmesan Style Grated Topping
1 teaspoon Italian seasoning
¾ cup shredded Kraft reduced-fat mozzarella cheese
2 cups hot cooked spaghetti, rinsed and drained

In an 8-cup microwave-safe mixing bowl, combine green beans, carrots, onion, and undrained mushrooms. Cover and microwave on HIGH (100% power) for 5 minutes, stirring after 3 minutes. In a medium bowl, combine mushroom soup, dry milk powder, and water. Stir in Parmesan cheese, Italian seasoning, and mozzarella cheese. Add soup mixture to vegetable mixture. Mix well to combine. Stir in spaghetti. Re-cover and continue to microwave on HIGH for 6 to 8 minutes, or until mixture is hot and bubbly, stirring after every 3 minutes. Place bowl on counter, uncover, and let set for 2 minutes. Mix well before serving.

HINT: Usually 1½ cups broken uncooked spaghetti cooks to about 2 cups.

Each serving equals:

HE: 2½ Vegetable • 1¼ Protein • 1 Bread •
¼ Fat Free Milk • ½ Slider • 1 Optional Calorie

275 Calories • 7 gm Fat • 15 gm Protein •
38 gm Carbohydrate • 609 mg Sodium •
365 mg Calcium • 6 gm Fiber

DIABETIC EXCHANGES: 2½ Vegetable • 1½ Starch •
1 Meat

Spaghetti-Stuffed Peppers

In the mood for stuffed peppers, but a glance at your pantry or cabinet shelf shows you no rice to be found? Well, who says you have to pack your peppers with the usual? I felt like a real "Mother of Invention" when I decided to use up some cooked spaghetti in this tangy, tasty, and innovative dish! ● Serves 4

> 4 (large-sized) green bell peppers
> 1 (8-ounce) can Hunt's Tomato Sauce
> ¼ cup Kraft Reduced Fat Parmesan Style Grated
>   Topping
> ½ teaspoon Italian seasoning
> 2 teaspoons dried onion flakes
> 1 teaspoon Splenda Granular
> 2 cups cooked spaghetti, rinsed and drained
> ¾ cup shredded Kraft reduced-fat mozzarella cheese ☆

Cut a thin slice from stem end of each green pepper. Remove seeds and membrane. Rinse peppers. Place peppers in an 8-by-8-inch microwave-safe baking dish. Cover and microwave on HIGH (100% power) for 3 minutes. Place baking dish on counter, uncover, and let peppers set while preparing filling. In a large bowl, combine tomato sauce, Parmesan cheese, Italian seasoning, onion flakes, and Splenda. Stir in spaghetti and ½ cup mozzarella cheese. Evenly spoon about ⅔ cup spaghetti mixture into each green pepper. Continue to microwave on HIGH for 6 minutes, turning dish after every 2 minutes. Place baking dish on counter and sprinkle 1 tablespoon mozzarella cheese over top of each. Let set 2 minutes before serving.

HINT: Usually 1½ cups broken uncooked spaghetti cooks to about 2 cups.

Each serving equals:

HE: 2 Vegetable • 1¼ Protein • 1 Bread

229 Calories • 5 gm Fat • 12 gm Protein •
34 gm Carbohydrate • 548 mg Sodium •
213 mg Calcium • 5 gm Fiber

DIABETIC EXCHANGES: 2 Vegetable • 1½ Starch •
1 Protein

Broccoli Lasagna

Perfecting a recipe for a satisfying veggie lasagna has been one of my goals recently, and I think this one does an amazing job of blending lots of luscious ingredients into an entrée that truly satisfies both tummy and taste buds! The aroma of the cheeses joining hands and bubbling away is irresistible. ☻ Serves 6

> 3 cups chopped fresh broccoli
> 1 cup chopped onion
> 1½ cups fat-free cottage cheese
> 1 egg, slightly beaten, or equivalent in egg substitute
> 1 (8-ounce) can Hunt's Tomato Sauce
> 1 (15-ounce) can diced tomatoes, drained
> 1 teaspoon Italian seasoning
> 1 tablespoon Splenda Granular
> 3 cups cooked mini lasagna noodles, rinsed and drained ☆
> ¾ cup shredded Kraft reduced-fat Cheddar cheese ☆
> ¾ cup shredded Kraft reduced-fat mozzarella cheese ☆

In an 8-cup microwave-safe mixing bowl, combine broccoli and onion. Cover and microwave on HIGH (100% power) for 10 minutes or just until broccoli is tender. Drain, if necessary, and return to bowl. Stir in cottage cheese and egg. In a medium bowl, combine tomato sauce, tomatoes, Italian seasoning, and Splenda. Evenly spoon 1 cup sauce mixture into an 8-by-12-inch microwave-safe baking dish. Spoon 1½ cups noodles over sauce. Evenly spoon broccoli mixture over noodles. Sprinkle ½ cup Cheddar cheese and ½ cup mozzarella cheese over broccoli mixture. Layer remaining 1½ cups noodles over cheese and spoon remaining tomato sauce mixture over noodles. Cover and microwave on HIGH for 12 minutes, turning dish after 6 minutes. Sprinkle remaining ¼ cup Cheddar cheese and ¼ cup mozzarella cheese over top. Continue to microwave, uncovered, on HIGH for

2 to 3 minutes or until cheeses are melted. Place baking dish on counter and let set for 5 minutes. Divide into 6 servings.

HINT: Usually 2½ cups uncooked mini lasagna noodles cook to about 3 cups.

Each serving equals:

HE: 2½ Vegetable • 2 Protein • 1 Bread •
1 Optional Calorie

---

295 Calories • 7 gm Fat • 22 gm Protein •
36 gm Carbohydrate • 764 mg Sodium •
287 mg Calcium • 5 gm Fiber

DIABETIC EXCHANGES: 2 Vegetable • 2 Meat •
1½ Starch/Carbohydrate

Cheesy Pizza Potatoes

If you're a potato lover who's fantasized even for a minute about a "hash browns pizza," this is your lucky day! Imagine, all those flavors you adore, combined with your best-loved potatoes. This makes a terrific Sunday supper dish on a brisk February night, but anytime is the right time if you love it.

○ Serves 4 (¾ cup)

1 (8-ounce) can Hunt's Tomato Sauce
¼ cup water
2 teaspoons pizza or Italian seasoning
1 teaspoon Splenda Granular
4½ cups frozen loose-packed shredded hash brown potatoes, thawed
1 (4-ounce) can sliced mushrooms, drained and finely chopped
¼ cup sliced ripe olives
¾ cup shredded Kraft reduced-fat Cheddar cheese
¾ cup shredded Kraft reduced-fat mozzarella cheese

In an 8-cup microwave-safe mixing bowl, combine tomato sauce, water, pizza seasoning, and Splenda. Stir in potatoes, mushrooms, and olives. Cover and microwave on HIGH (100% power) for 10 minutes, stirring after 5 minutes. Stir in Cheddar cheese and mozzarella cheese. Continue to microwave on HIGH for 5 minutes or until mixture is bubbly and cheeses are melted, stirring after 3 minutes. Place bowl on counter and let set for 5 minutes. Mix well before serving.

HINT: Mr. Dell's frozen shredded potatoes are a good choice or raw shredded potatoes, rinsed and patted dry, may be used in place of frozen potatoes.

Each serving equals:

HE: 2 Protein • 1½ Vegetable • ¾ Bread • ¼ Fat •
1 Optional Calorie

225 Calories • 9 gm Fat • 15 gm Protein •
21 gm Carbohydrate • 623 mg Sodium •
361 mg Calcium • 3 gm Fiber

DIABETIC EXCHANGES: 1½ Meat • 1 Vegetable •
1 Starch

Salmon Scallop

There are so many healthy nutrients in salmon, but many cooks can't figure out what to do with the canned kind besides using it in a salad. Here, the eggs and milk blossom in the microwave's heat and rise, rise, rise—not unlike a soufflé. Served with a green salad, it's a pretty and pleasurable lunch. ☻ Serves 6

> 1 (14¾-ounce) can pink salmon, packed in water, drained, boned, and flaked
> ¾ cup dried fine bread crumbs
> ¾ cup finely chopped celery
> ⅔ cup Carnation Nonfat Dry Milk Powder
> ¾ cup water
> 2 eggs, beaten, or equivalent in egg substitute
> 2 teaspoons lemon juice

Spray an 8-by-8-inch microwave-safe baking dish with butter-flavored cooking spray. In a large bowl, combine salmon, bread crumbs, and celery. In a small bowl, combine dry milk powder and water. Add eggs and lemon juice. Mix well to combine. Stir milk mixture into salmon mixture. Pat mixture into prepared baking dish. Microwave on HIGH (100% power) for 6 to 8 minutes or until mixture is set in center. Place baking dish on counter and let set for 5 minutes. Cut into 6 servings.

Each serving equals:

HE: 2⅓ Protein • ⅔ Bread • ⅓ Fat Free Milk • ¼ Vegetable

---

160 Calories • 4 gm Fat • 17 gm Protein •
14 gm Carbohydrate • 601 mg Sodium •
208 mg Calcium • 1 gm Fiber

DIABETIC EXCHANGES: 2½ Meat • 1 Starch

Catalina Isle Fish Fillets

There's almost nothing easier than preparing fish in your microwave. It bakes up beautifully moist, and the crumb topping in this recipe adds to the pleasing texture and taste. Add a bright and tangy sauce, and you're ready to set sail! ☕ Serves 4

> *¼ cup Kraft Fat Free Catalina Dressing*
> *10 Ritz Reduced Fat Crackers, made into fine crumbs*
> *16 ounces white fish, cut into 4 pieces*
> *1 tablespoon + 1 teaspoon chopped fresh parsley*

Spray an 8-by-8-inch microwave-safe baking dish with butter-flavored cooking spray. Place Catalina dressing and cracker crumbs in separate saucers. Dip fish pieces, first in dressing, then in cracker crumbs. Evenly arrange coated fish pieces in prepared baking dish. Drizzle any remaining dressing or crumbs evenly over top. Microwave on HIGH (100% power) for 6 to 8 minutes or until fish flakes easily, turning fish over after 3 minutes. Place baking dish on counter and let set for 2 minutes. When serving, sprinkle 1 teaspoon fresh parsley over top of each.

HINT: A self-seal sandwich bag works great for crushing crackers.

Each serving equals:

HE: 2¼ Protein • ½ Bread • 17 Optional Calories

---

156 Calories • 4 gm Fat • 21 gm Protein •
9 gm Carbohydrate • 294 mg Sodium •
45 mg Calcium • 0 gm Fiber

DIABETIC EXCHANGES: 3 Meat • ½ Starch

Mushroom Lemon Fish

This was inspired by a wonderful fish dish that I tasted while I was traveling the country on a book tour. What makes all the difference? Fresh mushrooms, and just enough lemon pepper to enchant your taste buds. ☻ Serves 4

16 ounces frozen fish fillets, thawed, cut into 4 pieces
2 tablespoons I Can't Believe It's Not Butter! Light Margarine
1 cup sliced fresh mushrooms
2 tablespoons sliced green onion
⅓ cup Carnation Nonfat Dry Milk Powder
½ cup water
1 tablespoon all-purpose flour
1 teaspoon lemon pepper
1 teaspoon dried parsley flakes

Spray an 8-by-8-inch microwave-safe baking dish with butter-flavored cooking spray. Evenly arrange fish pieces in prepared baking dish. In an 8-cup microwave-safe mixing bowl, combine margarine, mushrooms, and onion. Microwave on HIGH (100% power) for 4 minutes or until onion is partially cooked. In a small bowl, combine dry milk powder and water. Add flour, lemon pepper, and parsley flakes. Mix well to combine. Stir milk mixture into mushroom mixture. Cover and continue to microwave on HIGH for 6 to 8 minutes or until mixture bubbles, stirring after every 3 minutes. Spoon sauce mixture evenly over fillets. Cover and microwave on HIGH for 8 to 10 minutes or until fish flakes easily. Place baking dish on counter, uncover, and let set for 3 minutes. When serving, evenly spoon sauce mixture over fish pieces.

Each serving equals:

HE: 2¼ Protein • ¾ Fat • ½ Vegetable • ¼ Fat Free Milk • 8 Optional Calories

132 Calories • 4 gm Fat • 19 gm Protein • 5 gm Carbohydrate • 285 mg Sodium • 111 mg Calcium • 0 gm Fiber

DIABETIC EXCHANGES: 3 Meat • 1 Fat • ½ Vegetable

Abie's Tuna Noodle Casserole

Did you know you could freeze your tuna noodle casserole and lose none of its beguiling charms when it's reheated later on? You can! You might want to divide what's left over into individual portions so you never have to warm more than you need. (That makes my grandson Abie happy when he comes to visit!)

● Serves 4 (1 scant cup)

¼ cup finely chopped onion
¾ cup finely chopped celery
1 (2-ounce) jar diced pimiento, undrained
1 (10¾-ounce) can Healthy Request Cream of Mushroom Soup
½ cup Kraft fat-free mayonnaise

1 teaspoon dried parsley flakes
⅛ teaspoon black pepper
1 (6-ounce) can white tuna, packed in water, drained and flaked
2 cups cooked noodles, rinsed and drained

In an 8-cup microwave-safe mixing bowl, combine onion, celery, and undrained pimiento. Microwave on HIGH (100% power) for 5 minutes. Stir in mushroom soup, mayonnaise, parsley flakes, and black pepper. Add tuna and noodles. Mix well to combine. Continue to microwave on HIGH for 5 minutes. Place bowl on counter and let set for 5 minutes. Mix well before serving.

HINT: Usually 1¾ cups uncooked noodles cooks to about 2 cups.

Each serving equals:

HE: 1 Bread • 1 Protein • ½ Vegetable • ¾ Slider • 1 Optional Calorie

225 Calories • 5 gm Fat • 15 gm Protein • 30 gm Carbohydrate • 622 mg Sodium • 91 mg Calcium • 2 gm Fiber

DIABETIC EXCHANGES: 1½ Starch • 1½ Meat • ½ Vegetable

"Hooked" on Tuna Casserole

Tuna was always a good value when it came to crafting thrifty meals, but over time, many tuna fans have wearied of the same old tuna casseroles their moms used to make. So for you, here's a fun new version to get "hooked" on, complete with colorful carrots and luscious creamed corn.   ☕   Serves 6

1 cup grated carrots
1 cup finely chopped celery
¼ cup finely chopped onion
2 (6-ounce) cans white tuna, packed in water,
     drained and flaked
⅔ cup uncooked Minute Rice
1 (8-ounce) can cream-style corn
¼ cup Land O Lakes Fat Free Half & Half
2 tablespoons Land O Lakes no-fat sour cream
1 teaspoon dried parsley flakes
14 small fat-free saltine crackers, made into crumbs

Spray an 8-by-8-inch microwave-safe baking dish with butter-flavored cooking spray. In a large bowl, combine carrots, celery, onion, and tuna. Stir in uncooked rice, corn, half & half, sour cream, and parsley flakes. Spread mixture into prepared baking dish. Cover and microwave on HIGH (100% power) for 10 minutes, stirring after 5 minutes. Evenly sprinkle cracker crumbs over top. Lightly spray top with butter-flavored cooking spray. Continue to microwave on HIGH for 2 minutes. Place baking dish on counter and let set for 3 minutes. Divide into 6 servings.

HINT: A self-seal sandwich bag works great for crushing crackers.

Each serving equals:

HE: 1½ Protein • 1 Bread • ¾ Vegetable •
11 Optional Calories

174 Calories • 2 gm Fat • 14 gm Protein •
25 gm Carbohydrate • 421 mg Sodium •
43 mg Calcium • 2 gm Fiber

DIABETIC EXCHANGES: 2 Protein • 1 Starch •
1 Vegetable

Impossible Tuna Cheese Pie

There's a long tradition of "impossible"-themed baked entrees that start out in liquid form and seem unlikely to end up edible—but they do! You'll be delightfully surprised by how well this dish sets up, and maybe you'll decide to reevaluate other things in your life that seem impossible but might not be. ☻ Serves 6

1 cup chopped celery

½ cup chopped onion

1½ cups shredded Kraft reduced-fat Cheddar cheese ☆

1 (6-ounce) can white tuna, packed in water,
    drained and flaked

1 (12-fluid-ounce) can Carnation Evaporated
    Fat Free Milk

3 eggs or equivalent in egg substitute

½ cup + 1 tablespoon Bisquick Reduced Fat Baking Mix

1 teaspoon dried onion flakes

1 teaspoon dried parsley flakes

¼ teaspoon paprika

Spray a 10-inch microwave-safe deep dish pie plate with butter-flavored cooking spray. In prepared pie plate, combine celery and onion. Cover and microwave on HIGH (100% power) for 3 minutes. Evenly sprinkle 1 cup Cheddar cheese and tuna over vegetables. Sprinkle remaining ½ cup Cheddar cheese over tuna. In a blender container, combine evaporated milk, eggs, baking mix, onion flakes, and parsley flakes. Cover and process on BLEND for 30 seconds or until mixture is smooth. Pour mixture evenly over cheese. Evenly sprinkle paprika over top. Continue to microwave on MEDIUM-HIGH (70% power) for 14 to 16 minutes or until center springs back when lightly touched. Place pie plate on counter and let set for 5 minutes. Cut into 6 servings.

Each serving equals:

HE: 2½ Protein • ½ Fat Free Milk • ½ Bread •
½ Vegetable

236 Calories • 8 gm Fat • 22 gm Protein •
19 gm Carbohydrate • 506 mg Sodium •
387 mg Calcium • 1 gm Fiber

DIABETIC EXCHANGES: 2½ Meat •
1 Starch/Carbohydrate • ½ Fat Free Milk

Tuna and More Casserole

Here's a veggie-stuffed concoction that fairly bursts with tastes and textures you'll love! It's important to thaw and drain the frozen vegetables, even patting them with paper towels so you don't end up with a soggy dinner. Instead of a traditional topping like crackers, I've opted for crisp-and-crunchy noodles—enjoy!

● Serves 6 (1 cup)

> *1½ cups frozen peas, thawed*
> *1½ cups frozen sliced carrots, thawed*
> *1½ cups frozen chopped cauliflower, thawed*
> *½ cup chopped onion*
> *1 tablespoon Land O Lakes Fat Free Half & Half*
> *1 (10¾-ounce) can Healthy Request Cream of Mushroom Soup*
> *¾ cup diced Velveeta Light processed cheese*
> *1 (6-ounce) can white tuna, packed in water, drained and flaked*
> *1 (4-ounce) can sliced mushrooms, drained*
> *⅛ teaspoon black pepper*
> *¾ cup coarsely broken chow mein noodles*

In an 8-cup microwave-safe mixing bowl, combine peas, carrots, cauliflower, onion, and half & half. Cover and microwave on HIGH (100% power) for 2 minutes. Stir in mushroom soup and Velveeta cheese. Add tuna, mushrooms, and black pepper. Mix well to combine. Re-cover and continue to microwave on HIGH for 10 to 12 minutes or until vegetables are tender and mixture is heated through, stirring after every 5 minutes. Place bowl on counter, uncover, and stir in chow mein noodles. Let set for 2 minutes. Mix well before serving.

HINT: Thaw vegetables by placing in a colander and rinsing under hot water for 1 minute.

Each serving equals:

HE: 1½ Vegetable • 1¼ Protein • ¾ Bread •
¼ Slider • 9 Optional Calories

194 Calories • 6 gm Fat • 14 gm Protein •
21 gm Carbohydrate • 617 mg Sodium •
161 mg Calcium • 3 gm Fiber

DIABETIC EXCHANGES: 2 Meat • 1½ Vegetable •
1 Starch

Tuna Patties with Cucumber Sauce

Cucumber has such a delicate flavor, you might never have considered using it as the centerpiece of a sauce . . . until now. Combined with other spices, it provides a splendid contrast to the baked tuna patties. This would make a pretty, light lunch or relaxed weekend supper.   ◐   Serves 6

½ cup Land O Lakes no-fat sour cream
¾ cup peeled and finely chopped cucumber
2 teaspoons dried onion flakes
½ teaspoon dried dill weed
2 (6-ounce) cans white tuna, packed in water,
    drained and flaked
3 slices reduced-calorie white bread, made into
    fine crumbs
1 egg, slightly beaten, or equivalent in egg substitute
2 tablespoons Kraft fat-free mayonnaise
¼ cup Land O Lakes Fat Free Half & Half
1 teaspoon Worcestershire sauce
1 teaspoon lemon juice

In a small bowl, combine sour cream, cucumber, onion flakes, and dill weed. Refrigerate while preparing patties. In a large bowl, combine tuna, bread crumbs, egg, mayonnaise, half & half, Worcestershire sauce, and lemon juice. Mix well to combine. Using a ½ cup measuring cup as a guide, form into 6 patties. Evenly arrange patties on a large microwave-safe plate. Cover and microwave on HIGH (100% power) for 5 minutes or until center is set, turning dish after 3 minutes. Place plate on counter, uncover, and let set for 2 minutes. When serving, top each patty with full 2 tablespoons cucumber sauce.

Each serving equals:

HE: 1½ Protein • ¼ Bread • ¼ Vegetable • ¼ Slider • 10 Optional Calories

127 Calories • 3 gm Fat • 15 gm Protein • 10 gm Carbohydrate • 343 mg Sodium • 64 mg Calcium • 0 gm Fiber

DIABETIC EXCHANGES: 2 Meat • ½ Starch/Carbohydrate

Uptown Chicken Bake

Can't decide between beef and chicken for dinner? You don't have to! Mae West was once quoted as saying "Too much of a good thing can be wonderful," and I think she's right—especially when it comes to a protein-rich recipe like this one. ☻ Serves 4

> 16 ounces skinned and boned uncooked chicken breast, cut into 4 pieces
>
> 1 (2.5-ounce) package sliced Carl Buddig 90% lean beef
>
> 2 cups sliced fresh mushrooms
>
> 1 (10¾-ounce) can Healthy Request Cream of Mushroom Soup
>
> 2 tablespoons Land O Lakes no-fat sour cream
>
> 2 tablespoons slivered almonds
>
> 2 cups hot cooked noodles, rinsed and drained

Spray an 8-by-8-inch microwave-safe baking dish with butter-flavored cooking spray. Place chicken pieces between waxed paper and flatten with a meat mallet or by rolling a soup can over chicken. Place ¼ of beef slices on each chicken piece. Roll up chicken and secure with a wooden toothpick. Evenly arrange chicken pieces in prepared baking dish. Microwave on HIGH (100% power) for 5 minutes. In a medium bowl, combine mushrooms, mushroom soup, sour cream, and almonds. Spoon soup mixture evenly over partially cooked chicken pieces. Cover and continue to microwave on HIGH for 5 minutes or until chicken is cooked through. Place baking dish on counter, uncover, and let set for 2 minutes. For each serving, place ½ cup noodles on a plate, arrange 1 piece chicken breast over noodles, and evenly spoon mushroom sauce over top.

HINTS: 1. Usually 1¾ cups uncooked noodles cooks to about 2 cups.

2. Don't forget to remove toothpicks before serving.

Each serving equals:

HE: 3¾ Protein • 1 Bread • 1 Vegetable • ¼ Fat •
½ Slider • 8 Optional Calories

316 Calories • 8 gm Fat • 32 gm Protein •
29 gm Carbohydrate • 620 mg Sodium •
107 mg Calcium • 1 gm Fiber

DIABETIC EXCHANGES: 3½ Meat • 1½ Starch •
1 Vegetable

Sunday Best Chicken

You don't have to dress for dinner, unless you're in the mood for a little more glamour than usual. But if you're looking for a sumptuous weekend meal that tastes and looks spectacular, this gets my vote. Even if you're not celebrating an occasion, you still deserve "the best." ☻ Serves 4

½ cup finely chopped onion

1 cup finely chopped celery

1 (2-ounce) jar chopped pimiento, undrained

1 (10¾-ounce) can Healthy Request Cream of Chicken Soup

¼ cup Land O Lakes no-fat sour cream

1 teaspoon dried parsley flakes

⅛ teaspoon black pepper

16 ounces skinned and boned uncooked chicken breast, cut into 4 pieces

In a medium microwave-safe mixing bowl, combine onion, celery, and undrained pimiento. Cover and microwave on HIGH (100% power) for 5 minutes. Stir in chicken soup, sour cream, parsley flakes, and black pepper. Evenly arrange chicken pieces in an 8-by-8-inch microwave-safe baking dish. Spoon chicken soup mixture evenly over chicken pieces. Cover and microwave on HIGH for 5 minutes. Turn dish and continue to microwave on HIGH for 10 to 14 minutes or until chicken is cooked through. Place baking dish on counter, uncover, and let set for 3 minutes. When serving, place 1 piece chicken on a plate and evenly spoon sauce mixture over top.

Each serving equals:

HE: 3 Protein • ¾ Vegetable • ¾ Slider

204 Calories • 4 gm Fat • 29 gm Protein •
13 gm Carbohydrate • 381 mg Sodium •
59 mg Calcium • 1 gm Fiber

DIABETIC EXCHANGES: 3 Meat • 1 Vegetable •
½ Other Carbohydrate

Grande Potatoes and Chicken

This scrumptious chicken casserole sparkles with just enough fiesta flavor to soothe the hunger in your belly—and light a fire in your soul! Served alongside a crunchy salad, it's an ideal meal for a busy family. ◐ Serves 6

1¾ cups water
¼ cup finely chopped onion
1⅓ cups instant potato flakes
¼ cup Land O Lakes no-fat sour cream
1 (8-ounce) can whole-kernel corn, rinsed and drained
1½ cups diced cooked chicken breast
1 (10¾-ounce) can Healthy Request Cream of Chicken Soup
½ cup chunky salsa (mild, medium, or hot)
1 teaspoon dried parsley flakes
⅛ teaspoon black pepper
¾ cup shredded Kraft reduced-fat Cheddar cheese

Spray an 8-by-12-inch microwave-safe baking dish with butter-flavored cooking spray. In an 8-cup microwave-safe mixing bowl, combine water and onion. Microwave on HIGH (100% power) for 2 minutes. Stir in potato flakes. Add sour cream and corn. Mix well to combine. Fold in chicken. Spread mixture evenly into prepared baking dish. In a medium bowl, combine chicken soup, salsa, parsley flakes, and black pepper. Spread soup mixture evenly over potato mixture. Microwave on HIGH for 4 minutes. Evenly sprinkle Cheddar cheese over top. Continue to microwave on HIGH for 2 to 3 minutes or until cheese melts. Place baking dish on counter and let set for 2 minutes. Divide into 6 servings.

HINT: If you don't have leftovers, purchase a chunk of cooked chicken breast from your local deli.

Each serving equals:

HE: 2 Protein • 1 Bread • ¼ Vegetable • ¼ Slider • 10 Optional Calories

221 Calories • 5 gm Fat • 19 gm Protein • 25 gm Carbohydrate • 611 mg Sodium • 127 mg Calcium • 2 gm Fiber

DIABETIC EXCHANGES: 2 Meat • 1½ Starch

Green Bean and Chicken Bake

Talk about cozy comfort food that's ready in just minutes—this casserole is easy to fix and downright delectable! This will appeal to anyone on a busy schedule, from young people in their first apartments to lifelong cooks who don't want to spend a lot of time in the kitchen anymore.   ☻   Serves 4

> 2 cups frozen cut green beans, thawed
> 1 tablespoon water
> 1 cup cubed Velveeta Light processed cheese
> 1 cup diced cooked chicken breast
> 1 teaspoon dried onion flakes
> 1 (10¾-ounce) can Healthy Request Cream of Chicken
>   Soup
> 10 Ritz Reduced Fat Crackers, made into crumbs

Evenly arrange green beans in an 8-by-8-inch microwave-safe baking dish. Drizzle water over top. Cover and microwave on HIGH (100% power) for 5 to 7 minutes or just until green beans are tender. Drain and return green beans to baking dish. Evenly sprinkle Velveeta cheese and chicken over green beans. Stir onion flakes into chicken soup. Spoon soup mixture evenly over chicken. Sprinkle cracker crumbs evenly over top. Lightly spray top with butter-flavored cooking spray. Microwave, uncovered, on HIGH for 5 minutes or until mixture is heated through. Place baking dish on counter and let set for 3 minutes. Divide into 4 servings.

HINTS: 1. Thaw green beans by placing in a colander and rinsing under hot water for 1 minute.

2. If you don't have leftovers, purchase a chunk of cooked chicken breast from your local deli.

Each serving equals:

HE: 2¼ Protein • 1 Vegetable • ½ Bread • ½ Slider • 5 Optional Calories

214 Calories • 6 gm Fat • 20 gm Protein • 20 gm Carbohydrate • 801 mg Sodium • 218 mg Calcium • 2 gm Fiber

DIABETIC EXCHANGES: 2 Meat • 1 Vegetable • 1 Starch/Carbohydrate

Speedy Chicken and Dumplings

Sure, you could spend all day Sunday making chicken and dumplings the old-fashioned way, and it would be delicious, I'm sure. But if you've got lots to do—why not try my "fast and fabulous" version? ☻   Serves 6 (1 cup)

> 1 tablespoon I Can't Believe It's Not Butter! Light Margarine
> ¾ cup finely chopped onion
> 1 (10¾-ounce) can Healthy Request Cream of Chicken Soup
> ½ cup Land O Lakes Fat Free Half & Half
> 2 full cups chopped cooked chicken breast
> ¾ cup frozen peas
> 1 teaspoon dried parsley flakes
> 1 (7.5-ounce) can Pillsbury refrigerated buttermilk biscuits

In an 8-cup microwave-safe mixing bowl, combine margarine and onion. Cover and microwave on HIGH (100% power) for 3 minutes. Stir in chicken soup, half & half, and chicken. Re-cover and continue to microwave on HIGH for 5 minutes, stirring after 3 minutes. Stir in peas and parsley flakes. Separate biscuits and cut each into 4 pieces. Add biscuit pieces to hot chicken mixture. Mix gently to combine. Re-cover and continue to microwave on HIGH for 6 minutes, stirring after every 3 minutes. Place covered bowl on counter and let set for 5 minutes. Mix gently before serving.

HINT: If you don't have leftovers, purchase a chunk of cooked chicken breast from your local deli.

Each serving equals:

HE: 2 Protein • 1½ Bread • ¼ Fat • ¼ Vegetable • ½ Slider • 1 Optional Calorie

249 Calories • 5 gm Fat • 23 gm Protein • 28 gm Carbohydrate • 541 mg Sodium • 42 mg Calcium • 1 gm Fiber

DIABETIC EXCHANGES: 2 Meat • 2 Starch/Carbohydrate

Creamy Chicken and Rice

We've got so many choices in the frozen vegetable aisle now, it's possible to make this dish with whatever combination sounds exciting on a given day. I tested this with the classic stir-fry veggies, but variety keeps life interesting. ☻ Serves 4 (1 cup)

1 (10¾-ounce) can Healthy Request Cream of Chicken Soup
½ cup fat-free milk
⅛ teaspoon black pepper
⅔ cup uncooked Minute Rice
2 cups diced cooked chicken breast
2 cups purchased stir-fry vegetables (fresh or frozen, thawed)

In an 8-cup microwave-safe mixing bowl, combine chicken soup, milk, and black pepper. Stir in uncooked rice. Add chicken and vegetables. Mix well to combine. Cover and microwave on HIGH (100% power) for 10 to 12 minutes or until rice and vegetables are tender, stirring after every 5 minutes. Place bowl on counter, uncover, and let set for 5 minutes. Mix well before serving.

HINTS: 1. If you don't have leftovers, purchase a chunk of cooked chicken breast from your local deli.
2. Thaw frozen vegetables by placing in a colander and rinsing under hot water for 1 minute.

Each serving equals:

HE: 2½ Protein • 1 Vegetable • ½ Bread • ½ Slider • 16 Optional Calories

268 Calories • 4 gm Fat • 28 gm Protein • 30 gm Carbohydrate • 664 mg Sodium • 99 mg Calcium • 3 gm Fiber

DIABETIC EXCHANGES: 2½ Meat • 1½ Starch/Carbohydrate • 1 Vegetable

Chicken ala King Supreme

You don't need to call the Supreme Court to get a verdict on this updated version of a traditional delight—just ask your family and friends! Its silken splendor turns an occasion for serving leftovers into a flavorful feast. ☺ Serves 4 (1 cup)

1 (10¾-ounce) can Healthy Request Cream of Chicken Soup
⅓ cup Carnation Nonfat Dry Milk Powder
½ cup water
¼ cup Land O Lakes Fat Free Half & Half
2 cups diced cooked chicken breast
1 (2.5-ounce) jar sliced mushrooms, finely chopped and drained
1 (2-ounce) jar sliced pimiento, drained
½ cup frozen peas, thawed
1 teaspoon dried onion flakes
1 teaspoon dried parsley flakes
⅛ teaspoon black pepper
1 hard-boiled egg, chopped

In an 8-cup microwave-safe mixing bowl, combine chicken soup, dry milk powder, water, and half & half. Stir in chicken, mushrooms, and pimiento. Add peas, onion flakes, parsley flakes, and black pepper. Mix well to combine. Cover and microwave on HIGH (100% power) for 5 minutes. Place bowl on counter and let set for 3 minutes. Stir in chopped egg. Serve at once.

HINTS: 1. If you don't have leftovers, purchase a chunk of cooked chicken breast from your local deli.
2. Thaw peas by placing in a colander and rinsing under hot water for 1 minute.
3. Good served over potatoes, rice, pasta, toast or English muffins.

Each serving equals:

HE: 2¾ Protein • ¼ Fat Free Milk • ¼ Bread •
¼ Vegetable • ½ Slider • 14 Optional Calories

---

221 Calories • 5 gm Fat • 28 gm Protein •
16 gm Carbohydrate • 473 mg Sodium •
115 mg Calcium • 1 gm Fiber

DIABETIC EXCHANGES: 3 Meat • 1 Starch/Carbohydrate

Chicken Stew Pot Pie

I remember when jars of fat-free gravy first appeared on store shelves. I looked at them in wonder, then grabbed an armful to start creating recipes! I think it makes all the difference in this happily homemade recipe for a comfy family meal. ☻ Serves 6

1 cup finely chopped celery
1½ cups frozen sliced carrots, thawed
½ cup chopped onion
1 (12-ounce) jar Heinz Fat Free Chicken Gravy ☆
2 full cups diced cooked chicken breast
½ cup frozen peas, thawed
⅛ teaspoon black pepper
1 (7.5-ounce) can Pillsbury refrigerated buttermilk biscuits
1 teaspoon dried parsley flakes
½ teaspoon paprika

In an 8-by-8-inch microwave-safe baking dish, combine celery, carrots, onion, and ¼ cup chicken gravy. Cover and microwave on HIGH (100% power) for 9 to 10 minutes or until vegetables are tender, stirring after 5 minutes. Stir in chicken, peas, remaining chicken gravy, and black pepper. Re-cover and continue to microwave on HIGH for 4 minutes. Separate biscuits and cut each into 4 pieces. Evenly sprinkle biscuit pieces over stew. Sprinkle parsley flakes and paprika evenly over top. Lightly spray top with butter-flavored cooking spray. Microwave, uncovered, on HIGH for 4 to 6 minutes or until biscuits spring back when lightly touched. Place baking dish on counter and let set for 3 minutes. Divide into 6 servings.

HINTS: 1. If you don't have leftovers, purchase a chunk of cooked chicken breast from your local deli.
2. Thaw peas by placing in a colander and rinsing under hot water for 1 minute.

Each serving equals:

HE: 2 Protein • 1½ Bread • 1 Vegetable • ¼ Slider • 5 Optional Calories

219 Calories • 3 gm Fat • 22 gm Protein • 26 gm Carbohydrate • 702 mg Sodium • 34 mg Calcium • 1 gm Fiber

DIABETIC EXCHANGES: 2 Meat • 1½ Starch/Carbohydrate • 1 Vegetable

Brunswick Pot Pie

The original Brunswick stew recipe came from the great state of Virginia around 1828, according to legend, and featured squirrel instead of chicken, but today a hearty blend of meat and veggies, flavored with a tangy sauce, is still a favorite for family reunions and church fund-raisers. I decided to make a biscuit-topped pot pie on a Brunswick theme—and all my taste-testers voted it a winner!

☺ Serves 6

1 (10¾-ounce) can Healthy Request Tomato Soup
1 cup chopped onion
3 tablespoons Oscar Mayer or Hormel Real Bacon Bits
1½ teaspoons Worcestershire sauce
⅛ teaspoon black pepper
1 cup frozen green lima beans, thawed
1¼ cups frozen whole-kernel corn, thawed
2 full cups diced cooked chicken breast
1 (7.5-ounce) can Pillsbury refrigerated buttermilk biscuits
1 teaspoon dried parsley flakes
Dash paprika

In an 8-by-8-inch microwave-safe baking dish, combine tomato soup and onion. Cover and microwave on HIGH (100% power) for 3 minutes. Stir in bacon bits, Worcestershire sauce, and black pepper. Add lima beans, corn, and chicken. Mix well to combine. Re-cover and microwave on HIGH for 5 minutes. Separate biscuits and cut each into 4 pieces. Evenly sprinkle biscuit pieces over hot chicken mixture. Sprinkle parsley flakes and paprika evenly over top. Lightly spray top with butter-flavored cooking spray. Microwave, uncovered, on HIGH for 4 to 6 minutes or until biscuits spring back when lightly touched. Place baking dish on counter and let set for 3 minutes. Divide into 6 servings.

HINTS: 1. Thaw lima beans and corn by placing in a colander and rinsing under hot water for 1 minute.
2. If you don't have leftovers, purchase a chunk of cooked chicken breast from your local deli.

Each serving equals:

HE: 2 Protein • 1½ Bread • ⅔ Vegetable • ½ Slider • 2 Optional Calories

288 Calories • 4 gm Fat • 25 gm Protein • 38 gm Carbohydrate • 654 mg Sodium • 25 mg Calcium • 3 gm Fiber

DIABETIC EXCHANGES: 2 Starch/Carbohydrate • 2 Meat • ½ Vegetable

Stuffed Red Peppers

I was swept away by a display of truly gorgeous red peppers in the farmer's market one day, and I carried home far more than I needed. (Or so I thought!) These naturally nutritious veggies are very high in vitamin C, they taste oh-so-sweet, and when you find them on sale, buy a bunch—and make this recipe!

❤ Serves 6

> 6 (medium-sized) red bell peppers
> 16 ounces extra lean ground sirloin beef or turkey breast
> 1 cup uncooked Minute Rice
> ½ cup chopped onion
> 1 (8-ounce) can tomatoes, finely chopped and undrained
> ⅛ teaspoon black pepper
> 1 (10¾-ounce) can Healthy Request Tomato Soup
> 1 teaspoon dried basil
> 6 tablespoons shredded Kraft reduced-fat Cheddar cheese

Cut a thin slice from stem end of each red pepper. Remove seeds and membrane. Rinse peppers. In a large bowl, combine meat, uncooked rice, onion, undrained tomatoes, and black pepper. Evenly spoon meat mixture into red peppers. Arrange filled peppers evenly in an 8-by-12-inch microwave-safe baking dish. In a small bowl, combine tomato soup and basil. Spoon soup mixture evenly over peppers. Cover and microwave on HIGH (100% power) for 18 to 22 minutes. Uncover and sprinkle 1 tablespoon Cheddar cheese over top of each pepper. Continue to microwave on HIGH for 1 minute or until cheese melts. Place baking dish on counter and let set for 3 minutes. When serving, evenly spoon soup mixture over top.

Each serving equals:

HE: 2⅓ Protein • 1½ Vegetable • ½ Bread • ¼ Slider • 10 Optional Calories

246 Calories • 6 gm Fat • 19 gm Protein • 29 gm Carbohydrate • 284 mg Sodium • 75 mg Calcium • 4 gm Fiber

DIABETIC EXCHANGES: 2 Meat • 1½ Vegetable • 1 Starch

Savory Stuffed Peppers

When I was a child, I always loved stuffed peppers, because it felt like I was getting to open a "surprise package" when I dug in to eat the filling. While tradition holds that peppers are usually filled with meat and rice, it's the unknown added ingredients that make each version so very special. ● Serves 4

4 (medium-sized) firm green bell peppers
8 ounces extra-lean ground sirloin beef or turkey breast
½ cup finely chopped onion
1 (8-ounce) can Hunt's Tomato Sauce ☆
½ teaspoon Worcestershire sauce
1 (8-ounce) can whole-kernel corn, rinsed and drained
¾ cup shredded Kraft reduced-fat Cheddar cheese
1 teaspoon Splenda Granular
1 teaspoon dried parsley flakes

Cut a thin slice from stem end of each green pepper. Remove seeds and membrane. Rinse peppers. Place peppers cut side up in an 8-by-8-inch microwave-safe baking dish. Cover and microwave on HIGH (100% power) for 3 minutes. Remove from microwave and set aside. Place meat and onion in a plastic colander and place colander in a glass pie plate. Cover and microwave on HIGH for 6 minutes, stirring after 3 minutes. In a large bowl, combine ½ cup tomato sauce, Worcestershire sauce, and corn. Add Cheddar cheese and browned meat mixture. Mix well to combine. Evenly spoon meat mixture into green peppers. Stir Splenda and parsley flakes into remaining ½ cup tomato sauce. Spoon about 2 tablespoons sauce mixture over top of each stuffed pepper. Continue to microwave on HIGH for 8 minutes, turning dish after 4 minutes. Place baking dish on counter and let set for 3 minutes before serving.

Each serving equals:

HE: 2½ Protein • 2¼ Vegetable • ½ Bread

239 Calories • 7 gm Fat • 20 gm Protein •
24 gm Carbohydrate • 704 mg Sodium •
168 mg Calcium • 5 gm Fiber

DIABETIC EXCHANGES: 2 Meat • 2 Vegetable • ½ Starch

Momma's Stuffed Green Peppers

As long ago as I can remember, moms have been serving this old-fashioned dish to their families—but even the very best dishes leave room for a little culinary "tinkering." These look as appetizing as they taste! ☻ Serves 4

4 (medium-sized) green bell peppers
8 ounces extra lean ground sirloin beef or turkey breast
½ cup chopped onion
1 (8-ounce) can tomatoes, finely chopped and undrained
¼ cup reduced-sodium ketchup
1 cup cooked rice
¾ cup shredded Kraft reduced-fat mozzarella cheese ☆
1 teaspoon Italian seasoning

Cut a thin slice from stem end of each green pepper. Remove seeds and membrane. Rinse peppers. Place peppers cut side up in an 8-by-8-inch glass baking dish. Cover and microwave on HIGH (100% power) for 3 minutes. Place baking dish on counter, uncover, and let set while preparing filling. Crumble meat into a plastic colander. Stir in onion. Place colander in a glass pie plate. Microwave on HIGH for 3 to 4 minutes, stirring after 2 minutes. Place browned meat mixture in a large bowl. Stir in undrained tomatoes, ketchup, rice, ½ cup mozzarella cheese, and Italian seasoning. Evenly spoon meat mixture into green peppers. Re-cover and microwave on HIGH for 8 to 10 minutes, turning dish after every 4 minutes. Uncover and sprinkle 1 tablespoon mozzarella cheese over top of each. Place baking dish on counter and let set for 2 minutes before serving.

HINT: Usually ⅔ cup uncooked instant rice or ½ cup uncooked regular rice cooks to about 1 cup.

Each serving equals:

HE: 2½ Protein • 1¾ Vegetable • ½ Bread •
15 Optional Calories

---

226 Calories • 6 gm Fat • 20 gm Protein •
23 gm Carbohydrate • 252 mg Sodium •
169 mg Calcium • 4 gm Fiber

DIABETIC EXCHANGES: 2 Meat • 2 Vegetable • 1 Starch

Easy Italian Sandwiches

If you haven't tried cooking ground meat in your microwave yet, you're in for such a treat. The fat drains off, and the meat shrinks less than in a frying pan. When you add the rest of the ingredients, you've got a super-duper dish! ☻ Serves 6

> 16 ounces extra-lean ground sirloin beef or
>   turkey breast
> 1/2 cup chopped onion
> 1/2 cup chopped green bell pepper
> 1 (15-ounce) can diced tomatoes, drained
> 2 tablespoons reduced-sodium ketchup
> 1 1/2 teaspoons Italian seasoning
> 1/3 cup sliced ripe olives
> 6 tablespoons shredded Kraft reduced-fat
>   mozzarella cheese
> 6 small hamburger buns

Crumble meat into a plastic colander. Stir in onion and green pepper. Place colander in a glass pie plate. Microwave on HIGH (100% power) for 5 to 7 minutes or until meat is browned, stirring after every 3 minutes. In an 8-cup microwave-safe mixing bowl, combine browned meat mixture, tomatoes, ketchup, Italian seasoning, and olives. Microwave on HIGH for 6 to 8 minutes, stirring after every 3 minutes. Place bowl on counter, stir in mozzarella cheese, and let set for 2 minutes. For each sandwich, spoon about 2/3 cup meat mixture between a hamburger bun.

HINT: Also good spooned inside a pita half and topped with
    1 tablespoon fat-free sour cream.

Each serving equals:

HE: 2⅓ Protein • 1 Bread • 1 Vegetable • ¼ Fat •
10 Optional Calories

---

218 Calories • 6 gm Fat • 20 gm Protein •
21 gm Carbohydrate • 404 mg Sodium •
82 mg Calcium • 3 gm Fiber

DIABETIC EXCHANGES: 2 Meat • 1 Starch • 1 Vegetable

Micro Bacon Cheeseburgers

Here's the thing—when you put the cheese and bacon on top of a burger, the ketchup has nowhere to go! So I decided to "hide" my bacon and cheese inside my burger instead. If you don't share this secret before anyone takes a bite, you're likely to hear cries of delight on finding the surprise inside. ☻   Serves 6

16 ounces extra-lean ground sirloin beef or turkey breast
3 tablespoons dried fine bread crumbs
1 teaspoon dried parsley flakes
⅛ teaspoon black pepper
3 (¾-ounce) slices Kraft reduced-fat American cheese
¼ cup Oscar Mayer or Hormel Real Bacon Bits
6 small hamburger buns

In a large bowl, combine meat, bread crumbs, parsley flakes, and black pepper. Mix well to combine. Using about 3 tablespoons as a guide, form into 12 patties. Cut cheese slices in half. Evenly arrange cheese pieces on 6 patties. Sprinkle 1 tablespoon bacon bits over top of each. Top each with another patty. Press patties together with the tines of a fork to seal edges. Place patties on a microwave-safe plate. Cover and microwave on HIGH (100% power) for 5 to 6 minutes or until meat is no longer pink, turning plate after every 2 minutes. Place plate on counter, uncover, and let set for 3 minutes. For each serving, place 1 burger between a hamburger bun.

Each serving equals:

HE: 2½ Protein • 1 Bread • ¼ Slider •
12 Optional Calories

219 Calories • 7 gm Fat • 22 gm Protein •
17 gm Carbohydrate • 595 mg Sodium •
86 mg Calcium • 1 gm Fiber

DIABETIC EXCHANGES: 2½ Meat • 1 Starch

Mom's Meat Loaf

Every family has its favorites when it comes to this all-American standard, but it's the little variations from home to home that make each one unique. This version revives the flavors of my mom's meat loaf—just the way my dad liked it! ☕ Serves 6

> 16 ounces extra-lean ground sirloin beef or turkey breast
> 6 slices reduced-calorie white bread, made into crumbs
> 1 cup finely chopped onion
> 1 (8-ounce) can Hunt's Tomato Sauce ☆
> 1 tablespoon Splenda Granular
> 1 teaspoon dried parsley flakes
> 1½ teaspoons prepared yellow mustard
> ⅛ teaspoon black pepper

In a large bowl, combine meat, bread crumbs, onion, ⅓ cup tomato sauce, Splenda, parsley flakes, mustard, and black pepper. Mix well to combine. Pat mixture into a microwave baking ring. Evenly spoon remaining ⅔ cup tomato sauce over top. Cover and microwave on HIGH (100% power) for 16 minutes, turning after 8 minutes. Place baking ring on counter, uncover, and let set for 5 minutes. Cut into 6 servings.

HINT: If you don't have a microwave baking ring, place a custard cup upside down in center of a 9-inch glass pie plate and pat mixture around cup in pie plate.

Each serving equals:

HE: 2 Protein • 1 Vegetable • ½ Bread •
1 Optional Calorie

156 Calories • 4 gm Fat • 18 gm Protein •
12 gm Carbohydrate • 371 mg Sodium •
30 mg Calcium • 1 gm Fiber

DIABETIC EXCHANGES: 2 Meat • 1 Vegetable • ½ Starch

Rio Grande Meat Loaf

When you're ready to serve your own Blue Plate Special, you can't do better than to fix this piquant meat loaf. I like baking it in a ring instead of a loaf pan—it looks great on your table, and it helps the loaf hold its shape while it cooks. ◑ Serves 6

> ¾ cup finely chopped onion
> ¼ cup finely chopped green bell pepper
> 1 tablespoon water
> 16 ounces extra-lean ground sirloin beef or turkey breast
> ½ cup + 1 tablespoon shredded Kraft reduced-fat Cheddar cheese
> 15 Reduced Fat Ritz Crackers, made into fine crumbs
> 1½ teaspoons chili seasoning
> 1 (8-ounce) can Hunt's Tomato Sauce ☆
> 1 tablespoon Splenda Granular
> 1 teaspoon dried parsley flakes

In a small microwave-safe bowl, combine onion, green pepper, and water. Cover and microwave on HIGH (100% power) for 2 minutes. Drain, if necessary. In a large bowl, combine meat, Cheddar cheese, cracker crumbs, chili seasoning, ¼ cup tomato sauce, and drained vegetables. Pat mixture into a microwave baking ring. Microwave on HIGH (100% power) for 8 minutes. In a small bowl, combine remaining ¾ cup tomato sauce, Splenda, and parsley flakes. Evenly spoon mixture over top of meat loaf. Continue to microwave on HIGH for 4 minutes. Place baking ring on counter and let set for 5 minutes. Cut into 6 servings.

HINTS: 1. A self-seal sandwich bag works great for crushing crackers.
2. If you don't have a microwave baking ring, place a custard cup upside down in center of a 9-inch glass pie plate and pat mixture around cup in pie plate.

Each serving equals:

HE: 2½ Protein • 1 Vegetable • ½ Bread •
1 Optional Calorie

174 Calories • 6 gm Fat • 19 gm Protein •
11 gm Carbohydrate • 405 mg Sodium •
90 mg Calcium • 1 gm Fiber

DIABETIC EXCHANGES: 2½ Meat • 1 Vegetable •
½ Starch

Sour Cream Meat Loaf

If there was ever a clever way to make your meat loaf even more luscious than it always is, it's got to be adding a dollop of sour cream! It doesn't just moisten the meat mixture, it seems to add a wonderful velvety texture to the loaf. This also is chock-full of good-for-you veggies—almost a meal in just one dish!

◗ Serves 6

> ½ cup finely chopped celery
> ½ cup finely chopped onion
> ½ cup shredded carrots
> 2 tablespoons water
> 16 ounces extra-lean ground sirloin beef or turkey breast
> ½ cup Land O Lakes no-fat sour cream
> 21 small fat-free saltine crackers, made into crumbs
> 1 teaspoon dried parsley flakes
> ⅓ cup reduced-sodium ketchup

In an 8-cup microwave-safe mixing bowl, combine celery, onion, carrots, and water. Microwave on HIGH (100% power) for 3 minutes. Drain, if necessary. In a large bowl, combine meat, sour cream, cracker crumbs, parsley flakes, and drained vegetables. Mix well to combine. Pat mixture into a microwave baking ring. Microwave on HIGH for 14 minutes. Spoon ketchup evenly over top. Continue to microwave on HIGH for 2 minutes. Place baking ring on counter and let set for 5 minutes. Cut into 6 servings.

HINTS: 1. A self-seal sandwich bag works great for crushing crackers.
2. If you don't have a microwave baking ring, place a custard cup upside down in center of a 9-inch glass pie plate and pat mixture around cup in pie plate.

Each serving equals:

HE: 2 Protein • ½ Bread • ½ Vegetable • ¼ Slider •
13 Optional Calories

167 Calories • 3 gm Fat • 17 gm Protein •
18 gm Carbohydrate • 211 mg Sodium •
39 mg Calcium • 1 gm Fiber

DIABETIC EXCHANGES: 2 Meat • 1 Starch • ½ Vegetable

Savory Salisbury Supreme

You'll notice that many of my entrees serve four or six people, and if you're cooking for one or two, you may decide to turn the page and look elsewhere for dinner ideas. But this dish freezes beautifully, if you can't use it all the night you prepare it. It also reheats well—yes, in the microwave.   ☻   Serves 4

> 8 ounces extra-lean ground sirloin beef or turkey breast
> 1 (12-ounce) jar Heinz Fat Free Beef Gravy
> ¼ cup reduced-sodium ketchup
> 1 tablespoon dried onion flakes
> 1 (2.5-ounce) jar sliced mushrooms, undrained
> 1 tablespoon Worcestershire Sauce
> 2 teaspoons dried parsley flakes
> 2 tablespoons Land O Lakes no-fat sour cream
> 2 cups hot cooked noodles

Crumble meat into a plastic colander. Place colander in a glass pie plate. Microwave on HIGH (100% power) for 4 to 5 minutes or until meat is browned, stirring after every 2 minutes. In an 8-cup microwave-safe mixing bowl, combine browned meat, beef gravy, ketchup, onion flakes, undrained mushrooms, Worcestershire sauce, and parsley flakes. Cover and microwave on HIGH for 8 minutes, stirring after every 4 minutes. Place bowl on counter, uncover, stir in sour cream, and let set for 3 minutes. Mix well before serving. For each serving, place ½ cup noodles on a plate and spoon about ½ cup meat mixture over top.

HINT: Usually 1¾ cups uncooked noodles cooks to about 2 cups.

Each serving equals:

HE: $1\frac{1}{2}$ Protein • 1 Bread • $\frac{1}{4}$ Vegetable • $\frac{1}{2}$ Slider • 7 Optional Calories

236 Calories • 4 gm Fat • 16 gm Protein • 34 gm Carbohydrate • 615 mg Sodium • 33 mg Calcium • 2 gm Fiber

DIABETIC EXCHANGES: $1\frac{1}{2}$ Meat • $1\frac{1}{2}$ Starch/Carbohydrate

Stroganoff Casserole

Whenever I dine on a stroganoff recipe, I can't help thinking back to the magnificence of the Russian court I've seen in movies like *Nicholas and Alexandra*. Nothing was too opulent, and no dish was too rich for those royals! ☻ Serves 4 (1 cup)

> 8 ounces extra-lean ground sirloin beef or turkey breast
> 1 (10¾-ounce) can Healthy Request Cream of Mushroom Soup
> ¼ cup Land O Lakes Fat Free Half & Half
> 1 tablespoon dried onion flakes
> 1 (2.5-ounce) jar sliced mushrooms, drained
> 1 teaspoon Worcestershire sauce
> 1 teaspoon dried parsley flakes
> ½ cup Land O Lakes no-fat sour cream
> 1½ cups cooked noodles, rinsed and drained

Crumble meat into a plastic colander. Place colander in a glass pie plate. Microwave on HIGH (100% power) for 4 to 5 minutes or until meat is browned, stirring after every 2 minutes. Place browned meat in an 8-cup microwave-safe mixing bowl. Stir in mushroom soup and half & half. Add onion flakes, mushrooms, Worcestershire sauce, and parsley flakes. Mix well to combine. Cover and microwave on HIGH for 5 minutes. Stir in sour cream and noodles. Re-cover and continue to microwave on HIGH for 2 minutes or until mixture is heated through. Place bowl on counter, uncover, and let set for 5 minutes. Mix well before serving.

HINT: Usually 1¼ cups uncooked noodles cook to about 1½ cups.

Each serving equals:

HE: 1½ Protein • ¾ Bread • ¼ Vegetable •
¾ Slider • 18 Optional Calories

225 Calories • 5 gm Fat • 16 gm Protein •
29 gm Carbohydrate • 470 mg Sodium •
130 mg Calcium • 1 gm Fiber

DIABETIC EXCHANGES: 1½ Meat •
1½ Starch/Carbohydrate

Italian Beef and Noodles

It's astonishing just how much sumptuous flavor just a few spoonfuls of Parmesan cheese can give a dish, but this aged Italian cheese is POWERFUL culinary magic! It provides just the right finishing touch for this satisfying beef and pasta recipe.

☯ Serves 6 (1 cup)

> 16 ounces extra-lean ground sirloin beef or
> turkey breast
> ½ cup chopped onion
> 2½ cups uncooked noodles
> 1 (8-ounce) can Hunt's Tomato Sauce
> 1 (15-ounce) can diced tomatoes, undrained
> ½ cup water
> 1 teaspoon Splenda Granular
> 1 teaspoon Italian seasoning
> ⅛ teaspoon black pepper
> 6 tablespoons Kraft Reduced Fat Parmesan Style
> Grated Topping

Crumble meat into a plastic colander. Stir in onion. Place colander in a glass pie plate. Microwave on HIGH (100% power) for 5 to 7 minutes or until meat is browned, stirring after every 3 minutes. In an 8-cup microwave-safe mixing bowl, combine browned meat mixture, uncooked noodles, tomato sauce, and undrained tomatoes. Add water, Splenda, Italian seasoning, and black pepper. Mix well to combine. Cover and continue to microwave on HIGH for 15 minutes or until noodles are tender, stirring after every 5 minutes. Place bowl on counter, uncover, and let set for 5 minutes. Mix well before serving. When serving, top each serving with 1 tablespoon Parmesan cheese.

Each serving equals:

HE: 2¼ Protein • 1½ Vegetable • 1 Bread

197 Calories • 5 gm Fat • 18 gm Protein •
20 gm Carbohydrate • 441 mg Sodium •
69 mg Calcium • 2 gm Fiber

DIABETIC EXCHANGES: 2 Meat • 1½ Vegetable •
1 Starch

Pizza Noodle Casserole

Did you know that the colors of the Italian flag are red, white, and green? I only bring this up because those are also the colors of a saucy veggie pizza—which was my jumping-off point for this piquant pasta casserole. ☻ Serves 4 (1 cup)

> 8 ounces extra-lean ground sirloin beef or
>   turkey breast
> ½ cup chopped onion
> ½ cup chopped green bell pepper
> 1 (2.5-ounce) jar sliced mushrooms, drained
> 1 (8-ounce) can Hunt's Tomato Sauce
> 1 (15-ounce) can diced tomatoes, undrained
> 1 teaspoon Splenda Granular
> 1 teaspoon pizza or Italian seasoning
> 1¾ cups uncooked noodles
> ½ cup water
> ¾ cup shredded Kraft reduced-fat mozzarella cheese
> 6 tablespoons shredded Kraft reduced-fat Cheddar cheese

Crumble meat into a plastic colander. Stir in onion. Place colander in a glass pie plate. Microwave on HIGH (100% power) for 4 to 5 minutes or until meat is browned, stirring after every 2 minutes. In an 8-cup microwave-safe mixing bowl, combine browned meat mixture, green pepper, mushrooms, tomato sauce, and undrained tomatoes. Stir in Splenda, pizza seasoning, uncooked noodles, and water. Cover and continue to microwave on HIGH for 15 minutes or until noodles are tender, stirring after every 5 minutes. Place bowl on counter, uncover, stir in mozzarella and Cheddar cheeses, and let set for 5 minutes. Mix well before serving.

Each serving equals:

HE: 3 Protein • 2¾ Vegetable • 1 Bread

260 Calories • 8 gm Fat • 23 gm Protein •
24 gm Carbohydrate • 671 mg Sodium •
261 mg Calcium • 4 gm Fiber

DIABETIC EXCHANGES: 2½ Meat • 2 Vegetable •
1 Starch

Taco Macaroni Casserole

You don't need tortillas to have a terrific taco party—try this zesty recipe and see for yourself! In a way, you're making your own little taco salad, but in this case, you're also enjoying a South-of-the-Border macaroni marvel.   ☻   Serves 4

> 8 ounces extra lean ground sirloin beef or turkey breast
> ½ cup chopped onion
> 1 (10¾-ounce) can Healthy Request Tomato Soup
> 1 (15-ounce) can diced tomatoes, drained
> 1½ teaspoons taco seasoning
> 1½ cups cooked elbow macaroni, rinsed and drained
> 2 cups finely shredded lettuce
> 1 cup finely chopped fresh tomato
> 6 tablespoons shredded Kraft reduced-fat Cheddar cheese
> ¼ cup Land O Lakes no-fat sour cream

Crumble meat into a plastic colander. Stir in onion. Place colander in a glass pie plate. Microwave on HIGH (100% power) for 4 to 5 minutes or until meat is browned, stirring after every 2 minutes. In an 8-cup microwave-safe mixing bowl, combine browned meat mixture, tomato soup, tomatoes, and taco seasoning. Stir in macaroni. Cover and continue to microwave on HIGH for 10 minutes, stirring after 5 minutes. Place bowl on counter, uncover, and let set for 5 minutes. Mix well before serving. For each serving, place 1¼ cups casserole mixture on a plate, sprinkle ½ cup lettuce, ¼ cup fresh tomato, and 1½ tablespoons Cheddar cheese over casserole mixture, and top with 1 tablespoon sour cream.

HINT: Usually 1 cup uncooked macaroni cooks to about 1½ cups.

Each serving equals:

HE: 2 Protein • 2 Vegetable • ¾ Bread • ¾ Slider

286 Calories • 6 gm Fat • 20 gm Protein •
38 gm Carbohydrate • 557 mg Sodium •
131 mg Calcium • 4 gm Fiber

DIABETIC EXCHANGES: 2 Meat • 2 Vegetable •
1½ Starch/Carbohydrate

Oriental Pepper "Steaks"

One "added value" of cooking in your microwave is how it encourages veggies and spices to partner up in order to produce a dish that sizzles with unique regional flavors. Amazing how a little ginger and soy can lend true exotic taste to a simple beef and peppers dish.

☻ Serves 6

16 ounces extra-lean ground sirloin beef or turkey breast
6 tablespoons dried fine bread crumbs
1 tablespoon reduced-sodium soy sauce ☆
⅛ teaspoon black pepper
1 (8-ounce) can Hunt's Tomato Sauce ☆
¼ teaspoon ground ginger
1 cup chopped onion
1½ cups chopped green bell pepper

Spray an 8-by-12-inch microwave-safe baking dish with butter-flavored cooking spray. In a large bowl, combine meat, bread crumbs, 2 teaspoons soy sauce, black pepper, and ¼ cup tomato sauce. Using a ⅓ cup measuring cup as a guide, form into 6 patties. Place patties in prepared baking dish. Microwave on MEDIUM (50% power) for 6 minutes. In a medium bowl, combine remaining ¾ cup tomato sauce, ginger, and remaining 1 teaspoon soy sauce. Stir in onion and green pepper. Spoon sauce mixture evenly over meat patties. Cover and continue to microwave on MEDIUM for 8 to 10 minutes or until vegetables are tender. Place baking dish on counter, uncover, and let set for 5 minutes. When serving, evenly spoon sauce over patties.

Each serving equals:

HE: 2 Protein • 1½ Vegetable • ⅓ Bread

155 Calories • 3 gm Fat • 17 gm Protein •
15 gm Carbohydrate • 502 mg Sodium •
18 mg Calcium • 1 gm Fiber

DIABETIC EXCHANGES: 2 Meat • 1½ Vegetable

Tom's Nacho Cups

My son Tommy has just loved nachos ever since he was a little guy—something about their crunchy, cheesy, tangy flavor captured his heart and his taste buds long ago. So, Tom, these are for you—perfect one-serving pleasers that celebrate the tastes you adore.

● Serves 6

> 8 ounces extra lean ground sirloin beef or turkey breast
> ½ cup chopped onion
> 1 (8-ounce) can Hunt's Tomato Sauce
> 1 (15-ounce) can Bush's red kidney beans, rinsed and drained
> ½ cup chunky salsa (mild, medium, or hot)
> ⅓ cup sliced ripe olives
> 1½ cups (3 ounces) Dorito's Baked Corn Chips
> ¾ cup shredded Kraft reduced-fat Cheddar cheese

Crumble meat into a plastic colander. Stir in onion. Place colander in a glass pie plate. Microwave on HIGH (100% power) for 4 to 5 minutes, or until meat is browned, stirring after every 2 minutes. In an 8-cup microwave-safe mixing bowl, combine browned meat mixture, tomato sauce, kidney beans, salsa, and olives. Cover and continue to microwave on HIGH for 4 minutes, stirring after 2 minutes. Evenly divide corn chips between 6 (12-ounce) custard cups. Spoon about ⅔ cup hot meat mixture over each and top with 2 tablespoons Cheddar cheese. Let set for 2 minutes before serving.

Each serving equals:

HE: 2½ Protein • 1 Bread • 1 Vegetable • ¼ Fat

219 Calories • 7 gm Fat • 16 gm Protein •
23 gm Carbohydrate • 822 mg Sodium •
121 mg Calcium • 4 gm Fiber

DIABETIC EXCHANGES: 2 Meat • 1 Starch/Carbohydrate •
1 Vegetable

Chili Burger Casserole

Here's a real kid-pleaser, for kids of all ages! Anyone who can't resist a gooey cheeseburger is sure to jump on the bandwagon for this casserole that celebrates it. And while they're gobbling it down, they'll never notice that it also delivers lots of healthy veggies and protein. ☻ Serves 6

16 ounces extra-lean ground sirloin beef or turkey breast
1 cup frozen whole-kernel corn, thawed
1 (15-ounce) can Bush's red kidney beans, rinsed and drained
⅓ cup sliced ripe olives
1 (8-ounce) can Hunt's Tomato Sauce
1 (15-ounce) can diced tomatoes, undrained
1½ teaspoons chili seasoning
¾ cup coarsely crushed Dorito's Baked Corn Chips ☆
¾ cup shredded Kraft reduced-fat Cheddar cheese

Crumble meat into a plastic colander. Place colander in a glass pie plate. Microwave on HIGH (100% power) for 5 to 7 minutes or until meat is browned, stirring after every 3 minutes. In an 8-cup microwave-safe mixing bowl, combine browned meat, corn, kidney beans, and olives. Add tomato sauce, undrained tomatoes, and chili seasoning. Mix well to combine. Stir in ½ cup corn chips. Spray a microwave-safe 8-by-8-inch baking dish with butter-flavored cooking spray. Evenly spread mixture into prepared baking dish. Microwave on HIGH for 5 minutes, turning after 3 minutes. In a medium bowl, combine remaining corn chips and Cheddar cheese. Sprinkle mixture evenly over top of casserole. Continue to microwave on HIGH for 1 minute or until cheese melts. Place baking dish on counter and let set for 5 minutes. Divide into 6 servings.

HINT: Thaw corn by placing in a colander and rinsing under hot water for 1 minute.

Each serving equals:

HE: 3½ Protein • 1 Bread • 1 Vegetable

272 Calories • 8 gm Fat • 24 gm Protein •
26 gm Carbohydrate • 501 mg Sodium •
119 mg Calcium • 7 gm Fiber

DIABETIC EXCHANGES: 3 Meat • 1 Starch • 1 Vegetable

Mexicali Rice

Serve six people with just a pound of ground meat—what a smart and thrifty chef you'll be! No one will leave the table hungry, you can bet, with all the other goodies in this spicy blend of Mexican-style meat and veggies. ☽ Serves 6 (1 cup)

16 ounces extra-lean ground sirloin beef or turkey breast
1 cup finely chopped onion
1 cup chopped green bell pepper
1 cup uncooked Minute Rice
1 (15-ounce) can diced tomatoes, undrained
½ cup reduced-sodium V8 juice
1½ cups frozen whole-kernel corn, thawed
1 tablespoon Splenda Granular
1 teaspoon chili seasoning
⅛ teaspoon black pepper

Crumble meat into a plastic colander. Stir in onion and green pepper. Place colander in a glass pie plate. Microwave on HIGH (100% power) for 5 to 7 minutes or until meat is browned, stirring after every 3 minutes. In an 8-cup microwave-safe mixing bowl, combine browned meat mixture, uncooked rice, undrained tomatoes, V8 juice, and corn. Add Splenda, chili seasoning, and black pepper. Mix well to combine. Cover and continue to microwave on HIGH for 12 to 15 minutes or until rice and vegetables are tender, stirring after every 5 minutes. Place bowl on counter, uncover, and let set for 5 minutes. Mix well before serving.

HINT: Thaw corn by placing in a colander and rinsing under hot water for 1 minute.

Each serving equals:

HE: 2 Protein • 1½ Vegetable • 1 Bread •
1 Optional Calorie

220 Calories • 4 gm Fat • 18 gm Protein •
28 gm Carbohydrate • 153 mg Sodium •
30 mg Calcium • 3 gm Fiber

DIABETIC EXCHANGES: 2 Meat • 1½ Vegetable •
1 Starch

German Meatballs and Sauerkraut

If you've always believed that meatballs are primarily an Italian phenomenon (such as in spaghetti and . . .), you're in for a culinary surprise! Most cuisines have some kind of meatball, from the sweet 'n' sour type from eastern Europe to these hearty ones that rest on a bed of sauerkraut. Grab a beer (or a root beer) and dig in!

🌑 Serves 6

> 16 ounces extra lean ground sirloin beef or turkey breast
> 1 cup finely chopped onion
> ½ cup + 1 tablespoon dried fine bread crumbs
> 1 (8-ounce) can Hunt's Tomato Sauce ☆
> 1 (15-ounce) can Frank's Bavarian Style sauerkraut,
>   very well drained
> 1 (8-ounce) can tomatoes, finely chopped and undrained
> 1 tablespoon Splenda Granular
> ½ teaspoon pumpkin pie spice
> 1 teaspoon dried parsley flakes
> ⅛ teaspoon black pepper

In a large bowl, combine meat, onion, bread crumbs, and ¼ cup tomato sauce. Form into 24 (1-inch) meatballs. Arrange meatballs in an 8-by-12-inch microwave-safe baking dish. Cover and microwave on HIGH (100% power) for 8 minutes, turning after 4 minutes. Place covered baking dish on counter while preparing sauerkraut. In an 8-cup microwave-safe mixing bowl, combine sauerkraut, remaining ¾ cup tomato sauce, undrained tomatoes, Splenda, pumpkin pie spice, parsley flakes, and black pepper. Cover and microwave on HIGH for 5 minutes. Mix well. For each serving, place ½ cup sauerkraut mixture on a plate and spoon 4 meatballs over top.

HINTS: 1. If you can't find Bavarian sauerkraut, use regular sauerkraut, ½ teaspoon caraway seeds, and 1 teaspoon Splenda Granular.

2. Place sauerkraut in a colander and press juice out with a sturdy spoon.

Each serving equals:

HE: 2 Protein • 2 Vegetable • ½ Bread • 1 Optional Calorie

200 Calories • 4 gm Fat • 17 gm Protein • 24 gm Carbohydrate • 705 mg Sodium • 38 mg Calcium • 2 gm Fiber

DIABETIC EXCHANGES: 2 Meat • 2 Vegetable • ½ Starch

Superb Swiss Steak

I've grown tomatoes all my life, so I know how much tomatoes love the sun. But they also adore the heat of the microwave, which seems to bring out their sweetness and warmth as they bake. This dish spends a bit more time in the microwave than you may be used to, but enjoy the freedom as it cooks unattended.

● Serves 4

4 (4-ounce) lean tenderized minute or cube steaks
1 (15-ounce) can diced tomatoes, undrained
1 (10¾-ounce) can Healthy Request Tomato Soup
1 tablespoon all-purpose flour
1 (2.5-ounce) jar sliced mushrooms, drained
½ cup finely chopped onion
1½ teaspoons Italian seasoning

Evenly arrange steak pieces in an 8-by-8-inch microwave-safe baking dish. In a medium bowl, combine undrained tomatoes, tomato soup, and flour. Stir in mushrooms, onion, and Italian seasoning. Spoon tomato mixture evenly over steak. Cover and microwave on HIGH (100% power) for 5 minutes, then microwave on MEDIUM (50% power) for 25 to 30 minutes or until meat is tender. Place baking dish on counter, uncover, and let set for 5 minutes. When serving, evenly spoon sauce mixture over top of steaks.

Each serving equals:

HE: 3 Protein • 1½ Vegetable • ½ Slider •
12 Optional Calories

225 Calories • 5 gm Fat • 26 gm Protein •
19 gm Carbohydrate • 548 mg Sodium •
28 mg Calcium • 3 gm Fiber

DIABETIC EXCHANGES: 3 Meat • 1½ Vegetable •
½ Starch

Pronto Pizza Steaks

Keeping these slim steaks on hand just makes good sense, letting you fix a super-fast meal with just a few other ingredients. Tonight, enjoy two of your favorites in one savory dish, as you top your steak, instead of a crust, with sauce and cheese! ☻ Serves 4

2 tablespoons Kraft Fat Free Italian Dressing

4 (4-ounce) lean minute or cube steaks

1/2 cup onion slices

1 (10¾-ounce) can Healthy Request Tomato Soup

1 (2.5-ounce) jar sliced mushrooms, drained

1 teaspoon pizza seasoning

6 tablespoons shredded Kraft reduced-fat mozzarella cheese

Pour Italian dressing into an 8-by-8-inch microwave-safe baking dish. Coat steaks on both sides in dressing and then evenly arrange steaks in same baking dish. Cover and microwave on HIGH (100% power) for 3 minutes. Evenly sprinkle onion slices over steaks. In a medium bowl, combine tomato soup, mushrooms, and pizza seasoning. Spoon soup mixture evenly over top of steaks. Re-cover and microwave on MEDIUM (50% power) for 16 to 20 minutes or until meat is tender. Place baking dish on counter and evenly sprinkle mozzarella cheese over top. Let set for 5 minutes. When serving, evenly spoon any remaining sauce over top.

Each serving equals:

HE: 3½ Protein • ½ Vegetable • ½ Slider • 9 Optional Calories

233 Calories • 9 gm Fat • 24 gm Protein • 14 gm Carbohydrate • 591 mg Sodium • 80 mg Calcium • 1 gm Fiber

DIABETIC EXCHANGES: 3 Meat • ½ Starch • ½ Vegetable

Beef and Biscuits

This dish was inspired by the flavors of a hot roast beef sandwich, but I chose to use biscuit bits instead of bread, which doesn't stand up as well to all that tasty gravy! See why it's always good to have a chunk of cooked meat on hand? ☾ Serves 6

> 2 cups frozen mixed vegetables, thawed
> ½ cup chopped onion
> 1 (12-ounce) jar Heinz Fat Free Beef Gravy
> 2 full cups diced cooked lean roast beef
> 1 (2.5-ounce) can sliced mushrooms, drained
> 1 (7.5-ounce) can Pillsbury refrigerated buttermilk biscuits
> 1 teaspoon dried parsley flakes
> ½ teaspoon paprika

In an 8-by-8-inch microwave-safe baking dish, combine mixed vegetables and onion. Cover and microwave on HIGH (100% power) for 4 minutes. Add gravy, roast beef, and mushrooms. Mix well to combine. Re-cover and continue to microwave on HIGH for 6 to 8 minutes or until hot and bubbly, stirring after every 3 minutes. Separate biscuits and cut each into 4 pieces. Evenly sprinkle biscuit pieces over hot beef mixture. Sprinkle parsley flakes and paprika over top. Spray tops with butter-flavored cooking spray. Microwave, uncovered, on HIGH for 4 to 5 minutes or until biscuits spring back when lightly touched. Place baking dish on counter and let set for 3 minutes. Divide into 6 servings.

HINTS: 1. Thaw mixed vegetables by placing in a colander and rinsing under hot water for 1 minute.
2. If you don't have leftovers, purchase a chunk of cooked lean roast beef from your local deli.

Each serving equals:

HE: 2 Protein • 1½ Bread • ½ Vegetable •
14 Optional Calories

258 Calories • 6 gm Fat • 22 gm Protein •
29 gm Carbohydrate • 743 mg Sodium •
23 mg Calcium • 3 gm Fiber

DIABETIC EXCHANGES: 2 Meat • 1½ Starch •
1 Vegetable

Home Style Beef Hash

Remember that commercial that used to ask how to "handle" a man who's really hungry? This dish is one very good way! It's a hearty, true meat-and-potatoes combo that just can't be beat.

● Serves 4 (1¼ cups)

1 (12-ounce) jar Heinz Fat Free Beef Gravy☆
½ cup chopped onion
2 tablespoons reduced-sodium ketchup
1 tablespoon Worcestershire sauce
2 teaspoons dried parsley flakes
2 cups diced cooked lean roast beef
3 full cups diced cooked potatoes

In an 8-cup microwave-safe mixing bowl, combine ¼ cup gravy and onion. Microwave on HIGH (100% power) for 3 minutes. Stir in remaining gravy, ketchup, Worcestershire sauce, and parsley flakes. Add roast beef and potatoes. Mix well to combine. Cover and microwave on MEDIUM (50% power) for 12 to 14 minutes or until mixture is hot. Place bowl on counter, uncover, and let set for 5 minutes. Mix well before serving.

HINT: If you don't have leftovers, purchase a chunk of cooked lean roast beef from your local deli.

Each serving equals:

HE: 2½ Protein • 1 Bread • ¼ Vegetable • ¼ Slider • 9 Optional Calories

256 Calories • 4 gm Fat • 24 gm Protein •
31 gm Carbohydrate • 630 mg Sodium •
25 mg Calcium • 2 gm Fiber

DIABETIC EXCHANGES: 2½ Meat • 1½ Starch

Creole Pork Tenders

The Creoles were Europeans, many of them second sons, who settled the country around New Orleans in the late seventeenth century. They brought with them Spanish and French cuisine that combined with New World ingredients and became something new. The blend of onion, pepper, and celery used in almost all Creole and Cajun dishes is sometimes known as "the Holy Trinity."

● Serves 4

4 (4-ounce) lean tenderized pork tenderloins	1 (8-ounce) can Hunt's Tomato Sauce
½ cup chopped onion	1 tablespoon Splenda Granular
½ cup chopped green bell pepper	2 teaspoons dried parsley flakes
½ cup chopped celery	⅛ teaspoon black pepper
	2 to 3 drops Tabasco sauce

Evenly arrange pork pieces in an 8-by-8-inch microwave-safe baking dish. Sprinkle onion, green pepper, and celery evenly over meat. In a small bowl, combine tomato sauce, Splenda, parsley flakes, black pepper, and Tabasco sauce. Evenly spoon sauce mixture over top. Cover and microwave on HIGH (100% power) for 5 minutes, then microwave on MEDIUM (50% power) for 15 to 20 minutes or until meat is tender. Place baking dish on counter, uncover, and let set for 2 minutes. When serving, evenly spoon sauce over pork pieces.

HINT: Wonderful served with hot rice.

Each serving equals:

HE: 3 Protein • 1¾ Vegetable • 1 Optional Calorie

189 Calories • 5 gm Fat • 27 gm Protein •
9 gm Carbohydrate • 421 mg Sodium •
29 mg Calcium • 2 gm Fiber

DIABETIC EXCHANGES: 3 Meat • 1 Vegetable

German-Style Pork Tenders and Kraut

Cooking with beer is an inventive but long-lived tradition that delivers an astounding amount of flavor in a meat dish like this one. Even a non-alcoholic beer is full-bodied and adds just the right tangy touch to a simple preparation. ☻ Serves 4

> 4 (4-ounce) lean pork tenderloins or cutlets
> ½ cup chopped onion
> 1 (15-ounce) can Frank's Bavarian Style sauerkraut, drained
> ¼ cup non-alcoholic beer or water

Evenly arrange pork pieces in an 8-by-8-inch microwave-safe baking dish. Sprinkle onion and sauerkraut evenly over meat. Pour beer evenly over top. Cover and microwave on HIGH (100% power) for 5 minutes, then on MEDIUM (50% power) for 15 to 20 minutes or until meat is tender. Place baking dish on counter, uncover, and let set for 3 minutes. Evenly divide into 4 servings.

HINT: If you can't find Bavarian sauerkraut, use regular sauerkraut, ½ teaspoon caraway seeds, and 1 teaspoon Splenda Granular.

Each serving equals:

HE: 3 Protein • 1¼ Vegetable • 3 Optional Calories

192 Calories • 4 gm Fat • 23 gm Protein •
16 gm Carbohydrate • 663 mg Sodium •
10 mg Calcium • 0 gm Fiber

DIABETIC EXCHANGES: 3 Meat • 1 Vegetable

Bountiful Jambalaya

Traditional jambalaya can take up to several hours on the stove, which means that for most of us, we don't make it because we don't have that kind of time. But it's such a mouthwatering dish, so I decided there had to be a way to speed it up by using the microwave. Try it and see just how good it can be!

Serves 4 (1 cup)

½ cup chopped onion
½ cup chopped green bell
    pepper
½ teaspoon dried minced garlic
½ cup water ☆
1 (10¾-ounce) can Healthy
    Request Tomato Soup
1 cup uncooked Minute Rice

1 cup diced Dubuque 97% fat-
    free ham or any extra-
    lean ham
1 (6-ounce) package frozen
    cooked shrimp, thawed
1 teaspoon dried parsley flakes
2 to 3 drops Tabasco sauce

In an 8-cup microwave-safe mixing bowl, combine onion, green pepper, garlic, and 2 tablespoons water. Microwave on HIGH (100% power) for 3 to 4 minutes or until vegetables are tender. Stir in tomato soup and remaining 6 tablespoons water. Add uncooked instant rice, ham, shrimp, parsley flakes, and Tabasco sauce. Mix well to combine. Cover and continue to microwave on HIGH for 8 to 10 minutes or until rice and vegetables are tender, stirring after every 4 minutes. Place bowl on counter, uncover, and let set for 5 minutes. Mix well before serving.

Each serving equals:

HE: 2½ Protein • ¾ Bread • ½ Vegetable •
½ Slider • 5 Optional Calories

223 Calories • 3 gm Fat • 18 gm Protein •
31 gm Carbohydrate • 680 mg Sodium •
35 mg Calcium • 2 gm Fiber

DIABETIC EXCHANGES: 2½ Meat • 1 Starch •
½ Vegetable

Broccoli Cordon Bleu

Okay, so my husband, Cliff, wouldn't award the "blue ribbon" to any dish that contained broccoli, but I'm willing to bet that you will, once you taste this scrumptious supper dish that echoes the flavors of the original French dish (chicken, cheese, ham) but takes it a step or two further! ☻ Serves 4

> 4 slices reduced-calorie rye bread
> 1 cup diced cooked chicken breast
> 1 full cup diced Dubuque 97% fat-free ham or any extra-lean
>   ham
> 1 (10-ounce) package frozen cut broccoli, thawed
> 1 (10¾-ounce) can Healthy Request Cream of Mushroom Soup
> 1 teaspoon dried onion flakes
> 4 (¾-ounce) slices Kraft reduced-fat Swiss cheese

Spray an 8-by-8-inch microwave-safe baking dish with butter-flavored cooking spray. Place bread slices in prepared baking dish. In a large bowl, combine chicken, ham, and broccoli. Add mushroom soup and onion flakes. Mix well to combine. Evenly spoon mixture over bread. Arrange Swiss cheese slices evenly over top. Cover and refrigerate for at least 4 hours or overnight. When ready to cook, uncover and microwave on MEDIUM (50% power) for 20 to 22 minutes, turning baking dish after every 5 minutes. Place baking dish on counter and let set for 5 minutes. Divide into 4 servings.

HINTS: 1. If you don't have leftovers, purchase a chunk of cooked chicken breast from your local deli.
2. Thaw broccoli by placing in a colander and rinsing under hot water for 1 minute.

Each serving equals:

HE: 3¼ Protein • 1 Vegetable • ½ Bread • ½ Slider • 1 Optional Calorie

277 Calories • 9 gm Fat • 29 gm Protein • 20 gm Carbohydrate • 973 mg Sodium • 314 mg Calcium • 2 gm Fiber

DIABETIC EXCHANGES: 3 Meat • 1 Vegetable • 1 Starch

Alfredo Ham and Broccoli Dish

These ingredients are such a natural for the microwave—they "bloom" together in the speedy heat without losing their shape or getting mushy. This lush and creamy combo makes a delightful quick meal. ❂ Serves 4 (1 cup)

> 2 cups frozen cut broccoli, thawed
> 1½ cups diced Dubuque 97% fat-free ham or any extra-lean ham
> 2 cups cooked fettuccine or noodles
> 1 teaspoon lemon pepper
> ½ cup Land O Lakes Fat Free Half & Half
> 2 tablespoons fat-free milk
> ½ cup Kraft Reduced Fat Parmesan Style Grated Topping

In an 8-cup microwave-safe mixing bowl, combine broccoli and ham. Cover and microwave on HIGH (100% power) for 4 minutes. Drain, if necessary. Add fettuccine, lemon pepper, half & half, milk, and Parmesan cheese. Mix well to combine. Re-cover and continue to microwave on HIGH for 2 minutes. Place bowl on counter, uncover, and let set for 3 minutes. Mix well before serving.

HINTS: 1. Thaw broccoli by placing in a colander and rinsing under hot water for 1 minute.
2. Usually 1½ cups uncooked fettuccine cooks to about 2 cups.

Each serving equals:

HE: 2 Protein • 1 Bread • 1 Vegetable • ¼ Slider • 1 Optional Calorie

---

262 Calories • 6 gm Fat • 19 gm Protein • 33 gm Carbohydrate • 850 mg Sodium • 163 mg Calcium • 3 gm Fiber

---

DIABETIC EXCHANGES: 2 Meat • 1½ Starch • 1 Vegetable

Asparagus and Ham Pasta Dish

When you're cooking pasta for a family meal, it's a great idea to cook more than you need, so you've got an extra cup or two for a recipe like this one. Cooked pasta will keep in the refrigerator for up to three days, according to the National Pasta Association. And it reheats beautifully!   ☻   Serves 4 (1¼ cups)

> 1 (12-fluid-ounce) can Carnation Evaporated Fat Free Milk
> 2 tablespoons water
> 3 tablespoons all-purpose flour
> ¾ cup shredded Kraft reduced-fat mozzarella cheese
> 2 cups finely chopped fresh asparagus
> 1 teaspoon lemon pepper
> 1½ cups cooked rotini pasta, rinsed and drained
> 1½ cups diced Dubuque 97% fat-free ham or any extra-lean ham

In an 8-cup microwave-safe mixing bowl, combine evaporated milk and flour. Mix well using a wire whisk. Cover and microwave on HIGH (100% power) for 3 minutes, stirring after every minute. Stir in mozzarella cheese, asparagus, and lemon pepper. Add rotini pasta and ham. Mix well to combine. Re-cover and continue to microwave on HIGH for 5 minutes or until asparagus is tender and mixture is hot. Place bowl on counter, uncover, and let set for 3 minutes. Mix well before serving.

HINT: Usually a full 1 cup uncooked rotini pasta cooks to about 1½ cups.

Each serving equals:

HE: 2½ Protein • 1 Bread • 1 Vegetable • ¾ Fat Free Milk

---

302 Calories • 6 gm Fat • 28 gm Protein • 34 gm Carbohydrate • 884 mg Sodium • 433 mg Calcium • 2 gm Fiber

---

DIABETIC EXCHANGES: 2½ Meat • 1 Starch • 1 Vegetable • 1 Fat Free Milk

Creamed Ham and Cabbage

I always try to keep some extra cooked potatoes in the fridge for recipes like this one. As long as you've got them already made, this meal will come together in just minutes—but it doesn't taste as if you rushed.   ☺   Serves 4 (1 cup)

> 1 (12-fluid-ounce) can Carnation Evaporated Fat Free Milk
> 3 tablespoons all-purpose flour
> 4 cups purchased coleslaw mix
> 1½ cups diced cooked potatoes
> 1½ cups diced Dubuque 97% fat-free ham or any extra-lean ham
> 1 teaspoon dried parsley flakes
> ⅛ teaspoon black pepper

In an 8-cup microwave-safe mixing bowl, combine evaporated milk and flour. Mix well using a wire whisk. Cover and microwave on HIGH (100% power) for 3 minutes, stirring after every minute. Add coleslaw mix, potatoes, ham, parsley flakes, and black pepper. Mix well to combine. Re-cover and continue to microwave on HIGH for 8 to 10 minutes or until cabbage is tender, stirring after every 4 minutes. Place bowl on counter, uncover, and let set for 3 minutes. Mix well before serving.

HINT: 3¼ cups shredded cabbage and ¾ cup shredded carrots may be used in place of purchased coleslaw mix.

Each serving equals:

HE: 1½ Protein • 1 Vegetable • ¾ Fat Free Milk • ¾ Bread

239 Calories • 3 gm Fat • 19 gm Protein • 34 gm Carbohydrate • 647 mg Sodium • 286 mg Calcium • 3 gm Fiber

DIABETIC EXCHANGES: 1½ Meat • 1 Vegetable • 1 Fat Free Milk • 1 Starch

Ham and Cabbage Hot Dish

You've got choices when it comes to cabbage, but most people will use traditional green cabbage in this aromatic supper dish. If you love red cabbage, you may want to try this recipe with that veggie instead. ☻ Serves 4 (1 cup)

1 (8-ounce) can Hunt's Tomato Sauce

1½ teaspoons prepared yellow mustard

2 teaspoons Splenda Granular

1 (15-ounce) can diced tomatoes, undrained

½ cup chopped onion

1½ cups diced Dubuque 97% fat-free ham or any extra-lean ham

⅔ cup uncooked Minute Rice

3 cups coarsely chopped cabbage

1 teaspoon dried parsley flakes

⅛ teaspoon black pepper

In an 8-cup microwave-safe mixing bowl, combine tomato sauce, mustard, and Splenda. Stir in undrained tomatoes and onion. Add ham, uncooked rice, cabbage, parsley flakes, and black pepper. Mix well to combine. Cover and microwave on HIGH (100% power) for 10 to 14 minutes or until cabbage and rice are tender, stirring after every 5 minutes. Place bowl on counter, uncover, and let set for 5 minutes. Mix well before serving.

Each serving equals:

HE: 3 Vegetable • 1½ Protein • ½ Bread •
1 Optional Calorie

186 Calories • 2 gm Fat • 14 gm Protein •
28 gm Carbohydrate • 939 mg Sodium •
67 mg Calcium • 3 gm Fiber

DIABETIC EXCHANGES: 3 Vegetable • 1½ Meat •
1 Starch

Green Bean, Mushroom, and Ham Casserole

People sometimes wonder why I use mushrooms in a jar instead of fresh, and here's what I tell them: pre-cooked mushrooms are a timesaver, they don't go bad if you don't use them for a few days, and unlike fresh mushrooms, which can get spongy if cooked in liquid, they work beautifully with other ingredients in a dish like this. ☉ Serves 4

> 1 (10¾-ounce) can Healthy Request Cream of Mushroom Soup
> 2 tablespoons Land O Lakes Fat Free Half & Half
> 1½ teaspoons dried onion flakes
> 2 (15-ounce) cans French-style green beans, rinsed and drained
> 1 (2.5-ounce) jar sliced mushrooms, drained
> 2 full cups diced Dubuque 97% fat-free ham or any extra-lean ham
> 10 Ritz Reduced Fat Crackers, made into crumbs
> 6 tablespoons shredded Kraft reduced-fat Cheddar cheese

Spray an 8-by-8-inch microwave-safe baking dish with butter-flavored cooking spray. In a large bowl, combine mushroom soup and half & half. Add onion flakes, green beans, mushrooms, and ham. Mix well to combine. Spread mixture evenly in prepared baking dish. In a small bowl, combine cracker crumbs and Cheddar cheese. Evenly sprinkle mixture over top. Spray top with butter-flavored cooking spray. Microwave on HIGH (100% power) for 12 to 15 minutes or until mixture is hot and bubbly, turning dish after every 5 minutes. Place baking dish on counter and let set for 5 minutes. Divide into 4 servings.

HINT: A self-seal sandwich bag works great for crushing crackers.

Each serving equals:

HE: 2½ Protein • 2¼ Vegetable • ½ Bread •
½ Slider • 7 Optional Calories

236 Calories • 8 gm Fat • 20 gm Protein •
21 gm Carbohydrate • 996 mg Sodium •
191 mg Calcium • 3 gm Fiber

DIABETIC EXCHANGES: 2 Meat • 2 Vegetable •
1 Starch/Carbohydrate

Beans and Ham Combo

If you're looking for a high-fiber meal that also provides great nutritional value, you can't do much better than a dish based on beans. Remember to rinse and drain all your canned beans, which gets rid of excessive sodium and makes them just taste fresher.

◑ Serves 4 (1 cup)

> 1 (15-ounce) can diced tomatoes, undrained
> ¼ cup reduced-sodium ketchup
> 1 teaspoon prepared yellow mustard
> ⅛ teaspoon black pepper
> 1 (15-ounce) can Bush's great northern beans, rinsed and drained
> ½ cup chopped onion
> 1½ cups diced Dubuque 97% fat-free ham or any extra-lean ham

In an 8-cup microwave-safe mixing bowl, combine undrained tomatoes, ketchup, mustard, and black pepper. Add great northern beans, onion, and ham. Mix well to combine. Cover and microwave on HIGH (100% power) for 10 to 12 minutes or until mixture is hot, stirring after every 5 minutes. Place bowl on counter, uncover, and let set for 5 minutes. Mix well before serving.

Each serving equals:

HE: 2¾ Protein • 1¼ Vegetable • ½ Bread

---

194 Calories • 2 gm Fat • 17 gm Protein •
27 gm Carbohydrate • 607 mg Sodium •
63 mg Calcium • 5 gm Fiber

DIABETIC EXCHANGES: 2 Meat • 1 Vegetable • 1 Starch

Southern Sweet Potato Ham Hash

It's a very Southern-style approach to cooking when you create a dish that combines "meat" and "sweet"! Here, the nuts and added fruits join hands with the potatoes and ham for a plantation party that lasts all night long. ◐   Serves 4 (1 full cup)

3 cups peeled and chopped raw sweet potatoes
1 tablespoon water
1 cup (1 medium) cored, peeled, and chopped cooking apples
¼ cup chopped dried apricots
2 tablespoons chopped pecans
2 full cups diced Dubuque 97% fat-free ham or any extra-lean
    ham
1½ tablespoons apricot spreadable fruit

In an 8-cup microwave-safe mixing bowl, combine sweet potatoes and water. Cover and microwave on HIGH (100% power) for 5 minutes. Add apples, apricots, pecans, and ham. Mix well to combine. Stir in spreadable fruit. Re-cover and continue to microwave on HIGH for 8 to 10 minutes or until sweet potatoes are tender and mixture is hot, stirring after every 4 minutes. Place bowl on counter, uncover, and let set for 5 minutes. Mix well before serving.

Each serving equals:

HE: 2 Protein • 1 Bread • 1 Fruit • ½ Fat

261 Calories • 5 gm Fat • 16 gm Protein •
38 gm Carbohydrate • 729 mg Sodium •
33 mg Calcium • 4 gm Fiber

DIABETIC EXCHANGES: 2 Meat • 1 Starch • 1 Fruit •
½ Fat

Ham-Rice Florentine

Squeeze that thawed spinach! Squeeze it good! You don't want any extra water in this fragrant casserole—just the goodness of creamy, cheesy ham contrasted with the dark-green bits of this iron-rich vegetable that is so good for you. ☺ Serves 4 (1¼ cups)

> 1 (15-ounce) can diced tomatoes, undrained
> ½ cup finely chopped onion
> 1½ cups cooked rice
> 1 (10-ounce) package frozen chopped spinach, thawed and well drained
> ¼ cup Kraft Reduced Fat Parmesan Style Grated Topping
> 1½ cups diced Dubuque 97% fat-free ham or any extra-lean ham
> ⅛ teaspoon black pepper
> ½ cup + 1 tablespoon shredded Kraft reduced-fat mozzarella cheese

In an 8-cup microwave-safe mixing bowl, combine undrained tomatoes and onion. Cover and microwave on HIGH (100% power) for 3 minutes. Stir in rice, spinach, Parmesan cheese, ham, and black pepper. Re-cover and continue to microwave on HIGH for 5 minutes. Add mozzarella cheese. Mix well to combine. Place bowl on counter and let set for 3 minutes. Mix gently before serving.

HINT: Usually 1 cup uncooked instant rice or ¾ cup uncooked regular rice cooks to about 1½ cups.

Each serving equals:

HE: 2½ Protein • 1¾ Vegetable • ¾ Bread

234 Calories • 6 gm Fat • 19 gm Protein •
26 gm Carbohydrate • 819 mg Sodium •
213 mg Calcium • 4 gm Fiber

DIABETIC EXCHANGES: 2½ Meat • 1 Vegetable •
1 Starch

German Mashed Potato Pie

I thought of this first as a kind of shepherd's pie, but when I decided not to put the potatoes on top of the rest but to mix all of the ingredients together, it needed its own name. Don't you love the sound of a "mashed potato pie"? YUM! ☻ Serves 4

1½ cups water

2 teaspoons dried onion flakes

1 (10¾-ounce) can Healthy Request Cream of Mushroom Soup

1⅓ cups instant potato flakes

⅓ cup Carnation Nonfat Dry Milk Powder

1 (8-ounce) can sauerkraut, well drained

8 ounces Oscar Mayer or Healthy Choice reduced-fat
frankfurters, diced

½ cup + 1 tablespoon shredded Kraft reduced-fat Cheddar cheese

Spray an 8-by-8-inch microwave-safe baking dish with butter-flavored cooking spray. In an 8-cup microwave-safe mixing bowl, combine water and dried onion flakes. Microwave on HIGH (100% power) for 60 seconds. Stir in mushroom soup, potato flakes, and dry milk powder. Add sauerkraut, frankfurters, and Cheddar cheese. Mix well to combine. Spread mixture into prepared baking dish. Microwave on HIGH for 8 to 10 minutes or until mixture is very hot. Place baking dish on counter and let set for 3 minutes. Divide into 4 servings.

Each serving equals:

HE: 2¼ Protein • 1 Bread • ½ Vegetable •
¼ Fat Free Milk • ½ Slider • 6 Optional Calories

266 Calories • 6 gm Fat • 17 gm Protein •
36 gm Carbohydrate • 982 mg Sodium •
265 mg Calcium • 3 gm Fiber

DIABETIC EXCHANGES: 2 Meat • 1½ Starch •
½ Vegetable

Layered Bavarian Bake

This impressively bountiful casserole fairly oozes with great flavors, from tangy Swiss cheese to zesty corned beef, and all of it mingled with the unique taste of sauerkraut spiced with caraway. What a terrific choice for a family Halloween bash or an after-the-game supper during football season! ☾ Serves 6

> 2 cups hot water
> ¼ cup finely chopped onion
> ¼ cup Land O Lakes Fat Free Half & Half
> 2 cups instant potato flakes
> 1 (14½-ounce) can Frank's Bavarian Style sauerkraut,
>   well drained
> 3 (2.5-ounce) packages Carl Buddig 90% lean corned beef,
>   shredded
> 6 (¾-ounce) slices Kraft reduced-fat Swiss cheese

Spray a deep-dish 10-inch microwave-safe pie plate with butter-flavored cooking spray. In an 8-cup microwave-safe mixing bowl, combine water and onion. Microwave on HIGH (100% power) for 60 seconds. Stir in half & half. Add potato flakes. Mix well to combine. Fold in sauerkraut. Spread ⅔ of potato mixture in prepared pie plate. Sprinkle shredded corned beef over potato layer. Arrange Swiss cheese slices evenly over corned beef. Carefully spread remaining potato mixture over top. Microwave on HIGH (100% power) for 12 minutes, turning dish after every 4 minutes. Place pie plate on counter and let set for 5 minutes. Divide into 6 servings.

HINTS: 1. If you can't find Bavarian sauerkraut, use regular sauer-kraut, ½ teaspoon caraway seeds, and 1 teaspoon Splenda Granular.
2. Place sauerkraut in a colander and press juice out with a sturdy spoon.

Each serving equals:

HE: 2¼ Protein • 1 Bread • ⅔ Vegetable •
6 Optional Calories

199 Calories • 7 gm Fat • 14 gm Protein •
20 gm Carbohydrate • 860 mg Sodium •
235 mg Calcium • 1 gm Fiber

DIABETIC EXCHANGES: 2 Meat • 1 Starch • 1 Vegetable

Kids-of-All-Ages Casserole

Feel like a kid again, or just dazzle the youngsters coming for one of your kid's birthday parties, with this lip-smacking-good dish of cheesy, creamy franks! Make sure you dice the hot dog pieces small enough to keep your littlest guests safe.

◐ Serves 6 (1 scant cup)

> 1 (10¾-ounce) can Healthy Request Cream of Mushroom Soup
> ⅓ cup Land O Lakes Fat Free Half & Half
> 1½ cups diced Velveeta Light processed cheese
> 8 ounces Oscar Mayer or Healthy Choice reduced-fat
>   frankfurters, diced
> 1 teaspoon dried parsley flakes
> ⅛ teaspoon black pepper
> 3 cups cooked elbow macaroni

In an 8-cup microwave-safe mixing bowl, combine mushroom soup, half & half, and Velveeta cheese. Microwave on HIGH (100% power) for 4 minutes, stirring after 2 minutes. Stir in frankfurters, parsley flakes, and black pepper. Add macaroni. Mix well to combine. Continue to microwave on HIGH for 5 minutes or until mixture is hot. Place bowl on counter and let set for 3 minutes. Mix well before serving.

HINT: Usually 2 cups uncooked elbow macaroni cooks to about
    3 cups.

Each serving equals:

> HE: 2 Protein • 1 Bread • ¼ Slider •
> 16 Optional Calories
>
> ---
>
> 238 Calories • 6 gm Fat • 15 gm Protein •
> 31 gm Carbohydrate • 949 mg Sodium •
> 222 mg Calcium • 1 gm Fiber
>
> ---
>
> DIABETIC EXCHANGES: 2 Meat •
> 1½ Starch/Carbohydrate

Desserts

From the very beginning of Healthy Exchanges, I've been known for my desserts, and I'm still as proud as ever about creating truly scrumptious taste treats that everyone, whatever their health concerns may be, can enjoy without GUILT!

I've always given some of the credit to the wonderful manufacturers of good-for-us convenience foods, and I'd also like to celebrate the appliances that make it fun and easy for busy people to bake. As innovations in the kitchen go, the microwave has invited cooks of all ages and experience to stir up healthy desserts that don't taste like "you're on a diet."

With this book, you'll be able to "bake up a storm" in your magnificent microwave, which is especially good for preparing fabulous fruity sauces (Rhubarb Orange Dessert Sauce), as well as exquisite old-fashioned delights such as Easy as Pie Apple Crisp and Pumpkin Patch Pie. I've given you lots of fun choices here, including puddings, cakes, and custards for all occasions. Whether you're planning a baby shower or a family potluck, a bake sale or a picnic, you'll have exactly what you need to make a culinary splash!

Rhubarb Orange Dessert Sauce

A great way to keep from getting bored with the same old, same old desserts is to pour a freshly made sauce over the top! This one is a luscious color, and it spreads sunshine everywhere you use it.

○ Serves 8 (½ cup)

1 (4-serving) package JELL-O sugar-free vanilla cook-and-serve
     pudding mix
1 cup unsweetened orange juice
¼ cup Splenda Granular
6 cups finely chopped fresh or frozen rhubarb, thawed
5 to 6 drops red food coloring

In an 8-cup microwave-safe mixing bowl, combine dry pudding mix, orange juice, and Splenda. Mix well using a wire whisk. Add rhubarb. Mix well to combine. Microwave on HIGH (100% power) for 8 minutes or just until mixture starts to boil, stirring after 4 minutes. Stir in red food coloring. Place bowl on counter and let set for 2 minutes. Mix well before serving.

HINT: Good served "as is" warm or cold, spooned over angel food cake, over sugar- and fat-free vanilla ice cream, or over pancakes.

Each serving equals:

HE: ¾ Vegetable • ¼ Fruit • 13 Optional Calories

44 Calories • 0 gm Fat • 1 gm Protein •
10 gm Carbohydrate • 61 mg Sodium •
81 mg Calcium • 1 gm Fiber

DIABETIC EXCHANGES: ½ Fruit

Creamy Fruit Parfait

Here's a delectable and easy dessert to make when you don't have fresh fruit in the house but still want that flavor. (It's another one of my creative ways to use Diet Mountain Dew, too!)

◐ Serves 4

1 (4-serving) package JELL-O sugar-free vanilla cook-and-serve pudding mix
⅔ cup Carnation Nonfat Dry Milk Powder
1 (15-ounce) can fruit cocktail, packed in fruit juice, undrained
½ cup Diet Mountain Dew
¼ cup Cool Whip Lite

In an 8-cup microwave-safe mixing bowl, combine dry pudding mix, dry milk powder, undrained fruit cocktail, and Diet Mountain Dew. Cover and microwave on HIGH (100% power) for 5 minutes or just until mixture starts to boil, stirring after every 2 minutes. Place bowl on counter, uncover, and let set for 5 minutes, stirring occasionally. Evenly spoon pudding mixture into 4 parfait or dessert dishes. Refrigerate for at least 30 minutes. When serving, top each with 1 tablespoon Cool Whip Lite.

Each serving equals:

HE: 1 Fruit • ½ Fat Free Milk • ¼ Slider • 10 Optional Calories

100 Calories • 0 gm Fat • 4 gm Protein • 21 gm Carbohydrate • 102 mg Sodium • 150 mg Calcium • 1 gm Fiber

DIABETIC EXCHANGES: 1 Fruit • ½ Fat Free Milk

Fruit-Topped Cheesecake Tarts

Why make mini-cheesecakes instead of one big one? I can think of a few reasons: they're easy to serve, they look luscious, and they give you the option of fewer servings in a small household (my cheesecakes serve eight). Enjoy!   ☻   Serves 4

> 6 (2½-inch) graham crackers, made into crumbs
> 1 (8-ounce) package Philadelphia fat-free cream cheese
> ⅓ cup Splenda Granular
> 1 egg or equivalent in egg substitute
> 1 tablespoon Land O Lakes no-fat sour cream
> 1 tablespoon lemon juice
> ½ teaspoon vanilla extract
> 6 tablespoons spreadable fruit (any flavor)

Evenly sprinkle graham cracker crumbs into 4 (8-ounce) custard cups. In a medium bowl, stir cream cheese with a sturdy spoon until soft. Add Splenda, egg, sour cream, lemon juice, and vanilla extract. Using a wire whisk, mix well until light and fluffy. Evenly spoon about ¼ cup mixture into each custard cup. Arrange custard cups in a circle in microwave. Microwave on MEDIUM (50% power) for 5 minutes or until center is almost set. Place custard cups on counter and let set for 5 minutes. Meanwhile, in a small bowl, stir spreadable fruit with a spoon until slightly softened. Top each cheesecake with 1½ tablespoons spreadable fruit. Refrigerate for at least 1 hour.

HINT: A self-seal sandwich bag works great for crushing graham crackers.

Each serving equals:

HE: 1¼ Protein • 1 Fruit • ½ Bread •
12 Optional Calories

---

178 Calories • 2 gm Fat • 10 gm Protein •
30 gm Carbohydrate • 366 mg Sodium •
174 mg Calcium • 0 gm Fiber

DIABETIC EXCHANGES: 1 Meat • 1 Fruit •
1 Starch/Carbohydrate

Lemon Cream and Chocolate Parfaits

What a delectably simple way to dazzle your dinner guests! These parfaits look just lovely, and they taste even better than they look. If you don't own a set of parfait glasses, put some on your wish list—or keep visiting yard sales until you score a set.

❂ Serves 4

> 1 (4-serving) package JELL-O sugar-free vanilla cook-and-serve pudding mix
> 1 (4-serving) package JELL-O sugar-free lemon gelatin
> ⅔ cup Carnation Nonfat Dry Milk Powder
> 2 tablespoons Splenda Granular
> 1¾ cups water
> 1 (8-ounce) package Philadelphia fat-free cream cheese
> 6 (2½-inch) chocolate graham crackers, made into crumbs
> 1 tablespoon + 1 teaspoon mini chocolate chips

In an 8-cup microwave-safe mixing bowl, combine dry pudding mix, dry gelatin, dry milk powder, Splenda, and water. Microwave on HIGH (100% power) for 5 minutes or just until mixture starts to boil, stirring after 3 minutes. Add cream cheese. Mix well using a wire whisk, until mixture is thoroughly blended. For each parfait, spoon about ¼ cup pudding mixture into 4 parfait dishes, sprinkle about 2 tablespoons graham cracker crumbs over pudding mixture, top with another ¼ cup pudding mixture, and sprinkle with 1 teaspoon chocolate chips. Refrigerate for at least 15 minutes.

HINT: A self-seal sandwich bag works great for crushing graham crackers.

Each serving equals:

HE: 1 Protein • ½ Fat Free Milk • ½ Bread •
¼ Slider • 15 Optional Calories

146 Calories • 2 gm Fat • 14 gm Protein •
18 gm Carbohydrate • 523 mg Sodium •
409 mg Calcium • 0 gm Fiber

DIABETIC EXCHANGES: 1 Meat • 1 Starch/Carbohydrate

Orange Marmalade Pecan Custard

I stood in the grocery store aisle thinking about what flavor I'd like to combine with my favorite nut, the pecan. So many choices, so little time—so I chose the tart 'n' sweet orange marmalade to create my collage of tastes and texture. ☺ Serves 4

> 1 (4-serving) package JELL-O sugar-free vanilla cook-and-serve
>   pudding mix
> ⅔ cup Carnation Nonfat Dry Milk Powder
> 1½ cups water
> 6 tablespoons orange marmalade spreadable fruit
> 2 tablespoons chopped pecans
> ¼ cup Cool Whip Lite

In an 8-cup microwave-safe mixing bowl, combine dry pudding mix, dry milk powder, and water. Stir in spreadable fruit and pecans. Microwave on HIGH (100% power) for 6 minutes or just until mixture starts to boil, stirring after 3 minutes. Place bowl on counter and let set for 5 minutes, stirring occasionally. Evenly spoon mixture into 4 dessert dishes. Refrigerate for at least 30 minutes. When serving, top each with 1 tablespoon Cool Whip Lite.

Each serving equals:

> HE: 1 Fruit • ½ Fat Free Milk • ½ Fat • ¼ Slider •
> 10 Optional Calories
>
> ---
>
> 151 Calories • 3 gm Fat • 4 gm Protein •
> 27 gm Carbohydrate • 169 mg Sodium •
> 155 mg Calcium • 0 gm Fiber
>
> ---
>
> DIABETIC EXCHANGES: 1 Fruit • ½ Fat Free Milk •
> ½ Fat

Pears Helene Pudding Treats

I can think of no better way to win a woman's heart than to name a luscious dessert creation after her! Good for you, Helene, whoever you were, whose passion for chocolate and pears allows us to share the love. ☺ Serves 4

> 1 (4-serving) package JELL-O sugar-free chocolate cook-and-serve
>   pudding mix
> ⅔ cup Carnation Nonfat Dry Milk Powder
> 1 (15-ounce) can pear halves, packed in fruit juice, finely chopped
>   and drained, and ⅓ cup liquid reserved
> 1¼ cups water
> 2 tablespoons Land O Lakes Fat Free Half & Half
> ½ teaspoon vanilla extract
> ¼ cup chopped walnuts
> ¼ cup Cool Whip Lite
> 1 tablespoon + 1 teaspoon mini chocolate chips

In an 8-cup microwave-safe mixing bowl, combine dry pudding mix, dry milk powder, reserved pear liquid, water, and half & half. Mix well using a wire whisk. Cover and microwave on HIGH (100% power) for 6 minutes or just until mixture starts to boil, stirring after 3 minutes. Stir in vanilla extract, chopped pears, and walnuts. Place bowl on counter, uncover, and let set for 5 minutes, stirring occasionally. Evenly spoon mixture into 4 dessert dishes. Refrigerate for at least 30 minutes. When serving, top each with 1 tablespoon Cool Whip Lite and 1 teaspoon chocolate chips.

Each serving equals:

HE: 1 Fruit • ½ Fat Free Milk • ½ Fat • ¼ Protein •
½ Slider • 11 Optional Calories

196 Calories • 6 gm Fat • 6 gm Protein •
30 gm Carbohydrate • 178 mg Sodium •
181 mg Calcium • 3 gm Fiber

DIABETIC EXCHANGES: 1 Fruit • 1 Fat •
½ Fat Free Milk • ½ Other Carbohydrate

Pears with Raspberry Sauce

It's simple but sensational to top a pale pear with an irresistibly gorgeous, rosy-red raspberry sauce—and with this recipe, it couldn't be easier! Perfect for a card party or ladies' luncheon, I'd say.

● Serves 4

> 1 (15-ounce) can pear halves, packed in fruit juice, coarsely chopped, drained, and ½ cup liquid reserved
> 1 (4-serving) package JELL-O sugar-free vanilla cook-and-serve pudding mix
> 1 (4-serving) package JELL-O sugar-free raspberry gelatin
> 1 cup water
> 1½ cups frozen unsweetened raspberries, thawed and juice reserved
> ¼ cup Cool Whip Lite
> 1 tablespoon + 1 teaspoon slivered almonds

Evenly divide pear pieces between 4 dessert dishes. In an 8-cup microwave-safe mixing bowl, combine dry pudding mix, dry gelatin, reserved pear liquid, and water. Microwave on HIGH (100% power) for 5 minutes or just until mixture starts to boil, stirring after 3 minutes. Stir in raspberries with juice. Place bowl on counter and let set for 10 minutes, stirring occasionally. Evenly spoon about ½ cup raspberry mixture over pears in dessert dishes. Refrigerate for at least 1 hour. When serving, top each with 1 tablespoon Cool Whip Lite and 1 teaspoon almonds.

Each serving equals:

HE: 1½ Fruit • ⅓ Fat • ¼ Slider •
10 Optional Calories

122 Calories • 2 gm Fat • 2 gm Protein •
24 gm Carbohydrate • 82 mg Sodium •
28 mg Calcium • 5 gm Fiber

DIABETIC EXCHANGES: 1½ Fruit • ½ Fat

Strawberries and Cream Pudding

I'll probably never get to watch Wimbledon in person (truth: I'm not that big a tennis fan), but I love the look of the tournament when I see it on television. The players still must wear white, the courts are grass green, and instead of fast food, the fans are devouring plates of strawberries and cream! This is my "toast" to tennis!

○ Serves 4

3 cups frozen unsweetened strawberries

½ cup Splenda Granular

2 teaspoons cornstarch

1 (4-serving) package JELL-O sugar-free vanilla cook-and-serve pudding mix

⅔ cup Carnation Nonfat Dry Milk Powder

1 cup water

¼ cup Land O Lakes Fat Free Half & Half

In an 8-cup microwave-safe mixing bowl, combine strawberries and Splenda. Microwave on HIGH (100% power) for 2 minutes. Stir in cornstarch. Continue to microwave on HIGH for 4 minutes. Place bowl on counter. In another 8-cup microwave-safe mixing bowl, combine dry pudding mix, dry milk powder, water, and half & half. Microwave on HIGH for 5 minutes or just until mixture starts to boil, stirring after 3 minutes. Place bowl on counter and let set for 10 minutes, stirring occasionally. For each serving, spoon ¼ cup strawberries into 4 parfait dishes and spoon ¼ cup pudding mixture over strawberries. Repeat layers. Refrigerate for at least 1 hour.

Each serving equals:

HE: ¾ Fruit • ½ Fat Free Milk • ½ Slider • 2 Optional Calories

132 Calories • 0 gm Fat • 5 gm Protein • 28 gm Carbohydrate • 107 mg Sodium • 197 mg Calcium • 3 gm Fiber

DIABETIC EXCHANGES: ½ Fruit • ½ Fat Free Milk • ½ Other Carbohydrate

Fireside Pudding

Even if you never spent a week at Girl Scout Camp, you'll quickly adore this pudding version of the classic cookout treat, s'mores. Has it been more than a few years since you roasted marshmallows under the stars? This dish will bring back plenty of happy memories!   ● Serves 4

> 1 (4-serving) package JELL-O sugar-free vanilla cook-and-serve
>   pudding mix
> 1 (12-fluid-ounce) can Carnation Evaporated Fat Free Milk
> ½ cup Land O Lakes no-fat sour cream
> ¼ cup purchased graham cracker crumbs or 4 (2½-inch) graham
>   cracker squares, made into crumbs
> ¼ cup miniature marshmallows
> ¼ cup Hershey's Lite Chocolate Syrup

In an 8-cup microwave-safe mixing bowl, combine dry pudding mix and evaporated milk. Microwave on HIGH (100% power) for 4 minutes or just until mixture starts to boil, stirring after 2 minutes. Place bowl on counter and let set for at least 15 minutes, stirring occasionally. Fold in sour cream. Evenly spoon mixture into 4 dessert dishes. Sprinkle 1 tablespoon cracker crumbs and 1 tablespoon marshmallows over top of each. Drizzle 1 tablespoon chocolate syrup over marshmallows. Refrigerate for at least 30 minutes.

HINT: A self-seal sandwich bag works great for crushing graham crackers.

Each serving equals:

HE: ¾ Fat Free Milk • ⅓ Bread • ¾ Slider •
11 Optional Calories

173 Calories • 1 gm Fat • 8 gm Protein •
33 gm Carbohydrate • 345 mg Sodium •
284 mg Calcium • 1 gm Fiber

DIABETIC EXCHANGES: 1 Fat Free Milk •
1 Starch/Carbohydrate

Coconut Custard Dessert

There's just something about coconut that carries us away to South Sea islands where the only decision we need to make is "Pina colada or strawberry daiquiri?" This light dessert is a perfect end to a meaty main course.   ☻   Serves 4

> 1 (4-serving) package JELL-O sugar-free vanilla cook-and-serve
>   pudding mix
> ⅔ cup Carnation Nonfat Dry Milk Powder
> 1¾ cups water
> 1 teaspoon rum extract
> 1 teaspoon coconut extract
> 4 teaspoons flaked coconut

In an 8-cup microwave-safe mixing bowl, combine dry pudding mix, dry milk powder, water, rum extract, and coconut extract. Microwave on HIGH (100% power) for 4 minutes or just until mixture starts to boil, stirring after every 2 minutes. Place bowl on counter and let set for 5 minutes, stirring occasionally. Evenly spoon mixture into 4 dessert dishes. Sprinkle 1 teaspoon coconut evenly over each. Refrigerate for at least 2 hours.

Each serving equals:

HE: ½ Fat Free Milk • ¼ Slider • 5 Optional Calories

---

69 Calories • 1 gm Fat • 4 gm Protein •
11 gm Carbohydrate • 182 mg Sodium •
151 mg Calcium • 0 gm Fiber

DIABETIC EXCHANGES: ½ Fat Free Milk

Southern-Style
Banana Meringue Pudding

Wherever you travel in the southern United States, you'll find banana pudding on the menu. It's the favorite of boys and girls throughout the region, so I thought I'd try to make my own version of this frothy, creamy treat. ☻ Serves 4

> 1 (4-serving) package JELL-O sugar-free vanilla cook-and-serve
>   pudding mix
> ⅔ cup Carnation Nonfat Dry Milk Powder
> 1¾ cups water
> 6 (2½-inch) graham cracker squares ☆
> 2 cups (2 medium) diced bananas
> 3 egg whites
> 1 teaspoon vanilla extract
> ¼ cup Splenda Granular

In an 8-cup microwave-safe mixing bowl, combine dry pudding mix, dry milk powder, and water. Microwave on HIGH (100% power) for 5 minutes or just until mixture starts to boil, stirring after 3 minutes. Coarsely crush 3 graham crackers. Stir in bananas and graham cracker pieces. Evenly spoon mixture into four (8-ounce) microwave-safe custard cups. In a medium bowl, beat egg whites with an electric mixer on HIGH until soft peaks form. Add vanilla extract and Splenda. Continue beating on HIGH for 3 minutes or until stiff peaks form. Evenly spoon meringue on top of puddings. Finely crush remaining 3 graham crackers. Evenly sprinkle crumbs over tops of meringue. Arrange custard cups in a circle in microwave. Microwave on HIGH for 3 minutes or until a knife inserted into meringue comes out clean. Place custard cups on counter and let set for 10 minutes. Refrigerate for at least 30 minutes.

HINT: A self-seal sandwich bag works great for crushing graham
    crackers.

Each serving equals:

HE: 1 Fruit • ½ Fat Free Milk • ½ Bread •
¼ Protein • ¼ Slider • 3 Optional Calories

177 Calories • 1 gm Fat • 8 gm Protein •
34 gm Carbohydrate • 197 mg Sodium •
159 mg Calcium • 2 gm Fiber

DIABETIC EXCHANGES: 1 Fruit • ½ Fat Free Milk •
½ Starch

Maple Pumpkin Pudding

Canned pumpkin is a great pantry helper—a terrifically moist addition to breads and cakes, and the ideal centerpiece for a creamy pudding that celebrates the special flavors of New England in the fall! ☻ Serves 6

> 1 (15-ounce) can Libby's solid-pack pumpkin
> ⅔ cup Carnation Nonfat Dry Milk Powder
> 1 cup water
> 1 (4-serving) package JELL-O sugar-free vanilla cook-and-serve pudding mix
> ½ cup Log Cabin Sugar Free Maple Syrup
> 1 teaspoon pumpkin pie spice
> 3 tablespoons chopped pecans
> 6 tablespoons Cool Whip Lite

In an 8-cup microwave-safe mixing bowl, combine pumpkin, dry milk powder, water, dry pudding mix, and maple syrup. Add pumpkin pie spice. Mix well to combine. Cover and microwave on MEDIUM (50% power) for 10 minutes or just until mixture starts to boil, stirring with a wire whisk after every 4 minutes. Stir in pecans. Place bowl on counter, uncover, and let set for 5 minutes, stirring occasionally. Evenly spoon mixture into 6 dessert dishes. Refrigerate for at least 30 minutes. Just before serving, top each with 1 tablespoon Cool Whip Lite.

Each serving equals:

HE: ⅔ Vegetable • ½ Fat • ⅓ Fat Free Milk • ¼ Slider • 17 Optional Calories

---

111 Calories • 3 gm Fat • 4 gm Protein • 17 gm Carbohydrate • 154 mg Sodium • 126 mg Calcium • 3 gm Fiber

---

DIABETIC EXCHANGES: 1 Starch • ½ Fat

Springtime Tapioca Pudding

When spring comes to Iowa it brings the rhubarb, which inspires Iowa cooks to invent dishes like this one. I used frozen berries because the raspberry season and the rhubarb season don't coincide, alas. The good news is that frozen berries do a great job in this recipe!   ❤   Serves 4

> 1 (4-serving) package JELL-O sugar-free raspberry gelatin
> 3 tablespoons Quick Cooking Minute Tapioca
> ½ cup Splenda Granular
> ½ cup Diet Mountain Dew
> 3 cups finely chopped fresh or frozen rhubarb, thawed
> 1½ cups frozen raspberries, undrained

In an 8-cup microwave-safe mixing bowl, combine dry gelatin, tapioca, Splenda, and Diet Mountain Dew. Stir in rhubarb and undrained raspberries. Cover and microwave on HIGH (100% power) for 8 minutes or just until mixture starts to boil and rhubarb is tender, stirring after 5 minutes. Place bowl on counter, uncover, and let set for 5 minutes, stirring occasionally. Evenly spoon mixture into 4 dessert dishes. Refrigerate for at least 30 minutes.

Each serving equals:

HE: ¾ Vegetable • ½ Fruit • ½ Slider •
4 Optional Calories

88 Calories • 0 gm Fat • 2 gm Protein •
20 gm Carbohydrate • 62 mg Sodium •
90 mg Calcium • 4 gm Fiber

DIABETIC EXCHANGES: 1 Fruit • ½ Starch/Carbohydrate

Tapioca Pudding

Nothing could be simpler—or more lip-smacking good—than this classic tapioca made in the microwave. Make sure you use real vanilla, not an imitation extract. It's gotten more expensive, but this is a case when the real thing makes all the difference.

❂ Serves 6

> 3 cups fat-free milk
> 1 (4-serving) package JELL-O sugar-free vanilla cook-and-serve
>   pudding mix
> 3 tablespoons Quick Cooking Minute Tapioca
> 1 teaspoon vanilla extract

In an 8-cup microwave-safe mixing bowl, combine milk, dry pudding mix, tapioca, and vanilla extract. Let set for 5 minutes. Microwave on MEDIUM (50% power) for 15 minutes or just until mixture starts to boil, stirring after every 5 minutes. Place bowl on counter and let set for 5 minutes, stirring occasionally. Spoon mixture into 6 dessert dishes. Serve warm or cold.

Each serving equals:

HE: ½ Fat Free Milk • ¼ Slider • 8 Optional Calories

---

72 Calories • 0 gm Fat • 4 gm Protein •
14 gm Carbohydrate • 140 mg Sodium •
151 mg Calcium • 0 gm Fiber

DIABETIC EXCHANGES: ½ Fat Free Milk • ½ Starch

Apricot Rice Pudding

I like to think of the apricots in this dish as the "buried treasure," fun to find and even more fun to eat. They make a great addition to a creamy dessert, with their wrinkly texture and sweet flavor.

❂ Serves 6

> 1 (4-serving) package JELL-O sugar-free vanilla cook-and-serve
>   pudding mix
> 1 cup Carnation Nonfat Dry Milk Powder
> 3 cups water
> ½ cup chopped dried apricots
> 1 cup uncooked Minute Rice
> 1 teaspoon vanilla extract
> Dash ground nutmeg

In an 8-cup microwave-safe mixing bowl, combine dry pudding mix, dry milk powder, and water. Stir in chopped apricots and uncooked rice. Cover and microwave on HIGH (100% power) for 6 minutes or just until mixture starts to boil, stirring after 3 minutes. Add vanilla extract. Mix well to combine. Place bowl on counter, uncover, and let set for 5 minutes, stirring occasionally. Evenly spoon mixture into 6 dessert dishes. Sprinkle nutmeg over top of each. Refrigerate for at least 30 minutes.

Each serving equals:

HE: ½ Fat Free Milk • ½ Bread • ½ Fruit •
13 Optional Calories

128 Calories • 0 gm Fat • 5 gm Protein •
27 gm Carbohydrate • 143 mg Sodium •
160 mg Calcium • 1 gm Fiber

DIABETIC EXCHANGES: ½ Fat Free Milk • ½ Starch •
½ Fruit

Rice Raisin Pudding Treats

Even after all these years, every diner I know still serves rice pudding. Why fiddle with what works, right? Well, here is a classic comfort food dessert—and it still satisfies! ☻ Serves 4

> 1 (4-serving) package JELL-O sugar-free vanilla cook-and-serve
>   pudding mix
> 3 cups fat-free milk
> 2/3 cup uncooked Minute Rice
> 1/2 cup seedless raisins
> Dash cinnamon
> 1/4 cup Cool Whip Lite

In an 8-cup microwave-safe mixing bowl, combine dry pudding mix and milk. Stir in uncooked rice and raisins. Cover and microwave on HIGH (100% power) for 6 minutes or just until mixture starts to boil, stirring after 3 minutes. Place bowl on counter, uncover, and let set for 5 minutes, stirring occasionally. Evenly spoon pudding mixture into 4 dessert dishes and lightly sprinkle cinnamon over top of each. Refrigerate for at least 30 minutes. When serving, top each with 1 tablespoon Cool Whip Lite.

Each serving equals:

HE: 1 Fruit • 3/4 Fat Free Milk • 1/2 Bread • 1/4 Slider •
10 Optional Calories

185 Calories • 1 gm Fat • 8 gm Protein •
36 gm Carbohydrate • 113 mg Sodium •
181 mg Calcium • 1 gm Fiber

DIABETIC EXCHANGES: 1 Fruit • 1 Fat Free Milk •
1 Starch

Apple Harvest Rice Pudding

Coring apples used to be a frustrating kitchen assignment—the old apple corers weren't very easy to use. But now there are wonderful little tools that push the core right out, so you don't have to worry about breaking a nail or scraping a finger. Bring on the apple harvest! ● Serves 4

1 (4-serving) package JELL-O sugar-free vanilla cook-and-serve pudding mix
⅔ cup Carnation Nonfat Dry Milk Powder
1 cup unsweetened apple juice
1 cup water
1 cup (2 small) cored, peeled and diced cooking apples
⅔ cup uncooked Minute Rice
1 teaspoon apple pie spice
2 tablespoons chopped walnuts
¼ cup Cool Whip Lite

In an 8-cup microwave-safe mixing bowl, combine dry pudding mix, dry milk powder, apple juice, and water. Stir in apples and uncooked rice. Cover and microwave on HIGH (100% power) for 8 minutes or just until mixture starts to boil, stirring after 3 minutes. Stir in apple pie spice and walnuts. Place bowl on counter, uncover, and let set for 5 minutes, stirring occasionally. Evenly spoon pudding mixture into 4 dessert dishes. Refrigerate for at least 30 minutes. When serving, top each with 1 tablespoon Cool Whip Lite.

Each serving equals:

HE: 1 Fruit • ½ Fat Free Milk • ½ Bread • ½ Fat • ¼ Slider • 18 Optional Calories

179 Calories • 3 gm Fat • 6 gm Protein • 32 gm Carbohydrate • 123 mg Sodium • 165 mg Calcium • 1 gm Fiber

DIABETIC EXCHANGES: 1 Fruit • 1 Other Carbohydrate • ½ Fat Free Milk

Apple Dumpling Cups

These are fun food, according to my grandchildren, who saw the little custard cups cooling on the counter and said, "Please, can I taste that?" As soon as I said yes, they dove in—and the cheers that followed warmed this grandma's heart!   ☺   Serves 6

3 cups (6 small) cored, peeled, and sliced cooking apples
¾ cup Splenda Granular
¾ cup Bisquick Reduced Fat Baking Mix
2 tablespoons I Can't Believe It's Not Butter! Light Margarine
6 tablespoons chopped walnuts
¾ cup Land O Lakes Fat Free Half & Half
2 tablespoons purchased graham cracker crumbs or 2 (2½-inch)
    graham cracker squares, made into crumbs

In a large bowl, combine apples and Splenda. Evenly spoon mixture into six (8-ounce) microwave-safe custard cups. In a medium bowl, combine baking mix and margarine. Stir in walnuts. Sprinkle crumb mixture evenly over apples in custard cups. Drizzle 2 tablespoons half & half over top of each. Evenly sprinkle 1 teaspoon graham cracker crumbs over top. Arrange prepared custard cups in a circle in microwave. Microwave on HIGH (100% power) for 8 to 10 minutes or until apples are tender. Place custard cups on counter and let set for 2 minutes before serving.

Each serving equals:

HE: 1 Fruit • 1 Fat • ⅔ Bread • ¼ Protein •
¼ Slider • 17 Optional Calories

---

188 Calories • 8 gm Fat • 3 gm Protein •
26 gm Carbohydrate • 258 mg Sodium •
54 mg Calcium • 2 gm Fiber

DIABETIC EXCHANGES: 1 Fruit • 1 Fat •
1 Other Carbohydrate

Apple Bread Pudding

Over the years, I've developed a basic bread pudding recipe that really satisfies my taste for this old-fashioned delight, but I love to keep coming up with new "tweaks" of flavor and texture. This one will appeal to young and old alike! ○ Serves 4

> 1 (4-serving) package JELL-O sugar-free vanilla cook-and-serve
> pudding mix
> 2 cups fat-free milk
> 1 cup (2 small) cored, peeled, and diced cooking apples
> ¼ cup seedless raisins
> 1 teaspoon apple pie spice
> 1 teaspoon vanilla extract
> 4 slices reduced-calorie bread, cubed

In an 8-cup microwave-safe mixing bowl, combine dry pudding mix and milk. Cover and microwave on HIGH (100% power) for 5 minutes or just until mixture starts to boil, stirring after 2 minutes. Stir in apples, raisins, apple pie spice, and vanilla extract. Continue to microwave on HIGH for 2 minutes. Gently stir in bread cubes. Continue to microwave on HIGH for 1½ minutes. Place bowl on counter and let set for 5 minutes, stirring occasionally. Evenly spoon mixture into 4 dessert dishes. Good warm or cold.

Each serving equals:

HE: 1 Fruit • ½ Fat Free Milk • ½ Bread • ¼ Slider

157 Calories • 1 gm Fat • 7 gm Protein •
30 gm Carbohydrate • 294 mg Sodium •
175 mg Calcium • 1 gm Fiber

DIABETIC EXCHANGES: 1 Fruit • ½ Fat Free Milk •
½ Starch

South Seas Orange Squares

When I tasted this, I felt the seductive pull of those tropical breezes. Was it Tahiti calling my name, or just Cliff wondering if it was time for dinner?   ☻   Serves 6

12 (2½-inch) graham cracker squares ☆
1 (4-serving) package JELL-O sugar-free vanilla cook-and-serve pudding mix
1 (4-serving) package JELL-O sugar-free orange gelatin
⅔ cup Carnation Nonfat Dry Milk Powder
2 cups cold water
2 (11-ounce) cans mandarin oranges, rinsed and drained
½ teaspoon coconut extract
2 tablespoons flaked coconut
1 tablespoon Splenda Granular
6 tablespoons Cool Whip Lite

Evenly arrange 8 graham cracker squares in an 8-by-8-inch microwave-safe baking dish, breaking as necessary to fit. In an 8-cup microwave-safe mixing bowl, combine dry pudding mix, dry gelatin, dry milk powder, and water. Microwave on HIGH (100% power) for 5 minutes or just until mixture starts to boil, stirring after 3 minutes. Place bowl on counter. Stir in mandarin oranges and coconut extract. Let set for 10 minutes, stirring occasionally. Carefully spoon mixture over graham cracker crust. Refrigerate for 1 hour. Crush remaining 4 graham crackers. In a small bowl, combine graham cracker crumbs, coconut, and Splenda. Evenly sprinkle crumb mixture over top of set filling. Cut into 6 servings. When serving, top each with 1 tablespoon Cool Whip Lite.

HINT: A self-seal sandwich bag works great for crushing graham crackers.

Each serving equals:

HE: ⅔ Bread • ⅔ Fruit • ⅓ Fat Free Milk •
¼ Slider • 16 Optional Calories

130 Calories • 2 gm Fat • 5 gm Protein •
23 gm Carbohydrate • 246 mg Sodium •
109 mg Calcium • 1 gm Fiber

DIABETIC EXCHANGES: 1 Starch/Carbohydrate • ½ Fruit

Cheery Cherry Cobbler

Remember the classic song promising that gray skies were going to clear up, so put on a happy face? Well, no matter what the weather looks like outside, you're bound to smile when you serve up this sweet and yummy dessert! ☺ Serves 6

> 1 (20-ounce) can Lucky Leaf No Sugar Added Cherry Pie Filling
> ³⁄₄ cup Bisquick Reduced Fat Baking Mix
> 6 tablespoons Splenda Granular ☆
> ½ teaspoon baking powder
> 2 tablespoons Land O Lakes Fat Free Half & Half
> 1 egg, slightly beaten, or equivalent in egg substitute
> 2 tablespoons I Can't Believe It's Not Butter! Light Margarine
> 6 tablespoons purchased graham cracker crumbs or 6 (2½-inch)
>   graham crackers, made into crumbs
> ½ teaspoon ground cinnamon

Evenly spread pie filling in a microwave-safe 10-inch pie plate. Cover and microwave on HIGH (100% power) for 3 minutes. Meanwhile, in a large bowl, combine baking mix, ¼ cup Splenda, and baking powder. Add half & half, egg, and margarine. Mix just until combined. Drop batter by tablespoonful over hot cherry pie filling to form 6 biscuits. In a small bowl, combine graham cracker crumbs, remaining 2 tablespoons Splenda, and cinnamon. Evenly sprinkle crumb mixture over top. Microwave, uncovered, for 3 to 5 minutes or until biscuits are done, turning dish after 2 minutes. Place pie plate on counter and let set for 5 minutes. Divide into 6 servings.

HINT: Good served warm with Wells' Blue Bunny sugar- and fat-free vanilla ice cream, or cold with Cool Whip Lite. If using, don't forget to count the additional calories.

Each serving equals:

HE: 1 Bread • ⅔ Fruit • ½ Fat • ¼ Slider •
1 Optional Calorie

---

152 Calories • 4 gm Fat • 3 gm Protein •
26 gm Carbohydrate • 308 mg Sodium •
39 mg Calcium • 1 gm Fiber

DIABETIC EXCHANGES: 1 Starch • 1 Fruit • ½ Fat

Easy-as-Pie Apple Crisp

Has the expression "easy as pie" lost its meaning for a generation that may never have learned to bake one? A friend insists it really means, "easy as eating pie"—and we're all good at that!

● Serves 4

> 1 (20-ounce) can Lucky Leaf No Sugar Added Apple Pie Filling
> ¾ cup Splenda Granular ☆
> 1 teaspoon lemon juice
> ¾ cup Quaker Quick Oats
> 1 tablespoon + 1 teaspoon I Can't Believe It's Not Butter! Light
>   Margarine

Spray four (8-ounce) microwave-safe custard cups with butter-flavored cooking spray. In a large bowl, combine apple pie filling, ¼ cup Splenda, and lemon juice. Evenly divide mixture between prepared custard cups. In a medium bowl, combine oats, remaining ½ cup Splenda, and margarine. Mix with a pastry blender or fork until mixture is crumbly. Evenly sprinkle about ¼ cup crumb mixture over top of each custard cup. Arrange custard cups in a circle in microwave. Microwave on HIGH (100% power) for 5 minutes. Place custard cups on counter and let set for 3 minutes before serving. Serve warm or cold.

HINT: Good served warm with Wells' Blue Bunny sugar- and fat-free vanilla ice cream, or cold with Cool Whip Lite. If using, be sure to count the additional calories.

Each serving equals:

HE: 1 Fruit • ¾ Bread • ½ Fat • 18 Optional Calories

139 Calories • 3 gm Fat • 2 gm Protein •
26 gm Carbohydrate • 47 mg Sodium •
8 mg Calcium • 3 gm Fiber

DIABETIC EXCHANGES: 1 Fruit • ½ Starch • ½ Fat

Pear Crisp

It's a perfect partnership—a truly old-fashioned dessert, prepared in one of the modern age's most helpful culinary inventions! Try this with different types of pears to see which you like best—Anjou, Bartlett, or something more exotic, depending on what your grocer has ordered. ● Serves 4

3 cups (6 small) cored, peeled, and sliced ripe pears
½ cup Quaker Quick Oats
3 tablespoons Bisquick Reduced Fat Baking Mix
½ cup Splenda Granular
½ teaspoon ground cinnamon
2 tablespoons I Can't Believe It's Not Butter! Light Margarine
2 tablespoons chopped walnuts

Spray four (8-ounce) microwave-safe custard cups with butter-flavored cooking spray. Evenly divide pears between prepared custard cups. In a medium bowl, combine oats, baking mix, Splenda, and cinnamon. Add margarine. Mix with a pastry blender or fork until mixture is crumbly. Stir in walnuts. Evenly sprinkle crumb mixture over pears. Arrange custard cups in a circle in microwave. Microwave on HIGH (100% power) for 5 minutes or until pears are tender. Place custard cups on counter and let set for at least 3 minutes before serving. Serve warm or cold.

Each serving equals:

HE: 1½ Fruit • 1 Fat • ¾ Bread •
19 Optional Calories

194 Calories • 6 gm Fat • 3 gm Protein •
32 gm Carbohydrate • 112 mg Sodium •
30 mg Calcium • 4 gm Fiber

DIABETIC EXCHANGES: 1½ Fruit • 1 Fat • 1 Starch

Pumpkin Patch Pie

A friend who teaches fourth grade e-mailed me not long ago: "JoAnna, we're growing terrariums in the classroom, and you should see the vines we're getting from pumpkin seeds. Who'd have thunk it?" Too bad she teaches in a city neighborhood with no room for a pumpkin patch! In your honor, Marcia, I've created a festive pumpkin pie. ☻ Serves 8

1 Pillsbury refrigerated unbaked 9-inch pie crust
1 (15-ounce) can Libby's solid-pack pumpkin
2 eggs or equivalent in egg substitute
1 (12-fluid-ounce) can Carnation Evaporated Fat Free Milk
¾ cup Splenda Granular
⅓ cup Carnation Nonfat Dry Milk Powder
1 tablespoon + 1 teaspoon all-purpose flour
1½ teaspoons pumpkin pie spice

Place pie crust in a deep-dish microwave-safe 10-inch pie plate. Flute edges and prick bottom and sides with tines of a fork. Place a large piece of waxed paper over crust. Set a 9-inch microwave-safe pie plate over waxed paper inside crust. Microwave on HIGH (100% power) for 5 minutes. Place on counter, remove 9-inch pie plate and allow to cool while preparing filling. In an 8-cup microwave-safe mixing bowl, combine pumpkin, eggs, and evaporated milk. Add Splenda, dry milk powder, flour, and pumpkin pie spice. Mix well to combine. Microwave on HIGH for 8 minutes, stirring after 5 minutes. Spread hot mixture into prepared pie crust. Microwave on MEDIUM (50% power) for 15 to 18 minutes or until center is just set, turning pie plate every 5 minutes. Place pie plate on counter and let set for 10 minutes. Refrigerate for at least 1 hour. Cut into 8 servings.

Each serving equals:

HE: 1 Bread • ½ Fat Free Milk • ½ Fat •
½ Vegetable • ¼ Protein • 15 Optional Calories

212 Calories • 8 gm Fat • 7 gm Protein •
28 gm Carbohydrate • 195 mg Sodium •
175 mg Calcium • 2 gm Fiber

DIABETIC EXCHANGES: 1½ Starch/Carbohydrate •
1 Fat • ½ Fat Free Milk

Majestic Sour Cream Raisin Pie

My husband, Cliff, said this was good enough to serve to royalty! I'm not planning on inviting Her Majesty the Queen of England over for supper anytime soon, but it's good to know I've got the perfect dessert should her Rolls-Royce break down in DeWitt.

○ Serves 8

2 (4-serving) packages JELL-O sugar-free vanilla cook-and-serve
    pudding mix

1⅓ cups Carnation Nonfat Dry Milk Powder

2 cups water

¾ cup Land O Lakes no-fat sour cream

¾ cup seedless raisins

1 teaspoon ground cinnamon

1 (6-ounce) Keebler graham cracker pie crust

2 tablespoons purchased graham cracker crumbs or 2 (2½-inch)
    graham cracker squares, made into crumbs

1 tablespoon Splenda Granular

½ cup Cool Whip Lite

In an 8-cup microwave-safe mixing bowl, combine dry pudding mixes, dry milk powder, and water. Cover and microwave on HIGH (100% power) for 5 minutes or just until mixture starts to boil, stirring after 3 minutes. Add sour cream. Mix well to combine. Re-cover and microwave on HIGH for 30 seconds. Stir in raisins and cinnamon. Place bowl on counter, uncover, and let set for 10 minutes, stirring occasionally. Evenly spread mixture into pie crust. In a small bowl, combine graham cracker crumbs and Splenda. Evenly sprinkle crumb mixture over top of filling. Refrigerate for at least 1 hour. Cut into 8 servings. When serving, top each with 1 tablespoon Cool Whip Lite.

HINT: A self-seal sandwich bag works great for crushing graham crackers.

Each serving equals:

HE: 1 Bread • ¾ Fruit • ½ Fat Free Milk •
¼ Fat • ½ Slider • 1 Optional Calorie

---

222 Calories • 6 gm Fat • 6 gm Protein •
36 gm Carbohydrate • 251 mg Sodium •
193 mg Calcium • 1 gm Fiber

DIABETIC EXCHANGES: 1 Starch/Carbohydrate •
1 Fruit • ½ Fat Free Milk • ½ Fat

Cherry Hill Cheesecake

This spectacular treat requires a bit of extra effort (and more than one bowl) but a bite will tell you that it's more than worth it! It's lovely enough to serve for an anniversary or loved one's birthday.

☻ Serves 8

> 1 (4-serving) package JELL-O sugar-free vanilla cook-and-serve pudding mix
> 1 (4-serving) package JELL-O sugar-free cherry gelatin
> ½ cup water
> 1 (15-ounce) can tart red cherries, packed in water, undrained
> 1 teaspoon coconut extract ☆
> 1 (8-ounce) package Philadelphia fat-free cream cheese
> 1 egg or equivalent in egg substitute
> ⅓ cup Splenda Granular
> 1 (6-ounce) Keebler graham cracker pie crust
> ½ cup Cool Whip Lite
> 2 tablespoons flaked coconut
> 2 tablespoons purchased graham cracker crumbs or 2 (2½-inch) graham cracker squares, made into fine crumbs

In an 8-cup microwave-safe mixing bowl, combine dry pudding mix, dry gelatin, and water. Mix well using a wire whisk. Stir in undrained cherries. Cover and microwave on HIGH (100% power) for 5 minutes or just until mixture comes to a boil, stirring after 2 minutes. Stir in ½ teaspoon coconut extract. Place bowl on counter. Meanwhile, in another 8-cup microwave-safe mixing bowl, stir cream cheese with a sturdy spoon until soft. Add egg and Splenda. Mix well to combine. Cover and microwave on MEDIUM (50% power) for 6 minutes, stirring after 3 minutes. Stir in remaining ½ teaspoon coconut extract. Spread cream cheese mixture evenly into pie crust. Place filled pie crust on a wire rack and allow cream cheese mixture to cool for 15 minutes. Gently fold Cool Whip Lite into cooled cherry mixture. Spread cherry mixture evenly over cooled cream cheese filling. In a small bowl, combine coconut and graham cracker crumbs. Evenly sprinkle crumb mixture over top of cherry topping. Refrigerate for at least 2 hours. Cut into 8 servings.

HINT: A self-seal sandwich bag works great for crushing graham crackers.

Each serving equals:

HE: 1 Bread • ½ Protein • ½ Fruit • ¼ Fat • ½ Slider • 7 Optional Calories

---

191 Calories • 7 gm Fat • 7 gm Protein • 25 gm Carbohydrate • 347 mg Sodium • 90 mg Calcium • 2 gm Fiber

---

DIABETIC EXCHANGES: 1 Other Carb • 1 Fat • ½ Meat • ½ Fruit

Choco Brownie Cake

Are you a brownie fanatic who never met a brownie you didn't like? There are at least two schools of thought about this chocolate masterpiece—those who like it more like cake, and those who prefer it very close to fudge. I think I may have bridged the two in this luxurious delight! ☻ Serves 8

>1 cup + 2 tablespoons Bisquick Reduced Fat Baking Mix
>½ cup Splenda Granular
>¼ cup unsweetened cocoa powder
>½ teaspoon baking powder
>¼ cup Land O Lakes no-fat sour cream
>2 tablespoons + 2 teaspoons I Can't Believe It's Not Butter! Light Margarine
>½ cup water
>1 egg or equivalent in egg substitute
>2 teaspoons vanilla extract
>¼ cup chopped walnuts
>¼ cup mini chocolate chips

Spray an 8-by-8-inch microwave-safe baking dish with butter-flavored cooking spray. In a large bowl, combine baking mix, Splenda, cocoa powder, and baking powder. Add sour cream, margarine, water, egg, and vanilla extract. Mix gently just to combine. Fold in walnuts and chocolate chips. Microwave on MEDIUM (50% power) for 15 minutes or until center lightly springs back when touched. Place baking dish on a wire rack and let set for at least 10 minutes. Cut into 8 servings.

HINT: Good served warm with Wells' Blue Bunny sugar- and fat-free vanilla ice cream or cold with Cool White Lite. If using, don't forget to count the additional calories.

Each serving equals:

HE: ¾ Bread • ½ Fat • ¼ Protein • ¼ Slider •
19 Optional Calories

155 Calories • 7 gm Fat • 4 gm Protein •
19 gm Carbohydrate • 286 mg Sodium •
54 mg Calcium • 2 gm Fiber

DIABETIC EXCHANGES: 1½ Starch • ½ Fat

Golden Carrot Cake

I wish I could tell you that a piece of this cake is a good substitute for eating your vegetables, but I can't (although you do get lots of healthy nutrition from just one serving). The main reason to make it—it's just scrumptious! ☻   Serves 8

1½ cups Bisquick Reduced Fat Baking Mix

½ cup Splenda Granular

1 teaspoon baking powder

1 teaspoon apple pie spice

1 cup finely grated carrots

½ cup seedless raisins

¼ cup chopped walnuts

½ cup unsweetened orange juice

½ cup Musselman's "No Sugar Added" Applesauce

1 egg, beaten, or equivalent in egg substitute

2 tablespoons vegetable oil

1 teaspoon vanilla extract

Spray an 8-by-8-inch microwave-safe baking dish with butter-flavored cooking spray. In a large bowl, combine baking mix, Splenda, baking powder, and apple pie spice. Stir in carrots, raisins, and walnuts. Add orange juice, applesauce, egg, vegetable oil, and vanilla extract. Mix gently just to combine. Spread batter into prepared baking dish. Microwave on HIGH (100% power) for 8 minutes or just until top lightly springs back when touched, turning baking dish after every 2 minutes. Place baking dish on a wire rack and let set for at least 15 minutes. Cut into 8 servings.

HINT: Good served warm with Wells' Blue Bunny sugar- and fat-free vanilla ice cream or cold with Cool Whip Lite. If using, don't forget to count the additional calories.

Each serving equals:

HE: 1 Bread • 1 Fat • ¾ Fruit • ¼ Protein •
¼ Vegetable • 6 Optional Calories

208 Calories • 8 gm Fat • 4 gm Protein •
30 gm Carbohydrate • 328 mg Sodium •
73 mg Calcium • 1 gm Fiber

DIABETIC EXCHANGES: 1 Starch • 1 Fat • 1 Fruit

Pumpkin Pie Cake

Everyone makes pumpkin pie, so why not surprise your guests with a quick and tasty dessert? It's not quite a pie but yet it's not quite a cake either. I think it's the best of both worlds!

● Serves 8

> ½ cup cold water
> ⅔ cup Carnation Nonfat Dry Milk Powder
> ¾ cup Splenda Granular
> 18 (2½-inch) graham cracker squares, made into crumbs
> 1 (15-ounce) can Libby's solid-pack pumpkin
> 2 eggs or equivalent in egg substitute
> 2 teaspoons pumpkin pie spice

In a 2-cup microwave-safe measuring cup, combine water and dry milk powder until mixture makes a smooth paste. Cover and microwave on HIGH (100% power) for 45 to 60 seconds or until mixture is very hot, but not to the boiling point. Stir in Splenda. Mix well to combine. Cover and refrigerate for at least 2 hours before using. Spray a deep-dish microwave-safe 10-inch pie plate with butter-flavored cooking spray. In a large bowl, combine cooled milk mixture, graham cracker crumbs, pumpkin, eggs, and pumpkin pie spice. Mix gently to combine. Spread mixture into prepared pie plate. Microwave on MEDIUM (50% power) for 18 minutes or until center is still slightly soft but outside is firm, turning pie plate after 10 minutes. Place pie plate on a wire rack and let set for at least 30 minutes. Refrigerate for at least 1 hour. Cut into 8 servings.

HINT: A self-seal sandwich bag works great for crushing graham crackers.

Each serving equals:

HE: 1 Bread • ½ Vegetable • ¼ Fat Free Milk •
¼ Protein • 6 Optional Calories

131 Calories • 3 gm Fat • 5 gm Protein •
21 gm Carbohydrate • 145 mg Sodium •
97 mg Calcium • 3 gm Fiber

DIABETIC EXCHANGES: 1½ Starch/Carbohydrate

Walnut Snack Cake

There's always something new in nutrition research, but you've got to cheer whenever a study suggests that nuts are actually good for you! Walnuts are probably the best choice we've got—they're lower in fat than some other nuts, for one thing. Even more important, they transform a plain cake into a treat.   ☻   Serves 8

1 cup + 2 tablespoons Bisquick Reduced Fat Baking Mix
6 tablespoons purchased graham cracker crumbs
½ cup + 2 tablespoons Splenda Granular ☆
¼ cup chopped walnuts

¾ cup fat-free milk
1 egg or equivalent in egg substitute
2 tablespoons Land O Lakes no-fat sour cream
1 teaspoon vanilla extract
½ teaspoon ground cinnamon

Spray an 8-by-8-inch microwave-safe baking dish with butter-flavored cooking spray. In a large bowl, combine baking mix, graham cracker crumbs, ½ cup Splenda, and walnuts. Add milk, egg, sour cream, and vanilla extract. Mix gently to combine. Spread mixture into prepared baking dish. In a small bowl, combine remaining 2 tablespoons Splenda and cinnamon. Evenly sprinkle mixture over batter. Lightly spray top with butter-flavored cooking spray. Microwave on HIGH (100% power) for 5 to 7 minutes or just until center lightly springs back when touched, turning dish after 3 minutes. Place baking dish on a wire rack and let set for at least 10 minutes. Cut into 8 servings.

Each serving equals:

HE: 1 Bread • ¼ Protein • ¼ Fat •
12 Optional Calories

120 Calories • 4 gm Fat • 3 gm Protein •
18 gm Carbohydrate • 277 mg Sodium •
50 mg Calcium • 1 gm Fiber

DIABETIC EXCHANGES: 1 Starch • ½ Fat

Miscellaneous

I always end up with a chapter of goodies that aren't easily categorized but definitely need to be included in a cookbook of dishes that will help you eat well at every meal—and all year long. Too often, people watching their weight may decide to deny themselves the pleasure of socializing with friends because they don't want to be tempted. Others stick to the "straight and narrow" and eat all their meals "diet-style"—plain and simple and ultimately so boring they can't help hopping off the wagon.

So here are my little extras that make life worth living—and that make living healthy for a lifetime not only possible but downright pleasurable, too! Some are great to have on hand for planned snacks; others offer plentiful party platters perfect for serving to friends and family alike.

Start your day with mouthwatering muffins from the microwave such as my **Applesauce Surprise Muffins** *or a breakfast treat like my* **Maple Apple Puff Pancakes**— *and you'll discover that you've got renewed energy (and a satisfied tummy)! Dazzle your guests with* **Mexican Munch Mix** *and* **Grande Salsa**, *or serve a scrumptious, warm* **Bacon Cheese Dip** *with pita triangles or a favorite cracker. Looking for homemade holiday gifts? Go into the jam-making business this summer with* **Fresh Blueberry Jam**! *And keep a ready supply of* **Micro Cocoa Mix** *all winter long, so you'll never feel chilled to the bone again!*

Fluffy Scrambled Eggs

I wonder if the inventor of the microwave loved his scrambled eggs fluffy—you'd think so, considering how perfectly they emerge from the "magic box!" The half-and-half makes them extra-rich but doesn't add any fat.　　❂　　Serves 4 (½ cup)

> *6 eggs or equivalent in egg substitute*
> *¼ cup Land O Lakes Fat Free Half & Half*
> *½ teaspoon lemon pepper*
> *6 tablespoons shredded Kraft reduced-fat Cheddar cheese*

Spray an 8-cup microwave-safe mixing bowl with butter-flavored cooking spray. In prepared bowl, combine eggs, half & half, and lemon pepper. Stir in Cheddar cheese. Cover and microwave on HIGH (100% power) for 3 to 4 minutes or just until eggs are set, stirring after every minute with a fork. Place bowl on counter, uncover, and let set for 1 minute. Mix gently before serving.

Each serving equals:

HE: 2 Protein • 9 Optional Calories

---

146 Calories • 10 gm Fat • 12 gm Protein •
2 gm Carbohydrate • 166 mg Sodium •
129 mg Calcium • 0 gm Fiber

DIABETIC EXCHANGES: 2 Meat

Breakfast Omelet

This is really more of a frittata than an omelet, since I don't ask you to flip it! (Phew!) Eggs cook up beautifully creamy in this festive brunch dish. ❤ Serves 4

> 1½ cups frozen loose-packed shredded hash brown potatoes
> ½ cup finely chopped onion
> 1 tablespoon + 1 teaspoon I Can't Believe It's Not Butter! Light Margarine
> 4 eggs or equivalent in egg substitute
> ¼ cup Land O Lakes Fat Free Half & Half
> 1 teaspoon dried parsley flakes
> ½ teaspoon lemon pepper
> 1 full cup diced Dubuque 97% fat-free ham or any extra-lean ham

Spray a 9-inch microwave-safe pie plate with butter-flavored cooking spray. Evenly layer potatoes and onion in prepared pie plate. Dot top with margarine. Cover and microwave on HIGH (100% power) for 5 minutes. In a medium bowl, combine eggs, half & half, parsley flakes, and lemon pepper. Stir in ham. Pour mixture evenly over potatoes. Mix gently to combine. Re-cover and microwave on HIGH for 5 to 6 minutes or until omelet is firm, but moist, stirring after every 2 minutes. Place pie plate on counter, uncover, and let set for 2 minutes. Cut into 4 servings. Serve at once.

Each serving equals:

HE: 2 Protein • ½ Fat • ¼ Bread • ¼ Vegetable • 9 Optional Calories

168 Calories • 8 gm Fat • 15 gm Protein • 9 gm Carbohydrate • 514 mg Sodium • 49 mg Calcium • 1 gm Fiber

DIABETIC EXCHANGES: 2 Meat • ½ Fat • ½ Starch

Italian Omelet

Here's an easy way to prepare a lovely egg entree that uses handy ingredients and arrives at the table with all the excitement of a Venetian gondola ride! What a *bellissima* way to start the day.

☯ Serves 4

6 eggs or equivalent in egg substitute

1 teaspoon Italian seasoning

¼ teaspoon lemon pepper

½ cup fat-free cottage cheese

1 (8-ounce) can tomatoes, finely chopped and undrained

2 tablespoons reduced-sodium ketchup

¼ cup Kraft Reduced Fat Parmesan Style Grated Topping

Spray a 9-inch glass pie plate with olive oil–flavored cooking spray. In a medium bowl, combine eggs, Italian seasoning, and lemon pepper. Pour mixture into prepared pie plate. Cover and microwave on HIGH (100% power) for 4 minutes or until omelet is firm, but moist, stirring after every minute. In a small bowl, combine cottage cheese, undrained tomatoes, and ketchup. Evenly spoon mixture over omelet mixture. Sprinkle Parmesan cheese evenly over top. Continue to microwave on HIGH for 2 minutes. Place pie plate on counter and let set for 2 minutes. Cut into 4 servings. Serve at once.

Each serving equals:

HE: 2 Protein • 1 Vegetable • 8 Optional Calories

172 Calories • 8 gm Fat • 16 gm Protein •
9 gm Carbohydrate • 709 mg Sodium •
109 mg Calcium • 2 gm Fiber

DIABETIC EXCHANGES: 2 Meat • 1 Vegetable

Breakfast Burrito

Here's another bit of kitchen magic that produces a wonderful egg filling in no time at all! What a quick and easy meal this makes—and cleanup is simple. ☺ Serves 4

4 eggs, beaten, or equivalent in egg substitute
¼ cup chopped green onion
½ cup coarsely chopped cherry tomatoes
6 tablespoons shredded Kraft reduced-fat Cheddar cheese
4 (6-inch) flour tortillas
¾ cup chunky salsa (mild, medium, or hot)

Spray an 8-cup microwave-safe mixing bowl with butter-flavored cooking spray. In prepared bowl, combine eggs, green onion, and tomatoes. Microwave on HIGH (100% power) for 1 minute. Stir in Cheddar cheese and continue to microwave on HIGH for 1 minute longer. Spoon about ½ cup egg mixture in center of each tortilla. Roll each up and place in an 8-by-8-inch microwave-safe baking dish. Microwave on HIGH for 1 minute. For each serving, place 1 burrito on a plate and spoon 3 tablespoons salsa over top.

Each serving equals:

HE: 1½ Protein • 1 Bread • ¾ Vegetable

236 Calories • 8 gm Fat • 13 gm Protein •
28 gm Carbohydrate • 634 mg Sodium •
159 mg Calcium • 2 gm Fiber

DIABETIC EXCHANGES: 1½ Meat • 1 Starch •
1 Vegetable

Breakfast Raisin Oatmeal

Raisins have such an amazingly intense flavor, a few of them always seem like more! Here's a cozy-sweet way to start a winter's day.

○ Serves 2 (1 cup)

⅔ cup Quaker Quick Oats
¼ cup Splenda Granular
¼ teaspoon table salt
¼ cup seedless raisins
1½ cups water

In an 8-cup microwave-safe mixing bowl, combine oats, Splenda, salt, and raisins. Add water. Mix well to combine. Microwave on HIGH (100% power) for 4 to 5 minutes or until mixture starts to boil, stirring after every 2 minutes. Place bowl on counter and let set for 2 minutes. Mix well before serving. Serve at once.

Each serving equals:

HE: 1¼ Bread • 1 Fruit • 12 Optional Calories

166 Calories • 2 gm Fat • 4 gm Protein • 33 gm Carbohydrate • 293 mg Sodium • 21 mg Calcium • 3 gm Fiber

DIABETIC EXCHANGES: 1½ Starch • ½ Fruit

Maple Apple Puff Pancakes

Did you ever imagine you'd make pancakes in the microwave? This recipe is a revelation, an inventive way to offer brunch guests a special treat! And oh, that luscious baked apple aroma . . .

○ Serves 6

> ¼ cup Log Cabin Sugar Free Maple Syrup
> ½ teaspoon apple pie spice
> 2 cups (4 small) cored, peeled, and sliced cooking apples
> 1 cup + 2 tablespoons Bisquick Reduced Fat Baking Mix
> 1 cup water

Spray a 9-inch glass pie plate with butter-flavored cooking spray. In prepared pie plate, combine maple syrup and apple pie spice. Stir in apples. Cover and microwave on HIGH (100% power) for 3 to 4 minutes or until apples are tender. In a medium bowl, combine baking mix and water. Pour batter evenly over apples. Recover and microwave on HIGH for 3 to 5 minutes or until top springs back when lightly touched. Immediately invert onto a large serving plate. Let set on counter for at least 2 minutes. Cut into 6 servings.

Each serving equals:

HE: 1 Bread • ⅔ Fruit • 7 Optional Calories

---

117 Calories • 1 gm Fat • 4 gm Protein •
23 gm Carbohydrate • 306 mg Sodium •
139 mg Calcium • 4 gm Fiber

DIABETIC EXCHANGES: 1 Starch • ½ Fruit

Applesauce Surprise Muffins

The luscious aroma of cinnamon and apples might give away the "surprise" to anyone who wanders into the kitchen while these are baking. But what a tempting invitation they offer!

☻ Serves 6

¾ cup Bisquick Reduced Fat
    Baking Mix
2 tablespoons Splenda
    Granular
¼ teaspoon baking powder
½ teaspoon apple pie spice
¼ cup seedless raisins

¼ cup chopped walnuts
½ cup unsweetened applesauce
1 egg or equivalent in egg
    substitute
1 tablespoon Land O Lakes Fat
    Free Half & Half

Line a 6-well microwave muffin pan with paper liners. In a large bowl, combine baking mix, Splenda, baking powder, apple pie spice, raisins, and walnuts. Add applesauce, egg, and half & half. Mix gently just to combine. Spoon a scant ¼ cup batter into each prepared muffin cup. Microwave on HIGH (100% power) for 1 minute. Turn muffin ring halfway. Continue to microwave on HIGH for 1 to 1½ minutes or until tops spring back when lightly touched. Remove muffins from pan and place on a plate to cool for at least 2 minutes.

HINTS: 1. Good warm or cold.
      2. 6 (1-cup) glass custard cups lined with paper liners may be used instead of a muffin pan. Just be sure to arrange in a circle when microwaving.

Each serving equals:

HE: ⅔ Bread • ½ Fruit • ⅓ Protein • ⅓ Fat •
3 Optional Calories

---

133 Calories • 5 gm Fat • 3 gm Protein •
19 gm Carbohydrate • 207 mg Sodium •
43 mg Calcium • 1 gm Fiber

DIABETIC EXCHANGES: 1 Starch • ½ Fruit • ½ Fat

Cinnamon Maple Biscuits

No muss, no fuss—just a great example of how easily you can transform "store-bought" into "baked with love" at home.

● Serves 6

> 2 tablespoons + 2 teaspoons I Can't Believe It's Not Butter! Light Margarine
> ¼ cup Log Cabin Sugar Free Maple Syrup
> ¼ cup Splenda Granular
> ½ teaspoon ground cinnamon
> 1 (7.5-ounce) can Pillsbury refrigerated buttermilk biscuits
> ¼ cup chopped walnuts
> ¼ cup seedless raisins

Spray an 8-inch microwave-safe pie plate with butter-flavored cooking spray. In a small microwave-safe mixing bowl, combine margarine and maple syrup. Microwave on HIGH (100% power) for 20 seconds or until margarine is melted. Add Splenda and cinnamon. Mix well to combine. Separate biscuits and cut each into 4 pieces. Stir biscuit pieces into melted margarine mixture, making sure pieces are well coated. Arrange coated biscuit pieces in a circle in prepared pie plate. Sprinkle walnuts and raisins evenly over top. Microwave on HIGH for 3 minutes. Place pie plate on counter and let set for 2 minutes. Divide into 6 servings.

Each serving equals:

HE: 1¼ Bread • 1 Fat • ⅓ Fruit •
10 Optional Calories

---

166 Calories • 6 gm Fat • 4 gm Protein •
24 gm Carbohydrate • 380 mg Sodium •
10 mg Calcium • 1 gm Fiber

DIABETIC EXCHANGES: 1½ Starch/Carbohydrate • 1 Fat

Corny Cornbread Ring

Here's a captivating way to stir up and serve a cornbread just brimming with bits of corn! If you don't own a microwave-safe mold, why not treat yourself to a pretty one? It's a healthy living reward you surely deserve.   ☺   Serves 8

¾ cup Bisquick Reduced Fat Baking Mix

¾ cup yellow cornmeal

1 tablespoon Splenda Granular

1 teaspoon baking powder

1 cup frozen whole-kernel corn, thawed

2 eggs or equivalent in egg substitute

¼ cup Land O Lakes Fat Free Half & Half

¼ cup fat-free milk

¼ cup unsweetened applesauce

2 tablespoons + 2 teaspoons I Can't Believe It's Not Butter! Light Margarine

Spray a 6-cup microwave-safe ring mold with butter-flavored cooking spray. In a large bowl, combine baking mix, cornmeal, Splenda, and baking powder. Stir in corn. Add eggs, half & half, milk, applesauce, and margarine. Mix well to combine. Spread mixture into prepared mold. Microwave on HIGH (100% power) for 5 minutes or until center springs back when lightly touched. Immediately invert onto a large serving plate. Let set on counter for at least 5 minutes. Cut into 8 servings.

HINTS: 1. Thaw corn by placing in a colander and rinsing under hot water for 1 minute.

2. If you don't have a microwave-safe ring mold, place a custard cup in the center of a 9-inch glass pie plate sprayed with butter-flavored cooking spray and spread batter around cup in prepared pie plate.

3. Good served with warmed Log Cabin Sugar Free Maple Syrup. If using, be sure to count calories accordingly.

Each serving equals:

HE: 1½ Bread • ½ Fat • ¼ Protein •
11 Optional Calories

152 Calories • 4 gm Fat • 5 gm Protein •
24 gm Carbohydrate • 243 mg Sodium •
64 mg Calcium • 2 gm Fiber

DIABETIC EXCHANGES: 1½ Starch • ½ Fat

Quick Corn Bread

Watch for a sale on microwave-safe baking pans, or put them on your wish list for Christmas or your next birthday—they make healthy cooking so much easier, and lots of fun. This is a great "go-with" for all kinds of supper dishes. ☺ Serves 8

⅔ cup Carnation Nonfat Dry Milk Powder

1 cup water

1 tablespoon white distilled vinegar

1 cup all-purpose flour

1 cup yellow cornmeal

½ cup Splenda Granular

1 teaspoon baking powder

½ teaspoon baking soda

2 tablespoons + 2 teaspoons vegetable oil

2 eggs, slightly beaten, or equivalent in egg substitute

1 tablespoon Land O Lakes no-fat sour cream

Spray a 6-cup microwave-safe ring mold with butter-flavored cooking spray. In a small bowl, combine dry milk powder, water, and vinegar. Set aside. In a large bowl, combine flour, cornmeal, Splenda, baking powder, and baking soda. Add vegetable oil, eggs, sour cream, and milk mixture to flour mixture. Mix gently just to combine. Spread batter into prepared mold. Microwave on MEDIUM (50% power) for 6 to 8 minutes or until center springs back with lightly touched. Immediately invert onto a large serving plate. Let set on counter for at least 5 minutes. Cut into 8 servings.

HINT: If you don't have a microwave-safe ring mold, place a custard cup in center of 9-inch glass pie plate sprayed with butter-flavored cooking spray and spread batter around cup in prepared pie plate.

Each serving equals:

HE: 1⅔ Bread • 1 Fat • ¼ Fat Free Milk •
¼ Protein • 6 Optional Calories

194 Calories • 6 gm Fat • 7 gm Protein •
28 gm Carbohydrate • 187 mg Sodium •
118 mg Calcium • 2 gm Fiber

DIABETIC EXCHANGES: 2 Starch • 1 Fat

Orange Pecan Sticky Buns

Are you surprised to read this recipe title, thinking there's just no way to feast on sticky buns while eating healthy? I just loved the challenge of solving that particular culinary mystery, and I think I did it! These are irresistible—and one taste will win your loved ones over. ☺ Serves 5

> 3 tablespoons Splenda Granular
> 1/3 cup orange marmalade spreadable fruit
> 1/4 cup chopped pecans
> 1 (7.5-ounce) can Pillsbury refrigerated buttermilk biscuits

Spray a 9-inch glass pie plate with butter-flavored cooking spray. Separate biscuits and evenly arrange in prepared pie plate. In a small bowl, combine Splenda, spreadable fruit, and pecans. Evenly drizzle mixture over biscuits. Microwave on MEDIUM (50% power) for 3 minutes. Turn pie plate and microwave on HIGH (100% power) for 1 minute. Place pie place on counter and let set for 5 minutes. Divide into 5 servings.

Each serving equals:

HE: 1¼ Bread • ¾ Fruit • ¾ Fat •
4 Optional Calories

---

128 Calories • 4 gm Fat • 3 gm Protein •
20 gm Carbohydrate • 304 mg Sodium •
4 mg Calcium • 2 gm Fiber

DIABETIC EXCHANGES: 1 Starch • 1 Fruit • 1 Fat

Chunky Veggie Spaghetti Sauce

It's summer, and the zucchini is piled in sky-high stacks at every farmer's market you drive by. There's no better time to make a fresh, vegetable-based pasta sauce the whole family will love.

○ Serves 6 (1 scant cup)

> 3 cups chopped zucchini
> 2 cups sliced fresh mushrooms
> 1 cup chopped onion
> 1 tablespoon I Can't Believe It's Not Butter! Light Margarine
> 1 (8-ounce) can Hunt's Tomato Sauce
> 1 (15-ounce) can diced tomatoes, undrained
> 1 teaspoon Italian seasoning
> ¼ teaspoon dried minced garlic
> 1 tablespoon Splenda Granular

In an 8-cup microwave-safe mixing bowl, combine zucchini, mushrooms, onion, and margarine. Cover and microwave on HIGH (100% power) for 10 minutes, stirring after 5 minutes. Stir in tomato sauce, undrained tomatoes, Italian seasoning, garlic, and Splenda. Re-cover and microwave on HIGH for 6 to 8 minutes or just until vegetables are tender and mixture is hot, stirring after every 3 minutes. Place bowl on counter, uncover, and let set for 3 minutes. Mix well before serving.

Each serving equals:

HE: 3 Vegetable • ¼ Fat • 1 Optional Calorie

69 Calories • 1 gm Fat • 3 gm Protein •
12 gm Carbohydrate • 330 mg Sodium •
32 mg Calcium • 3 gm Fiber

DIABETIC EXCHANGES: 2 Vegetable

Grande Mild Salsa

There are so many salsas-in-a-jar in your supermarket, but there's just nothing better than homemade salsa made of ripe tomatoes from the garden! Here, I've combined the basic ingredients with some tangy taco seasoning for a little extra sizzle. Olé!

● Serves 6 (½ cup)

> *3 cups peeled and coarsely chopped fresh tomatoes*
> *1 cup chopped onion*
> *½ cup chopped green bell pepper*
> *1 tablespoon vegetable oil*
> *1 tablespoon white distilled vinegar*
> *1 tablespoon Splenda Granular*
> *1½ teaspoons taco seasoning*

In an 8-cup microwave-safe mixing bowl, combine tomatoes, onion, and green pepper. Add vegetable oil, vinegar, Splenda, and taco seasoning. Mix well to combine. Microwave on HIGH (100% power) for 15 minutes or until vegetables are tender and sauce slightly thickened, stirring after every 5 minutes. Place bowl on counter and let set for 10 minutes. Refrigerate for at least 1 hour. Mix well before serving.

HINT: This recipe was created for folks like me who *do not* like hot spicy foods! If you do, replace green pepper with hot chili peppers.

Each serving equals:

HE: 1½ Vegetable • ½ Fat • 1 Optional Calorie

50 Calories • 2 gm Fat • 1 gm Protein •
7 gm Carbohydrate • 43 mg Sodium •
16 mg Calcium • 2 gm Fiber

DIABETIC EXCHANGES: 1 Vegetable • ½ Fat

Classic Chunky Salsa

Why make your own salsa at home when the grocery store offers many tasty choices? First of all, it's usually a cost-cutter to do it yourself, but here are the best reasons I can think of: terrific fresh taste, a chance to use exactly the ingredients you like best, and a choice of how "chunky" you make it!　○　Serves 6 (½ cup)

> 1½ cups chopped onion
> ⅛ teaspoon dried minced garlic
> 1 (15-ounce) can diced tomatoes, undrained
> 1 (8-ounce) can Hunt's Tomato Sauce
> 1 (4-ounce) can chopped green chilies, drained
> 1 teaspoon ground cumin
> ½ teaspoon dried oregano

In an 8-cup microwave-safe mixing bowl, combine onion and garlic. Cover and microwave on HIGH (100% power) for 3 minutes or until onion is tender. Add undrained tomatoes, tomato sauce, and green chilies. Mix well to combine. Stir in cumin and oregano. Re-cover and continue to microwave on HIGH for 8 to 10 minutes or until mixture is hot, stirring after every 4 minutes. Place bowl on counter, uncover, and let set for 10 minutes. Refrigerate for at least 4 hours. Mix well before serving.

HINTS: 1. For those who prefer less "hot" salsa, use ½ cup chopped green or red bell pepper instead of green chilies.
2. If you prefer a sweeter salsa, stir in 1 or 2 tablespoons Splenda Granular just before refrigerating.

Each serving equals:

HE: 2 Vegetable

44 Calories • 0 gm Fat • 1 gm Protein •
10 gm Carbohydrate • 358 mg Sodium •
52 mg Calcium • 3 gm Fiber

DIABETIC EXCHANGES: 1½ Vegetable

Cliff's Hot Bacon Dressing

Did you ever think you'd make your own luscious bacon dressing? It appears often on restaurant menus, but it may have seemed too much trouble to re-create at home. Not any longer—here it is!

● Serves 6 (2 full tablespoons)

> 1 tablespoon I Can't Believe It's Not Butter! Light Margarine
> ¼ cup finely chopped onion
> 2 tablespoons Splenda Granular
> 1 tablespoon all-purpose flour
> ½ teaspoon prepared yellow mustard
> 1 tablespoon lemon juice
> ¾ cup water
> ¼ cup Kraft fat-free mayonnaise
> ¼ cup Oscar Mayer or Hormel Real Bacon Bits

In a 4-cup microwave-safe measuring cup, combine margarine and onion. Microwave on HIGH (100% power) for 2 minutes. Add Splenda, flour, mustard, lemon juice, and water. Mix well to combine. Continue to microwave on HIGH for 1½ to 2 minutes or until mixture thickens. Stir in mayonnaise and bacon bits. Drizzle hot dressing evenly over salads.

Each serving equals:

HE: ¼ Fat • ¼ Slider • 10 Optional Calories

42 Calories • 2 gm Fat • 2 gm Protein •
4 gm Carbohydrate • 253 mg Sodium •
4 mg Calcium • 0 gm Fiber

DIABETIC EXCHANGES: ½ Fat

Easy Hollandaise Sauce

This is another of those "restaurant-only" type sauces that few of us try to make at home. The good news is, this recipe is as easy as it is sumptuous when served over poached eggs or fresh asparagus in season. Enjoy!   ☻   Serves 8 (2 tablespoons)

> ½ cup Kraft fat-free mayonnaise
> ½ cup Land O Lakes no-fat sour cream
> 2 tablespoons Land O Lakes Fat Free Half & Half
> 1 tablespoon lemon juice
> 1 teaspoon prepared yellow mustard

In a 4-cup microwave-safe measuring cup, combine mayonnaise, sour cream, and half & half. Stir in lemon juice and mustard. Cover and microwave on MEDIUM (50% power) for 4 minutes, stirring after every minute. Place measuring cup on counter, uncover, and let set for 5 minutes. Refrigerate for at least 30 minutes.

HINT: Wonderful on asparagus and broccoli.

Each serving equals:

HE: ¼ Slider • 2 Optional Calories

---

24 Calories • 0 gm Fat • 0 gm Protein •
6 gm Carbohydrate • 152 mg Sodium •
24 mg Calcium • 0 gm Fiber

DIABETIC EXCHANGES: Free Food

Mustard Sauce

I enjoy making sauces in the microwave, and not just because I can do everything in one bowl. In this velvety blend, I've created a scrumptious, silky sauce that turns plain roasted meat into a marvelous meal! ☺ Serves 6 (⅓ cup)

> 2 tablespoons I Can't Believe It's Not Butter! Light Margarine
> 1 (12-fluid-ounce) can Carnation Evaporated Fat Free Milk
> 2 tablespoons all-purpose flour
> ¼ cup prepared yellow mustard
> 1 tablespoon Splenda Granular
> 1 tablespoon apple cider vinegar
> 1 teaspoon Worcestershire sauce

Spray a 4-cup microwave-safe measuring cup with butter-flavored cooking spray. Place margarine in prepared measuring cup. Microwave on HIGH (100% power) for 30 seconds or until margarine is melted. Add evaporated milk and flour. Mix well using a wire whisk. Microwave on HIGH for 2 to 3 minutes or until mixture thickens, stirring after every minute. Place measuring cup on counter. Stir in mustard, Splenda, vinegar, and Worcestershire sauce. Let set for at least 2 minutes. Mix well before serving.

HINTS: 1. Good served either warm or cold.
2. Wonderful served with ham or corned beef.

Each serving equals:

HE: ½ Fat Free Milk • ½ Fat • 10 Optional Calories

82 Calories • 2 gm Fat • 5 gm Protein •
11 gm Carbohydrate • 238 mg Sodium •
169 mg Calcium • 0 gm Fiber

DIABETIC EXCHANGES: ½ Fat Free Milk • ½ Fat

Raisin Sauce

If your sugar- and fat-free vanilla ice cream is looking a little "naked," consider how out-of-this-world delicious it would be when served with a really good fruity sauce like this one!

◑ Serves 6 (2 full tablespoons)

> 1 cup unsweetened apple juice
> 1 tablespoon cornstarch
> ½ cup Splenda Granular
> ½ cup seedless raisins
> 1 teaspoon lemon juice
> ½ teaspoon pumpkin pie spice

In a 4-cup microwave-safe measuring cup, combine apple juice, cornstarch, and Splenda. Mix well using a wire whisk. Stir in raisins and lemon juice. Microwave on HIGH (100% power) for 3 to 4 minutes or until mixture thickens and starts to boil. Stir in pumpkin pie spice. Place measuring cup on counter and let set for 2 minutes. Mix well before serving.

HINT: Good served warm with ham or cold with custard or angel food cake.

Each serving equals:

HE: 1 Fruit • 13 Optional Calories

---

68 Calories • 0 gm Fat • 0 gm Protein •
17 gm Carbohydrate • 3 mg Sodium •
10 mg Calcium • 1 gm Fiber

DIABETIC EXCHANGES: 1 Fruit

Bacon-Celery Cheese Spread

Tangy and cheesy, smooth and spicy, this festive spread is perfect for family gatherings, but feel free to fix it when it's just you and a friend watching your favorite reality show on TV.

● Serves 8 (¼ cup)

> 1 (8-ounce) package Philadelphia fat-free cream cheese
> ¼ cup Land O Lakes Fat Free Half & Half
> 1 teaspoon prepared horseradish sauce
> 1½ cups diced Velveeta Light processed cheese
> ¾ cup finely chopped celery
> ¼ cup finely chopped onion
> ½ cup Oscar Mayer or Hormel Real Bacon Bits

In an 8-cup microwave-safe mixing bowl, stir cream cheese with a sturdy spoon until soft. Stir in half & half and horseradish sauce. Add Velveeta cheese, celery, and onion. Mix well to combine. Microwave on MEDIUM (50% power) for 5 to 6 minutes or until cheese melts, stirring after every 2 minutes. Place bowl on counter. Stir in bacon bits. Let set for at least 2 minutes.

HINT: Good warm or cold with fresh vegetables, crackers, or chips.

Each serving equals:

HE: 1½ Protein • ¼ Vegetable • ¼ Slider •
8 Optional Calories

104 Calories • 4 gm Fat • 11 gm Protein •
6 gm Carbohydrate • 727 mg Sodium •
218 mg Calcium • 0 gm Fiber

DIABETIC EXCHANGES: 2 Protein

Frozen Strawberry Jam

Are you surprised to learn that you can store homemade jam in the freezer? If you didn't grow up in a home where jam-making was a tradition, you might not know! Actually, the title of this recipe is a cheerful reminder that you can even make jam from frozen berries—isn't that great news? Go for it!

> 6 cups frozen unsweetened strawberries
> ½ cup Splenda Granular
> 1 (4-serving) package JELL-O sugar-free strawberry gelatin
> 1 (1.75-ounce) package Sure-Jell Fruit Pectin for Lower Sugar
> Recipes

In an 8-cup microwave-safe mixing bowl, microwave strawberries on HIGH (100% power) for 4 minutes. Gently stir. Continue to microwave on MEDIUM (50% power) for 6 minutes, stirring after every 2 minutes. Mash strawberries using a potato masher or a fork. Stir in Splenda and dry gelatin. Add dry Sure-Jell. Mix well to combine. Microwave on HIGH for 4 minutes, stirring after every 2 minutes. Place bowl on counter and let set for at least 15 minutes. Mix well to combine. Evenly spoon mixture into freezer containers. Will keep for up to 2 weeks in refrigerator or 3 months in freezer.

Per 1 tablespoon serving:

HE: 8 Optional Calories

8 Calories • 0 gm Fat • 0 gm Protein •
2 gm Carbohydrate • 0 mg Sodium • 2 mg Calcium •
0 gm Fiber

DIABETIC EXCHANGES: 1 Free Food

Fresh Blueberry Jam

If you've never made your own jam, this is the year to try it—and the microwave is the appliance that will make it possible! I've suggested other excellent options for homemade jams your family will love. They also make pretty holiday gifts.

> 2¼ cups chopped fresh blueberries
> ½ cup Splenda Granular
> 1 (4-serving) package JELL-O sugar-free lemon gelatin
> ¾ cup cold Diet Mountain Dew

In an 8-cup microwave-safe mixing bowl, combine blueberries and Splenda. Let set for 5 minutes. Microwave on HIGH (100% power) for 3 to 5 minutes or until mixture starts to boil, stirring after 3 minutes. Add dry gelatin. Mix well to combine. Stir in Diet Mountain Dew. Continue to microwave on HIGH for 1 minute. Place bowl on counter and let set for at least 15 minutes. Mix well to combine. Evenly spoon mixture into freezer containers. Will keep for up to 2 weeks in refrigerator or 3 months in freezer.

HINT: Other options: fresh raspberries with raspberry gelatin; fresh strawberries with strawberry gelatin; fresh peaches with lemon gelatin.

Per 1 tablespoon equals:

HE: 4 Optional Calories

---

4 Calories • 0 gm Fat • 0 gm Protein •
1 gm Carbohydrate • 7 mg Sodium • 1 mg Calcium •
0 gm Fiber

DIABETIC EXCHANGES: 1 Free Food

Let's Party! Mix

You can never have too many fun and flavorful snack ideas—so why not try this heated sauce to bathe some munchies in? It'll make your mouth water—and your taste buds oh-so-happy!

Serves 8 (1 cup)

> ½ cup Kraft Fat Free Italian Dressing
> 2 teaspoons Worcestershire sauce
> 2 cups Corn Chex
> 2 cups Wheat Chex
> 2 cups Rice Chex
> 2 cups thin pretzel sticks
> ½ cup dry-roasted peanuts

In a very large microwave-safe mixing bowl, combine Italian dressing and Worcestershire sauce. Microwave on HIGH (100% power) for 1 minute. Add Corn Chex, Wheat Chex, Rice Chex, and pretzels. Mix well to combine. Stir in peanuts. Microwave on HIGH for 6 minutes, stirring after every 2 minutes, until evenly toasted. Place mixing bowl on counter and allow to cool completely, stirring occasionally. Mix well before serving. Store in airtight container or Ziploc storage bags.

Each serving equals:

HE: 1 Bread • ½ Fat • ¼ Protein •
8 Optional Calories

---

140 Calories • 4 gm Fat • 4 gm Protein •
22 gm Carbohydrate • 534 mg Sodium •
82 mg Calcium • 2 gm Fiber

DIABETIC EXCHANGES: 1 Starch • 1 Fat

Mexican Munch Mix

Here's something new for your kids to snack on—a crunchy blend of snack foods made savory and spicy. Root for your favorite World Cup soccer team (whether or not it's Mexico!) and enjoy!

❂ Serves 8 (1 cup)

> 3 tablespoons I Can't Believe It's Not Butter! Light Margarine
> 2 teaspoons taco seasoning
> 3 cups Wheat Chex
> 3 cups Corn Chex
> 1 cup thin pretzel sticks
> ¼ cup dry-roasted peanuts

In a very large microwave-safe mixing bowl, combine margarine and taco seasoning. Microwave on HIGH (100% power) for 40 to 60 seconds or until margarine is melted. Stir in Wheat Chex, Corn Chex, pretzels, and peanuts. Mix well to coat. Microwave on HIGH for 3 to 5 minutes or until mixture is heated through, stirring after every minute. Place bowl on counter and allow to cool completely, stirring occasionally. Mix well before serving. Store in airtight container or Ziploc storage bags.

Each serving equals:

HE: 1 Bread • ¾ Fat • 2 Optional Calories

---

124 Calories • 4 gm Fat • 3 gm Protein •
19 gm Carbohydrate • 292 mg Sodium •
56 mg Calcium • 1 gm Fiber

DIABETIC EXCHANGES: 1 Starch • 1 Fat

Taco Corn Snack

Isn't it great to have so many choices now when it comes to healthy baked snack chips? Combined with popcorn and some zesty flavoring, they make a terrific lunchbox addition or take-along treat for car trips.   ☻   Serves 8 (1 cup)

6 cups air-popped popcorn
3 cups coarsely broken Doritos Baked Corn Chips
2 tablespoons + 2 teaspoons I Can't Believe It's Not Butter! Light
   Margarine
2 teaspoons taco seasoning

In a very large microwave-safe mixing bowl, combine popcorn and corn chips. In a 1-cup microwave-safe measuring cup, combine margarine and taco seasoning. Microwave on HIGH (100% power) for 30 seconds or until margarine is melted. Mix well, then drizzle over popcorn mixture. Gently stir until popcorn and corn chips are coated. Place bowl on counter and allow to cool completely, stirring occasionally. Mix well before serving. Store in airtight container or Ziploc storage bags.

HINT: Usually 4 tablespoons unpopped popcorn makes about 6 cups popped popcorn, if prepared in an air popper.

Each serving equals:

HE: 1 Bread • ½ Fat

122 Calories • 6 gm Fat • 2 gm Protein •
15 gm Carbohydrate • 118 mg Sodium •
24 mg Calcium • 1 gm Fiber

DIABETIC EXCHANGES: 1 Starch • ½ Fat

Micro Cocoa Mix

Imagine how handy it would be to have a premixed hot cocoa blend ideal for stirring up an enticing cup in your microwave—and with almost no fuss! Saves time, saves money, and it's always ready when you are.

4 cups Carnation Nonfat Dry Milk Powder
⅔ cup Carnation Coffee-Mate Fat Free Coffee Creamer
1½ cups Splenda Granular
¾ cup unsweetened cocoa powder
½ teaspoon table salt

In a large bowl, combine dry milk powder, coffee creamer, Splenda, cocoa powder, and salt. Mix well to combine. Store in an airtight container. To make 1 cup of hot cocoa, combine ¼ cup cocoa mix and 1 cup water in a large microwave-safe mug. Microwave on HIGH (100% power) for 60 seconds or until mixture is very hot. Mix well before serving.

Per ¼ cup dry mix:

HE: ½ Fat Free Milk • ¼ Slider • 3 Optional Calories

---

60 Calories • 0 gm Fat • 4 gm Protein •
11 gm Carbohydrate • 107 mg Sodium •
148 mg Calcium • 1 gm Fiber

DIABETIC EXCHANGES: ½ Fat Free Milk

Bacon and Tomato Pizza Bites

I love how the microwave melts cheese so beautifully—it makes an "anytime" delight like this one such a pleasure to prepare.

◐ Serves 4

¼ cup Kraft fat-free mayonnaise
¼ cup Oscar Mayer or Hormel Real Bacon Bits
1 teaspoon dried onion flakes
1 teaspoon dried parsley flakes
2 English muffins, halved
1 cup peeled and chopped fresh tomato
4 (¾-ounce) slices Kraft reduced-fat American cheese

In a small bowl, combine mayonnaise, bacon bits, onion flakes, and parsley flakes. Spread a full 1 tablespoon mayonnaise mixture evenly over each English muffin half. Evenly sprinkle ¼ cup chopped tomato over mayonnaise mixture. Top each with 1 slice American cheese. Place prepared muffins on a microwave-safe plate. Microwave on MEDIUM (50% power) for 3 to 4 minutes or until filling is hot and cheese starts to melt. Serve at once.

Each serving equals:

HE: 1 Bread • 1 Protein • ½ Vegetable • ¼ Slider •
15 Optional Calories

---

161 Calories • 5 gm Fat • 10 gm Protein •
19 gm Carbohydrate • 762 mg Sodium •
210 mg Calcium • 2 gm Fiber

DIABETIC EXCHANGES: 1½ Meat • 1 Bread •
½ Vegetable

Ham Canapés

The word *canapés* isn't used that much anymore to describe the little "bites" that hostesses offer their guests before dinner, but back in the 1950s, it was considered the height of sophistication. These spirited charmers are fun to make and even more fun to devour, so try them the next time you have visitors!

◑ Serves 6 (5 each)

1 full cup finely chopped Dubuque 97% fat-free ham or
    any extra-lean ham
6 tablespoons shredded Kraft reduced-fat Cheddar cheese
¼ cup Kraft fat-free mayonnaise
1 tablespoon sweet pickle relish
2 teaspoons dried onion flakes
1 hard-boiled egg, finely chopped
30 Melba toast rounds

In a medium bowl, combine ham, Cheddar cheese, mayonnaise, pickle relish, and onion flakes. Stir in chopped egg. Evenly spoon about ½ tablespoon ham mixture on each toast round. Arrange 15 canapés in a circle on a microwave-safe plate. Microwave on HIGH (100% power) for 30 seconds. Repeat with remaining 15 canapés. Serve warm.

Each serving equals:

HE: 1½ Protein • 1 Bread • 15 Optional Calories

---

128 Calories • 4 gm Fat • 9 gm Protein •
14 gm Carbohydrate • 452 mg Sodium •
72 mg Calcium • 1 gm Fiber

DIABETIC EXCHANGES: 1 Meat • 1 Starch

Appetizer Franks

What a sweet 'n' savory way to enjoy these classic cocktail party treat! Franks are a natural in the microwave, and perfect for teens to make themselves. ☻ Serves 8 (6 each)

    ½ cup apricot spreadable fruit
    1 tablespoon prepared yellow mustard
    1 teaspoon dried parsley flakes
    ½ teaspoon dried onion flakes
    16 ounces Oscar Mayer or Healthy Choice reduced-fat
        frankfurters, cut into 48 (1-inch) pieces

In a 9-inch glass pie plate, combine spreadable fruit, mustard, parsley flakes, and onion flakes. Stir frankfurter pieces into mixture. Cover and microwave on HIGH (100% power) for 5 minutes. Serve at once.

Each serving equals:

HE: 1½ Protein • 1 Fruit

101 Calories • 1 gm Fat • 8 gm Protein •
15 gm Carbohydrate • 602 mg Sodium •
4 mg Calcium • 0 gm Fiber

DIABETIC EXCHANGES: 1 Meat • 1 Fruit

Spinach Appetizer Balls

Looking for something original to launch your next dinner party? These provide a refreshing change from the usual salty snacks.

◐ Serves 4 (2 each)

> 1 (10-ounce) package frozen chopped spinach,
>   thawed and well drained
> 1 cup unseasoned dry bread cubes
> 1 egg, beaten, or equivalent in egg substitute
> 3 tablespoons Kraft Fat Free Italian Dressing
> ¼ cup Kraft Reduced Fat Parmesan Style Grated Topping
> 1 tablespoon dried onion flakes
> 1 teaspoon lemon pepper

In a large bowl, combine spinach, bread cubes, egg, Italian dressing, Parmesan cheese, onion flakes, and lemon pepper. Mix well to combine. Form mixture into 8 (1-inch) balls. Arrange balls in a large microwave-safe pie plate. Cover and microwave on HIGH (100% power) for 2 minutes or until balls are almost set, turning plate once. Place pie plate on counter, uncover, and let set for 1 minute. Serve at once.

HINTS: 1. Thaw spinach by placing in a colander and rinsing under hot water for 1 minute.
2. Pepperidge Farm bread cubes work great.

Each serving equals:

HE: ½ Protein • ½ Vegetable • ¼ Bread •
8 Optional Calories

---

115 Calories • 3 gm Fat • 6 gm Protein •
16 gm Carbohydrate • 572 mg Sodium •
131 mg Calcium • 2 gm Fiber

DIABETIC EXCHANGES: ½ Starch • ½ Meat •
½ Vegetable

Biscuit Bites

Using prepared biscuit dough saves lots of time and effort, but you'll see that these still taste oh-so-homemade. These pack an astonishing little kick!   ☻   Serves 6

> 3 tablespoons I Can't Believe It's Not Butter! Light Margarine
> 1/2 teaspoon chili seasoning
> 1 (7.5-ounce) package Pillsbury refrigerated buttermilk biscuits
> 1/2 cup + 1 tablespoon shredded Kraft reduced-fat Cheddar cheese
> 3 tablespoons Oscar Mayer or Hormel Real Bacon Bits
> 2 tablespoons chopped green onion

Spray an 8-inch microwave-safe pie plate with butter-flavored cooking spray. In a small microwave-safe mixing bowl, combine margarine and chili seasoning. Microwave on HIGH (100% power) for 20 seconds or until margarine is melted. Separate biscuits and cut each into 4 pieces. Stir biscuit pieces in melted margarine mixture, making sure pieces are well coated. Evenly arrange coated biscuit pieces in prepared pie plate. Sprinkle Cheddar cheese, bacon bits, and onion evenly over top. Microwave on HIGH for 3 minutes or until cheese melts. Place pie plate on counter and let set for 2 minutes. Divide into 6 servings.

Each serving equals:

HE: 1 1/4 Bread • 1 Fat • 1/2 Protein •
12 Optional Calories

---

150 Calories • 6 gm Fat • 7 gm Protein •
17 gm Carbohydrate • 462 mg Sodium •
83 mg Calcium • 1 gm Fiber

DIABETIC EXCHANGES: 1 Starch • 1 Fat • 1/2 Meat

Convection Oven

Recipes

This bonus chapter of recipes for your convection oven seemed perfect for this book because both the microwave and convection reduce cooking time through innovative technology. Wait until you see how juicy your meat dishes will turn out, and how beautifully your baked goods rise and brown. The secret: Hot air that circulates through the oven ensures even cooking! This heated air and the special way the fan swirls it around inside the closed environment of your oven actually changes the way foods cook and bake. You can also use your convection oven to thaw, reheat, and dehydrate. And because your oven is specially insulated, the outside of the oven and your kitchen both stay cool!

So if you've been a little disappointed with the results of some of your favorite recipes in your convection oven, it may be because those recipes haven't been thoroughly tested in the convection oven environment. These recipes have—and they've come through with flying colors—and delicious aromas!

You'll discover a host of convection charmers in this chapter, from starters to finales, with an abundance of splendid main dishes for all occasions. Why not put Baked Sweet Potatoes and Apricots on the menu with a turkey entree, or serve up Saucy Oven Veggies with a pork roast? You can serve a different main dish "loaf" each week for a month, from Heartland Meat Loaf to Tomato and Dill Tuna Loaf, or add succulent fish to your list of favorites, with Nordic Fish Bake and Fillets Amandine. Top them off with Cherry Cheesecake Pie or Double Chocolate Pudding Cake, or pack Heavenly Lemon Bars in your child's lunchbox. This chapter will show you just how spectacular your convection oven can be!

Note: Because many people own the smaller, countertop combination toaster-oven/convection ovens, I've tested most of the recipes in this chapter in an 8-by-8-inch metal cake pan. However, if you have a larger unit and you want to use a 9-by-9-inch metal cake pan instead, your recipe will still turn out just as delicious. (You may want to check for doneness a few minutes early, as the mixture will not be quite as high in the pan and may finish cooking a bit sooner.) For baked goods (primarily cakes and such) that *require* a larger than 8-by-8-inch pan, I usually call for a 7-by-11-inch biscuit pan. If you don't have one, you can choose to use your 9-by-9-inch metal cake pan (if it fits in your oven) instead.

Rising Sun Munch Mix

In honor of those sweet-and-tangy Eastern specialties, I created this gift-from-the-East snack. It's full of crunch and texture in your mouth. If you love the contradiction of salty and sweet in one bite, this one's for you! ☾ Serves 6 (¾ cup)

5 cups Rice Chex
½ cup coarsely chopped walnuts
¼ cup reduced-sodium soy sauce
½ cup Splenda Granular

Preheat convection oven to 350 degrees. In a large bowl, combine Rice Chex and walnuts. In a small bowl, combine soy sauce and Splenda. Drizzle soy sauce mixture evenly over cereal mixture. Toss gently to coat. Spread mixture in an ungreased 8-by-8-inch cake pan. Bake in convection oven for 15 to 20 minutes or until crisp, stirring after every 5 minutes. Place pan on a wire rack and allow to cool completely, stirring occasionally. Mix well before serving. Store in airtight container or Ziploc storage bags.

Each serving equals:

HE: 1 Bread • ⅔ Fat • ⅓ Protein • 8 Optional Calories

158 Calories • 6 gm Fat • 3 gm Protein •
23 gm Carbohydrate • 528 mg Sodium •
78 mg Calcium • 1 gm Fiber

DIABETIC EXCHANGES: 1½ Starch • 1 Fat

Hot Tuna Dip

Kids love dipping carrot and celery sticks into this rich-and-creamy tuna blend, and it's also good with baked chips or crackers when you're having a few friends over to watch a movie or a NASCAR race. ♥ Serves 6 (¼ cup)

> 1 (8-ounce) package Philadelphia fat-free cream cheese
> 1 (6-ounce) can white tuna, packed in water, drained and flaked
> 2 tablespoons Land O Lakes Fat Free Half & Half
> 1 tablespoon dried onion flakes
> 1 teaspoon dried parsley flakes
> ⅛ teaspoon black pepper
> ¼ cup chopped almonds

Preheat convection oven to 350 degrees. Spray an 8-inch round cake pan with butter-flavored cooking spray. In prepared pan, stir cream cheese with a sturdy spoon until soft. Add tuna, half & half, onion flakes, parsley flakes, and black pepper. Mix well to combine. Stir in almonds. Bake in convection oven for 15 minutes or until mixture is hot. Mix well before serving. Serve at once.

HINT: Extra good with celery sticks.

Each serving equals:

HE: 1½ Protein • ⅓ Fat • 3 Optional Calories

99 Calories • 3 gm Fat • 14 gm Protein •
4 gm Carbohydrate • 344 mg Sodium •
194 mg Calcium • 1 gm Fiber

DIABETIC EXCHANGES: 1½ Meat • ½ Fat

Saucy Oven Veggies

How could any vegetable dish this scrumptious be good for you? Not only are you getting your daily veggies, you're also enjoying a sauce rich in calcium—but I bet you won't be thinking about any of these nutrition facts when you "ooh" and "aah" over the flavor!

● Serves 6

> ½ cup Kraft fat-free mayonnaise
> ½ cup fat-free milk
> ¼ cup Land O Lakes Fat Free Half & Half
> ¼ cup Kraft Reduced Fat Parmesan Style Grated Topping
> 1 tablespoon dried onion flakes
> 1 tablespoon dried parsley flakes
> ⅛ teaspoon black pepper
> 2 (10-ounce) packages frozen mixed vegetables, thawed
> 15 Ritz Reduced Fat Crackers, made into crumbs

Preheat convection oven to 350 degrees. Spray an 8-by-8-inch cake pan with butter-flavored cooking spray. In a large bowl, combine mayonnaise, milk, and half & half. Add Parmesan cheese, onion flakes, parsley flakes, and black pepper. Mix well to combine. Stir in mixed vegetables. Spread mixture evenly into prepared pan. Sprinkle cracker crumbs lightly over top. Lightly spray top with butter-flavored cooking spray. Bake in convection oven for 20 to 25 minutes or until mixture is hot and bubbly. Place pan on a wire rack and let set for 5 minutes. Divide into 6 servings.

HINTS: 1. Thaw mixed vegetables by placing in a colander and rinsing under hot water for 1 minute.
2. A self-seal sandwich bag works great for crushing crackers.

Each serving equals:

HE: 1 Bread • 1 Vegetable • ½ Slider •
2 Optional Calories

143 Calories • 3 gm Fat • 5 gm Protein •
24 gm Carbohydrate • 348 mg Sodium •
94 mg Calcium • 4 gm Fiber

DIABETIC EXCHANGES: 1½ Starch/Carbohydrate •
1 Vegetable

Mom's Creamed Green Beans

Here's more "magic" starring my husband's favorite vegetable, which has been the inspiration for so many recipes. Creamed veggies are truly cozy, old-fashioned comfort food—and they're just perfect for welcoming a loved one home from the road.

● Serves 4

> 3 cups frozen cut green beans, thawed
> 1 (12-fluid-ounce) can Carnation Evaporated Fat Free
> Milk
> 3 tablespoons all-purpose flour
> ⅛ teaspoon black pepper
> ½ cup + 1 tablespoon shredded Kraft reduced-fat
> Cheddar cheese
> 6 tablespoons dried bread crumbs

Preheat convection oven to 350 degrees. Spray an 8-by-8-inch cake pan with butter-flavored cooking spray. Evenly arrange green beans in prepared pan. In a covered jar, combine evaporated milk, flour, and black pepper. Shake well to blend. Pour mixture into a medium saucepan sprayed with butter-flavored cooking spray. Stir in Cheddar cheese. Cook over medium heat for 5 to 6 minutes or until mixture starts to thicken and cheese melts, stirring constantly. Drizzle hot mixture evenly over beans. Sprinkle bread crumbs evenly over top. Lightly spray top with butter-flavored cooking spray. Bake in convection oven for 30 to 35 minutes or until mixture is hot and bubbly. Place pan on a wire rack and let set for 5 minutes. Divide into 4 servings.

HINT: Thaw green beans by placing in a colander and rinsing under hot water for 1 minute.

Each serving equals:

HE: 1½ Vegetable • ¾ Fat Free Milk • ¾ Bread •
¾ Protein

---

203 Calories • 3 gm Fat • 14 gm Protein •
30 gm Carbohydrate • 337 mg Sodium •
414 mg Calcium • 4 gm Fiber

DIABETIC EXCHANGES: 1½ Vegetable •
1 Fat Free Milk • 1 Starch

Baked Celery Supreme

I'd bet that most people are used to eating their celery raw and crunchy, but this unique recipe will introduce it in an exciting new way. Even baking doesn't take away all the crispness of the water chestnuts and the almonds that help make this dish so original.

☺ Serves 4

> 3 cups sliced celery
> 1 (8-ounce) can sliced water chestnuts, chopped, rinsed, and
>   drained
> 1 (10¾-ounce) can Healthy Request Cream of Celery or
>   Mushroom Soup
> 1 (2-ounce) jar chopped pimiento, drained
> 1 tablespoon reduced-sodium soy sauce
> ⅛ teaspoon black pepper
> ¼ cup sliced almonds

Preheat convection oven to 350 degrees. Spray an 8-by-8-inch cake pan with butter-flavored cooking spray. In a large bowl, combine celery, water chestnuts, and celery soup. Stir in pimiento, soy sauce, and black pepper. Spread mixture evenly into prepared pan. Sprinkle almonds evenly over top. Bake in convection oven for 25 to 30 minutes or until celery is just tender and mixture is hot and bubbly. Place pan on wire rack and let set for 5 minutes. Divide into 4 servings.

Each serving equals:

HE: 2 Vegetable • ½ Fat • ¼ Protein • ½ Slider •
1 Optional Calorie

---

137 Calories • 5 gm Fat • 4 gm Protein •
19 gm Carbohydrate • 478 mg Sodium •
146 mg Calcium • 6 gm Fiber

DIABETIC EXCHANGES: 1½ Vegetable •
½ Other Carbohydrate • ½ Fat

Easy Scalloped Cabbage

This high-fiber dish tastes outrageously rich and luscious, but it's made with such a tiny amount of fat, you may be astonished! The fresh bread crumbs make all the difference, so take the time to toast the bread—the result is worth it. ☻ Serves 6

> 6 cups coarsely chopped cabbage
> 1 (10¾-ounce) can Healthy Request Cream of Mushroom Soup
> ¼ cup Land O Lakes Fat Free Half & Half
> 2 tablespoons I Can't Believe It's Not Butter! Light Margarine
> ⅛ teaspoon black pepper
> 3 slices reduced-calorie white bread, toasted and made into
>   crumbs

Preheat convection oven to 350 degrees. Spray an 8-by-8-inch cake pan with butter-flavored cooking spray. In a large skillet sprayed with butter-flavored cooking spray, sauté cabbage for 5 minutes. Add mushroom soup, half & half, margarine, and black pepper. Mix well to combine. Spread mixture evenly in prepared pan. Evenly sprinkle bread crumbs over cabbage mixture. Lightly spray top with butter-flavored cooking spray. Bake in convection oven for 20 minutes or until mixture is hot and bubbly. Place pan on a wire rack and let set for 5 minutes. Divide into 6 servings.

Each serving equals:

HE: 1 Vegetable • ½ Fat • ¼ Bread • ¼ Slider •
14 Optional Calories

91 Calories • 3 gm Fat • 3 gm Protein •
13 gm Carbohydrate • 330 mg Sodium •
102 mg Calcium • 2 gm Fiber

DIABETIC EXCHANGES: 1 Vegetable • ½ Fat • ½ Starch

Rice and Cheese Custard Bake

What is custard, really, but a heated combination of milk and eggs, flavored to please? This might remind you of the filling from a cheesy quiche, especially when you take your very first bite. It's light and hearty all at once.   ☻   Serves 6

 1 cup chopped onion
 ½ cup finely chopped celery
 1 (12-fluid-ounce) can Carnation Evaporated Fat Free Milk
 3 eggs, slightly beaten, or equivalent in egg substitute
 1 teaspoon Worcestershire sauce
 2 teaspoons dried parsley flakes
 2 cups cubed Velveeta Light processed cheese
 2 cups cooked rice
 6 tablespoons purchased dried fine bread crumbs
 ¼ cup Kraft Reduced Fat Parmesan Style Grated Topping

Preheat convection oven to 350 degrees. Spray an 8-by-8-inch cake pan with butter-flavored cooking spray. In a large skillet sprayed with butter-flavored cooking spray, sauté onion and celery for 6 to 8 minutes or just until tender. In a large bowl, combine milk, eggs, Worcestershire sauce, and parsley flakes. Add Velveeta cheese and rice. Mix well to combine. Stir in onion mixture. Spread mixture evenly into prepared pan. In a small bowl, combine bread crumbs and Parmesan cheese. Evenly sprinkle crumb mixture over rice mixture. Lightly spray top with butter-flavored cooking spray. Bake for 25 to 30 minutes or until mixture is hot and bubbly. Place pan on a wire rack and let set for 5 minutes. Divide into 6 servings.

HINT: Usually 1⅓ cups uncooked instant rice or 1 cup uncooked regular rice cooks to about 2 cups.

Each serving equals:

HE: 2 Protein • 1 Bread • ½ Fat Free Milk •
½ Vegetable

276 Calories • 8 gm Fat • 17 gm Protein •
34 gm Carbohydrate • 804 mg Sodium •
449 mg Calcium • 1 gm Fiber

DIABETIC EXCHANGES: 2 Meat • 1½ Starch •
½ Fat Free Milk • ½ Vegetable

Rice Siciliano

It's in Italy's southern regions that tomato-based dishes are most at home, and this is one of my recent favorites. This dish will truly deliver that Mediterranean warmth in every bite.

○ Serves 6

> 1 (15-ounce) can diced tomatoes, undrained
> 1¼ cups water
> 1 teaspoon Italian seasoning
> 1 tablespoon Splenda Granular
> 1 cup uncooked Minute Rice
> 1 cup chopped onion
> ½ cup chopped green bell pepper
> 1 cup + 2 tablespoons shredded Kraft reduced-fat mozzarella
>   cheese

Preheat convection oven to 350 degrees. Spray an 8-by-8-inch cake pan with olive oil–flavored cooking spray. In a large bowl, combine undrained tomatoes, water, Italian seasoning, and Splenda. Stir in uncooked rice, onion, and green pepper. Add mozzarella cheese. Mix well to combine. Spread mixture into prepared pan. Cover with foil and bake in convection oven for 25 minutes. Uncover and continue baking for 10 minutes or until rice is tender. Place pan on a wire rack and let set for 5 minutes. Divide into 6 servings.

Each serving equals:

HE: 1 Protein • 1 Vegetable • ½ Bread •
1 Optional Calorie

135 Calories • 3 gm Fat • 8 gm Protein •
19 gm Carbohydrate • 232 mg Sodium •
160 mg Calcium • 2 gm Fiber

DIABETIC EXCHANGES: 1 Meat • 1 Vegetable • 1 Starch

Country Noodles

This is the kind of dish you'd expect to find in some Old World restaurant, an array of creamy noodles with just the right amount of "kick" from the horseradish sauce and bacon. The aroma of Parmesan cheese will definitely give you and your dinner guests an appetite!   ☻   Serves 4

½ cup Land O Lakes no-fat
   sour cream
2 tablespoons Land O Lakes
   Fat Free Half & Half
¼ cup Kraft Reduced Fat
   Parmesan Style Grated
   Topping

1 tablespoon prepared
   horseradish sauce
¼ cup Oscar Mayer or Hormel
   Real Bacon Bits
1 teaspoon dried parsley flakes
1 teaspoon dried onion flakes
2 cups cooked noodles

Preheat convection oven to 350 degrees. Spray an 8-by-8-inch baking dish with butter-flavored cooking spray. In a large bowl, combine sour cream, half & half, Parmesan cheese, horseradish sauce, bacon bits, parsley flakes, and onion flakes. Add noodles. Mix gently to combine. Spread mixture into prepared baking dish. Bake in convection oven for 14 to 16 minutes or until mixture is hot and bubbly. Place pan on a wire rack and let set for 5 minutes. Divide into 4 servings.

HINT: Usually 1¾ cups uncooked noodles cooks to about 2 cups.

Each serving equals:

HE: 1 Bread • ¼ Protein • ½ Slider •
18 Optional Calories

172 Calories • 4 gm Fat • 8 gm Protein •
26 gm Carbohydrate • 416 mg Sodium •
87 mg Calcium • 2 gm Fiber

DIABETIC EXCHANGES: 1½ Starch/Carbohydrate •
½ Meat

Baked Sweet Potatoes and Apricots

Not every urge for something sweet has to be satisfied by a piece of cake! Here's a glorious way to please your taste buds's longing— and it's rich in vitamins and nutrients, not high in added sugar and fat. If you've got the sweet tooth, I've got the dish!

☺ Serves 4

1 (15-ounce) can vacuum-packed sweet potatoes, drained and
    coarsely chopped
1 (15-ounce) can apricot halves, packed in fruit juice, coarsely
    chopped, drained, and ⅓ cup liquid reserved
⅓ cup water
1 tablespoon cornstarch
½ cup Splenda Granular
½ teaspoon ground cinnamon

Preheat convection oven to 350 degrees. Spray an 8-by-8-inch cake pan with butter-flavored cooking spray. Evenly arrange sweet potatoes in prepared pan. Layer chopped apricots over top. In a small saucepan, combine reserved apricot juice, water, cornstarch, Splenda, and cinnamon. Cook over medium heat until mixture starts to thicken, stirring constantly. Drizzle hot mixture evenly over apricots. Bake in convection oven for 18 to 22 minutes or until mixture is hot and bubbly. Place pan on a wire rack and let set for 5 minutes. Divide into 4 servings.

Each serving equals:

HE: 1 Bread • 1 Fruit • 19 Optional Calories

136 Calories • 0 gm Fat • 2 gm Protein •
32 gm Carbohydrate • 67 mg Sodium •
34 mg Calcium • 3 gm Fiber

DIABETIC EXCHANGES: 1 Starch • 1 Fruit

Scalloped Potatoes with Celery

This recipe comes together so quickly, you can serve it on a weeknight when time is at a premium. Just stir it up, put it in to bake, take a relaxing shower, and dinner will soon be on the table.

○ Serves 6

> 1 (10¾-ounce) can Healthy Request Cream of Celery Soup
> 3 tablespoons Land O Lakes no-fat sour cream
> 1 teaspoon dried parsley flakes
> ⅛ teaspoon black pepper
> 4½ cups frozen loose-packed shredded hash brown potatoes
> 1 cup finely chopped celery
> ½ cup finely chopped onion
> 1½ cups shredded Kraft reduced-fat Cheddar cheese

Preheat convection oven to 350 degrees. Spray an 8-by-8-inch cake pan with butter-flavored cooking spray. In a large bowl, combine celery soup, sour cream, parsley flakes, and black pepper. Add hash browns, celery, and onion. Mix well to combine. Stir in Cheddar cheese. Evenly spread mixture into prepared pan. Cover with foil and bake in convection oven for 40 minutes. Uncover and continue baking for 15 minutes. Place pan on a wire rack and let set for 5 minutes. Divide into 6 servings.

HINT: Mr. Dell's frozen shredded potatoes are a good choice, or raw shredded potatoes, rinsed and patted dry, may be used in place of frozen potatoes.

Each serving equals:

HE: 1⅓ Protein • ½ Bread • ½ Vegetable •
¼ Slider • 18 Optional Calories

---

162 Calories • 6 gm Fat • 10 gm Protein •
17 gm Carbohydrate • 460 mg Sodium •
275 mg Calcium • 2 gm Fiber

DIABETIC EXCHANGES: 1 Starch/Carbohydrate •
1 Meat • ½ Vegetable

Italian Baked Potatoes and Onions

"Cooking" with dressing is a smart chef's time-saving technique I've celebrated often over the years. You get ready-made seasoning to stir into your dishes without having to keep a big stock of spices on hand, and the flavors bring simple ingredients like potatoes and onions to zesty life! ❤ Serves 4 (1 full cup)

> 4 cups diced raw potatoes
> 1 cup diced onion
> ¼ cup Kraft Fat Free Italian Dressing
> ¼ cup Kraft Reduced Fat Parmesan Style Grated Topping
> ¼ cup Land O Lakes no-fat sour cream

Preheat convection oven to 425 degrees. In an 8-by-8-inch cake pan sprayed with olive oil–flavored cooking spray, combine potatoes and onion. Add Italian dressing. Mix well to combine. Bake in convection oven for 30 to 45 minutes or until potatoes are almost tender. Evenly sprinkle Parmesan cheese over top and continue baking for 5 minutes. Place pan on a wire rack and let set for 5 minutes. When serving, top each portion with 1 tablespoon sour cream.

Each serving equals:

HE: 1 Bread • ½ Vegetable • ¼ Protein • ¼ Slider • 1 Optional Calorie

142 Calories • 2 gm Fat • 3 gm Protein • 28 gm Carbohydrate • 345 mg Sodium • 85 mg Calcium • 2 gm Fiber

DIABETIC EXCHANGES: 1½ Starch • ½ Vegetable

Cheesy Hash Browns

It feels like a dangerous splurge, to mix cheese into potatoes, but you'll be thrilled to discover that my Healthy Exchanges version isn't risky at all! This layered casserole can be served at any meal, from a dawn breakfast to a midnight supper. ☺ Serves 4

4½ cups frozen loose-packed shredded hash brown potatoes
3 tablespoons all-purpose flour
1 tablespoon dried onion flakes
1½ teaspoons dried parsley flakes

¾ cup shredded Kraft reduced-fat Cheddar cheese ☆
1 cup fat-free milk
2 tablespoons Land O Lakes Fat Free Half & Half
¼ teaspoon black pepper

Preheat convection oven to 325 degrees. Spray an 8-by-8-inch cake pan with butter-flavored cooking spray. In a large bowl, combine hash browns, flour, onion flakes, and parsley flakes. Stir in ¼ cup Cheddar cheese. Spread potato mixture in prepared pan. In a small bowl, combine milk, half & half, and black pepper. Pour mixture evenly over potatoes. Sprinkle remaining ½ cup Cheddar cheese evenly over top. Bake in convection oven for 45 to 50 minutes or until potatoes are tender and lightly browned. Place pan on a wire rack and let set for 5 minutes. Divide into 4 servings.

HINT: Mr. Dell's frozen shredded potatoes are a good choice, or raw shredded potatoes, rinsed and patted dry, may be used in place of frozen potatoes.

Each serving equals:

HE: 1 Bread • 1 Protein • ¼ Fat Free Milk • 3 Optional Calories

181 Calories • 5 gm Fat • 11 gm Protein • 23 gm Carbohydrate • 38 mg Sodium • 239 mg Calcium • 1 gm Fiber

DIABETIC EXCHANGES: 1½ Starch • 1 Meat

Grandma's Macaroni and Cheese with Green Beans

You may wonder, what is "evaporated fat free milk" anyway? It's a cooked version of regular fat-free milk, with half of the liquid removed and then canned to make it shelf-safe for months. I love cooking with it because, added to a little bit of flour, it makes a wonderful soup and sauce thickener.　　　　☻　　Serves 6

1 (12-fluid-ounce) can Carnation Evaporated Fat Free Milk
3 tablespoons all-purpose flour
1 tablespoon dried onion flakes
1 teaspoon prepared yellow mustard
1½ cups cubed Velveeta Light processed cheese
⅛ teaspoon black pepper
2 cups cooked elbow macaroni
1½ cups frozen cut green beans, thawed
2 slices reduced-calorie white bread, made into tiny crumbs

Preheat convection oven to 350 degrees. Spray an 8-by-8-inch cake pan with butter-flavored cooking spray. In a covered jar, combine evaporated milk and flour. Shake well to blend. Pour mixture into a medium saucepan sprayed with butter-flavored cooking spray. Stir in onion flakes, mustard, Velveeta cheese, and black pepper. Cook over medium heat for 5 to 6 minutes or until mixture thickens and cheese melts, stirring often. Meanwhile, in a large bowl, combine macaroni and green beans. Add hot cheese sauce. Mix well to combine. Spread mixture evenly into prepared pan. Sprinkle bread crumbs evenly over top. Lightly spray crumbs with butter-flavored cooking spray. Bake in convection oven for 25 to 30 minutes or until mixture is hot and bubbly. Place pan on a wire rack and let set for 5 minutes. Divide into 6 servings.

HINTS: 1. Usually 1⅓ cups uncooked elbow macaroni cooks to about 2 cups.

2. Thaw green beans by placing in a colander and rinsing under hot water for 1 minute.
3. 1 (15-ounce) can cut green beans, rinsed and drained, may be used in place of frozen.

Each serving equals:

HE: 1 Bread • 1 Protein • ½ Fat Free Milk • ½ Vegetable

220 Calories • 4 gm Fat • 14 gm Protein • 32 gm Carbohydrate • 578 mg Sodium • 347 mg Calcium • 2 gm Fiber

DIABETIC EXCHANGES: 1 Starch • 1 Meat • ½ Fat Free Milk • ½ Vegetable

Grande Macaroni and Cheese Bake

Talk about the beginning of a "beautiful friendship!" When a classic mac-and-cheese recipe joins hands with a little Mexican sizzle, the result is a meal with so much flavor, you have to call it "Grande." You'll almost hear the beat of *Tejano* music—just like that sung by the great late singer Selena! ☻ Serves 6

> 1 (10¾-ounce) can Healthy Request Tomato Soup
> ¾ cup chunky salsa (mild, medium, or hot)
> 1½ cups cubed Velveeta Light processed cheese
> 2½ cups cooked elbow macaroni, rinsed and drained
> 1½ teaspoons dried parsley flakes
> 1 teaspoon chili seasoning
> ⅛ teaspoon black pepper
> 5 Ritz Reduced Fat Crackers, made into crumbs

Preheat convection oven to 350 degrees. Spray an 8-by-8-inch cake pan with butter-flavored cooking spray. In a large saucepan, combine tomato soup, salsa, and Velveeta cheese. Cook over medium heat until mixture is heated through and cheese melts. Add macaroni, parsley flakes, chili seasoning, and black pepper. Mix well to combine. Spread mixture evenly into prepared pan. Evenly sprinkle cracker crumbs over top. Lightly spray top with butter-flavored cooking spray. Bake in convection oven for 20 to 25 minutes or until mixture is hot and bubbly. Place pan on a wire rack and let set for 5 minutes. Divide into 6 servings.

HINTS: 1. A self-seal sandwich bag works great for crushing crackers.
2. Usually 1⅔ cups uncooked elbow macaroni cooks to about 2½ cups.

Each serving equals:

HE: 1 Bread • 1 Protein • ¼ Vegetable • ¼ Slider •
10 Optional Calories

---

196 Calories • 4 gm Fat • 9 gm Protein •
31 gm Carbohydrate • 895 mg Sodium •
171 mg Calcium • 1 gm Fiber

DIABETIC EXCHANGES: 1½ Starch/Carbohydrate •
1 Meat

Sour Cream Dill Fish Bake

I realize that "white fish" is a huge category, especially these days, when our supermarkets seem more like specialty stores, and new types of fish keep turning up on the shelves. Recently, I've tasted basa, which is a Vietnamese catfish, and also tilapia, a farm-raised fish that originally came from Africa. Keep your menu varied when it comes to fish, and dinner will always be a treat!

❂ Serves 4

3 tablespoons all-purpose flour
1 teaspoon lemon pepper
16 ounces white fish, cut into 4 pieces
½ cup fat-free milk

¾ cup Land O Lakes no-fat sour cream
1 teaspoon dried onion flakes
½ teaspoon dried dill weed
6 tablespoons dried fine bread crumbs

Preheat convection oven to 375 degrees. Spray an 8-by-8-inch cake pan with butter-flavored cooking spray. In a shallow dish, combine flour and lemon pepper. Coat fish pieces in flour mixture. Evenly arrange coated fish pieces in prepared pan. Sprinkle any remaining flour mixture over top. Drizzle milk over coated fish pieces. Bake in convection oven for 15 to 20 minutes or until fish flakes easily with a fork. In a small bowl, combine sour cream, onion flakes, and dill weed. Evenly spoon mixture over top of fish pieces. Sprinkle bread crumbs evenly over top. Lightly spray crumbs with butter-flavored cooking spray. Continue to bake for 5 to 7 minutes or until crumbs are golden brown. Place pan on a wire rack and let set for 5 minutes.

Each serving equals:

HE: 2¼ Protein • ¾ Bread • ½ Slider • 15 Optional Calories

191 Calories • 3 gm Fat • 20 gm Protein • 21 gm Carbohydrate • 331 mg Sodium • 153 mg Calcium • 1 gm Fiber

DIABETIC EXCHANGES: 3 Meat • 1 Starch

Nordic Fish Bake

Okay, so the name "dill *weed*" sounds a bit odd, which may be one of the reasons you've never added this herb to your spice shelf. But the flavor this little plant imparts to creamy dishes is just spectacular—so give it a try! ☻ Serves 4

> *16 ounces white fish, cut into 4 pieces*
> *1 (10¾-ounce) can Healthy Request Cream of Mushroom Soup*
> *1 (2.5-ounce) can sliced mushrooms, drained*
> *¼ cup Land O Lakes no-fat sour cream*
> *1 teaspoon dried dill weed*

Preheat convection oven to 350 degrees. Spray an 8-by-8-inch cake pan with butter-flavored cooking spray. Evenly arrange fish pieces in prepared pan. In a medium bowl, combine mushroom soup, mushrooms, sour cream, and dill weed. Evenly spoon soup mixture over fish pieces. Bake in convection oven for 22 to 26 minutes or until fish flakes easily. Place pan on a wire rack and let set for 5 minutes. When serving, evenly spoon sauce over top of fish pieces.

Each serving equals:

HE: 2¼ Protein • ¼ Vegetable • ½ Slider •
16 Optional Calories

---

135 Calories • 3 gm Fat • 18 gm Protein •
9 gm Carbohydrate • 408 mg Sodium •
113 mg Calcium • 0 gm Fiber

DIABETIC EXCHANGES: 3 Meat • ½ Other Carbohydrate

Fillets Amandine

Simple food can be among the most elegant when you use good-quality ingredients. It doesn't take a long list of ingredients to make a delicious fish entree like this one. ☻ Serves 4

> 16 ounces white fish, cut into 4 pieces
> ¼ cup slivered almonds
> 1 tablespoon + 1 teaspoon I Can't Believe It's Not Butter! Light
>   Margarine, melted
> 2 teaspoons lemon juice

Preheat convection oven to 425 degrees. Spray an 8-by-8-inch cake pan with butter-flavored cooking spray. Evenly arrange fish pieces in prepared pan. Sprinkle 1 tablespoon almonds over top of each fish piece. In a small bowl, combine melted margarine and lemon juice. Drizzle mixture evenly over top of fish. Bake in convection oven for 8 to 10 minutes or until fish flakes easily with a fork. Place pan on a wire rack and let set for 3 minutes before serving.

Each serving equals:

HE: 2½ Protein • 1 Fat

---

130 Calories • 6 gm Fat • 18 gm Protein •
1 gm Carbohydrate • 107 mg Sodium •
50 mg Calcium • 0 gm Fiber

DIABETIC EXCHANGES: 3 Meat • 1 Fat

Tuna Cheese Melt

I know that eggs are an untraditional ingredient in a tuna melt, but that's one of the reasons I love creating new recipes. I can be just about anywhere, in the house, or walking through my gardens at Timber Ridge Farm, when I'll get a flash of inspiration and start crafting the dish in my mind. I've made loads of tuna melts over the years, and this is my latest! ❤ Serves 4

> 1 (6-ounce) can white tuna, packed in water, drained and flaked
> ½ cup + 1 tablespoon shredded Kraft reduced-fat Cheddar cheese
> ¼ cup Kraft fat-free mayonnaise
> ½ cup finely chopped celery
> 2 tablespoons finely chopped onion
> 2 hard-boiled eggs, chopped
> 4 small hamburger buns

Preheat convection oven to 475 degrees. In a large bowl, combine tuna, Cheddar cheese, and mayonnaise. Add celery and onion. Mix well to combine. Stir in chopped eggs. Evenly spoon about ½ cup tuna mixture between each bun. Wrap each bun in aluminum foil. Place wrapped buns in an 8-by-8-inch cake pan. Bake in convection oven to 10 to 12 minutes or until hot. Serve at once.

Each serving equals:

HE: 2¼ Protein • 1 Bread • ¼ Vegetable •
10 Optional Calories

220 Calories • 8 gm Fat • 19 gm Protein •
18 gm Carbohydrate • 617 mg Sodium •
134 mg Calcium • 2 gm Fiber

DIABETIC EXCHANGES: 2½ Meat • 1 Starch

Tomato and Dill Tuna Loaf

Looking for something a little different to do with those handy-dandy cans of tuna you got on sale? Here's a fiber-rich aromatic loaf that makes an impressive picnic sandwich. I made it with tomatoes from my garden, so it was even more special. ☻ Serves 6

2 (6-ounce) cans white tuna, packed in water, drained and flaked
¾ cup Quaker Quick Oats
1 cup finely chopped tomato
½ cup finely chopped onion
1 teaspoon dried dill weed
½ cup Land O Lakes no-fat sour cream

Preheat convection oven to 350 degrees. Spray a 9-by-5-inch loaf pan with butter-flavored cooking spray. In a large bowl, combine tuna, oats, tomato, onion, and dill weed. Add sour cream. Mix well to combine. Pat mixture into prepared pan. Bake in convection oven for 25 to 35 minutes or until center is firm and top is golden brown. Place pan on a wire rack and let set for 5 minutes. Divide into 6 servings.

HINT: Also makes good sandwiches when cold.

Each serving equals:

HE: 1½ Protein • ½ Bread • ½ Vegetable • ¼ Slider

122 Calories • 2 gm Fat • 14 gm Protein •
12 gm Carbohydrate • 208 mg Sodium •
43 mg Calcium • 1 gm Fiber

DIABETIC EXCHANGES: 2 Meat • ½ Starch •
½ Vegetable

Sweet Salmon Loaf

Sometimes, one ingredient makes an astonishing difference in a familiar recipe. In this updated salmon loaf, it's a wonderful dollop of sweet pickle relish that transforms good into superlative!

● Serves 6

> 1 (14¾-ounce) can pink salmon, drained, boned, and flaked
> 2 eggs or equivalent in egg substitute
> 15 Ritz Reduced Fat Crackers, made into crumbs
> ½ cup Kraft fat-free mayonnaise
> ¼ cup sweet pickle relish
> ¾ cup finely chopped celery
> 1 (2-ounce) jar chopped pimiento, drained
> ⅛ teaspoon black pepper

Preheat convection oven to 350 degrees. Spray a 9-by-5-inch loaf pan with butter-flavored cooking spray. In a large bowl, combine salmon, eggs, cracker crumbs, mayonnaise, and pickle relish. Add celery, pimiento, and black pepper. Mix well to combine. Pat mixture into prepared pan. Bake in convection oven for 25 to 35 minutes or until center is firm and top is golden brown. Place pan on a wire rack and let set for 5 minutes. Divide into 6 servings.

HINT: A self-seal sandwich bag works great for crushing crackers.

Each serving equals:

> HE: 2½ Protein • ½ Bread • ¼ Vegetable •
> ¼ Slider • 8 Optional Calories
> _____
> 189 Calories • 9 gm Fat • 15 gm Protein •
> 12 gm Carbohydrate • 610 mg Sodium •
> 130 mg Calcium • 1 gm Fiber
> _____
> DIABETIC EXCHANGES: 2½ Meat •
> 1 Starch/Carbohydrate

Oven Fried Chicken

From the diners in New York City's Harlem to the roomy kitchens of the American South, and from one coast to the other, you'll find more fried chicken recipes than you imagine! (Trust me, I've found hundreds over the years.) Every cook dips his or her chicken in a special series of mixes to make it "just right." This oven version is delectably moist and richly flavored—yum, yum, yum.

● Serves 4

> ⅓ cup Carnation Nonfat Dry Milk Powder
> ½ cup water
> 1 tablespoon white distilled vinegar
> ½ cup finely crushed cornflake crumbs
> ¼ cup Kraft Reduced Fat Parmesan Style Grated Topping
> 1 tablespoon dried parsley flakes
> 1 tablespoon dried onion flakes
> ⅛ teaspoon black pepper
> 16 ounces skinned and boned uncooked chicken breast,
>   cut into 4 pieces

Preheat convection oven to 375 degrees. Spray an 8-by-8-inch cake pan with butter-flavored cooking spray. In a shallow saucer, combine dry milk powder, water, and vinegar. Set aside. In another shallow saucer, combine cornflake crumbs, Parmesan cheese, parsley flakes, onion flakes, and black pepper. Dip chicken pieces first in milk mixture, then in crumb mixture. Evenly arrange coated chicken pieces in prepared pan. Drizzle any remaining milk and crumb mixture over top. Bake in convection oven for 35 to 45 minutes or until chicken is tender. Place pan on a wire rack and let set for 5 minutes.

Each serving equals:

HE: 3¼ Protein • ½ Bread • ¼ Fat Free Milk

229 Calories • 5 gm Fat • 30 gm Protein •
16 gm Carbohydrate • 281 mg Sodium •
138 mg Calcium • 0 gm Fiber

DIABETIC EXCHANGES: 3 Meat • 1 Starch

Easy Apricot Glazed Chicken

Spreadable fruit makes one of the best "instant" glazes I've ever tasted, but all on its own it's a little bit too sweet. Solution—just enough mustard to take the edge off! This dish looks utterly gorgeous when it arrives at the table, glistening and oh-so-juicy.

Serves 4

> 16 ounces skinned and boned uncooked chicken breast,
>   cut into 4 pieces
> 6 tablespoons apricot spreadable fruit
> 1 tablespoon Dijon Country Mustard
> 1 teaspoon dried parsley flakes

Preheat convection oven to 375 degrees. Spray an 8-by-8-inch cake pan with butter-flavored cooking spray. Place chicken pieces in prepared pan. In a small bowl, combine spreadable fruit, mustard, and parsley flakes. Evenly spread mixture over chicken pieces. Bake in convection oven for 25 to 35 minutes or until chicken is tender. Place pan on a wire rack and let set for 5 minutes. When serving, evenly drizzle any remaining sauce over chicken pieces.

Each serving equals:

HE: 3 Protein • 1 Fruit

---

188 Calories • 4 gm Fat • 23 gm Protein •
15 gm Carbohydrate • 145 mg Sodium •
12 mg Calcium • 1 gm Fiber

DIABETIC EXCHANGES: 3 Meat • 1 Fruit

Chicken Bake Supreme

If you've exhausted all your chicken ideas and are ready to wave the white flag, hold it right there! This high-protein, crunchy chicken concoction is a fresh and fun approach to serving your chicken leftovers. And don't you just love those chow mein noodles?

❂ Serves 4

1½ cups diced cooked chicken breast
½ cup chopped celery
1 (8-ounce) can sliced water chestnuts, rinsed and drained
1 (15-ounce) can French-style green beans, rinsed and drained
1 (10¾-ounce) can Healthy Request Cream of Chicken Soup
¾ cup shredded Kraft reduced-fat Cheddar cheese
1½ cups chow mein noodles ☆

Preheat convection oven to 350 degrees. Spray an 8-by-8-inch cake pan with butter-flavored cooking spray. In a large bowl, combine chicken, celery, water chestnuts, green beans, and chicken soup. Stir in Cheddar cheese and 1 cup noodles. Spread mixture evenly in prepared pan. Coarsely crush remaining ½ cup chow mein noodles and evenly sprinkle over top. Bake in convection oven for 25 to 30 minutes or until mixture is hot and bubbly. Place pan on a wire rack and let set for 5 minutes. Divide into 4 servings.

HINT: If you don't have leftovers, purchase a chunk of cooked chicken breast from your local deli.

Each serving equals:

HE: 3 Protein • 1½ Vegetable • 1 Bread • ½ Slider • 5 Optional Calories

299 Calories • 7 gm Fat • 27 gm Protein •
32 gm Carbohydrate • 841 mg Sodium •
186 mg Calcium • 5 gm Fiber

DIABETIC EXCHANGES: 3 Meat • 1½ Vegetable •
1 Other Carbohydrate • 1 Fat

Baked Chicken Salad

A chilled chicken salad is a perfect luncheon choice on a steamy summer afternoon, but on a frigid winter's day, who wouldn't prefer a bubbling hot version rich with melted cheese and the delicate crunch of almonds? ☕ Serves 4

> 1½ cups diced cooked chicken breast
> 1½ cups chopped celery
> 1 cup unseasoned dry bread cubes
> ½ cup Kraft fat-free mayonnaise
> ¼ cup finely chopped green onion
> ¼ teaspoon paprika
> ½ cup + 1 tablespoon shredded Kraft reduced-fat
>   Cheddar cheese
> ¼ cup slivered almonds

Preheat convection oven to 350 degrees. Spray an 8-inch round cake pan with butter-flavored cooking spray. In a large bowl, combine chicken, celery, and bread cubes. Add mayonnaise, green onion, and paprika. Mix well to combine. Stir in Cheddar cheese and almonds. Spread mixture evenly into prepared pan. Bake in convection oven for 10 to 15 minutes or until mixture is hot and bubbly. Place pan on a wire rack and let set for 5 minutes. Divide into 4 servings.

HINTS: 1. If you don't have leftovers, purchase a chunk of cooked chicken breast from your local deli.
2. Pepperidge Farm bread cubes work great.

Each serving equals:

HE: 3 Protein • ¾ Vegetable • ½ Fat • ¼ Bread •
¼ Slider

249 Calories • 9 gm Fat • 26 gm Protein •
16 gm Carbohydrate • 580 mg Sodium •
151 mg Calcium • 3 gm Fiber

DIABETIC EXCHANGES: 3 Meat • 1 Starch/Carbohydrate •
½ Vegetable • ½ Fat

Chicken Celery Calico

Nuts are a smart and healthy addition to almost any casserole dish, and it doesn't take a jarful to make your culinary "point." They provide a bit of protein and other good-for-you nutrients, and they make an everyday dish seem special. ☺ Serves 4

> 2 cups diced cooked chicken breast
> 1½ cups very thinly sliced celery
> 1 cup frozen whole-kernel corn, thawed
> ½ cup finely chopped onion
> ½ cup Kraft fat-free mayonnaise
> 1 teaspoon dried parsley flakes
> ¼ cup sliced almonds
> ½ cup cubed Velveeta Light processed cheese
> ¾ cup crushed Frito-Lay Baked Potato Chips

Preheat convection oven to 350 degrees. Spray an 8-by-8-inch cake pan with butter-flavored cooking spray. In a large bowl, combine chicken, celery, corn, and onion. Stir in mayonnaise and parsley flakes. Add almonds and Velveeta cheese. Mix well to combine. Spread mixture evenly in prepared pan. Sprinkle crushed potato chips evenly over top. Bake in convection oven to 22 to 26 minutes or until mixture is hot and bubbly. Place pan on a wire rack and let set 5 minutes. Divide into 4 servings.

HINTS: 1. If you don't have leftovers, purchase a chunk of cooked chicken breast from your local deli.
2. Thaw corn by placing in a colander and rinsing under hot water for 1 minute.

Each serving equals:

HE: 3 Protein • 1 Bread • 1 Vegetable • ½ Fat •
¼ Slider

305 Calories • 9 gm Fat • 29 gm Protein •
27 gm Carbohydrate • 612 mg Sodium •
151 mg Calcium • 4 gm Fiber

DIABETIC EXCHANGES: 3 Meat • 1 Starch •
1 Vegetable • ½ Fat

Turkey Cranberry Bake

Leftovers, leftovers—or as I like to think of them, the paints in my culinary palette! Instead of viewing the turkey remaining after Thanksgiving or a family gathering as an annoyance, I see it as the spark to yet another memorable recipe. This is so good, you may choose to make a turkey breast every couple of weeks just to enjoy it again. ☻ Serves 6

> 1 cup + 2 tablespoons Bisquick Reduced Fat Baking Mix
> ½ cup fat-free milk
> 2 tablespoons Land O Lakes Fat Free Half & Half
> 1 egg or equivalent in egg substitute
> 1 tablespoon prepared yellow mustard
> 2 cups diced cooked turkey breast
> 6 tablespoons dried cranberries or Craisins
> ¾ cup shredded Kraft reduced-fat Cheddar cheese
> 1 teaspoon dried onion flakes
> 1 teaspoon dried parsley flakes

Preheat convection oven to 350 degrees. Spray an 8-by-8-inch cake pan with butter-flavored cooking spray. In a large bowl, combine baking mix, milk, half & half, and egg. Stir in mustard. Add turkey, cranberries, Cheddar cheese, onion flakes, and parsley flakes. Mix well to combine. Spread mixture evenly into prepared pan. Bake in convection oven for 25 to 30 minutes or until top springs back when lightly touched. Place pan on a wire rack and let set for 5 minutes. Divide into 6 servings.

HINT: If you don't have leftovers, purchase a chunk of cooked turkey breast from your local deli.

Each serving equals:

HE: 2½ Protein • 1 Bread • ½ Fruit •
3 Optional Calories

225 Calories • 5 gm Fat • 21 gm Protein •
24 gm Carbohydrate • 460 mg Sodium •
158 mg Calcium • 1 gm Fiber

DIABETIC EXCHANGES: 2½ Meat • 1 Starch • ½ Fruit

Juicy Baked Burgers

These aren't only melt-in-your-mouth juicy, they also may be one of the zestiest versions I've ever prepared of a classic burger! The oven allows all the different flavors to mingle like mad—and baking is a great alternative to frying or grilling. ☻ Serves 6

> ½ cup fat-free milk
> 1 tablespoon dried onion flakes
> 1 tablespoon Worcestershire sauce
> 1 teaspoon prepared horseradish sauce
> ⅛ teaspoon black pepper
> 16 ounces extra-lean ground sirloin beef or turkey breast
> 3 tablespoons dried fine bread crumbs

Preheat convection oven to 375 degrees. Spray a 7-by-11-inch biscuit pan with butter-flavored cooking spray. In a large bowl, combine milk, onion flakes, Worcestershire sauce, horseradish sauce, and black pepper. Add meat and bread crumbs. Mix well to combine. Using a ⅓ cup measuring cup as a guide, form into 6 patties. Evenly arrange patties in prepared pan. Bake in convection oven for 25 to 30 minutes or until patties are baked to desired doneness. Place pan on a wire rack and let set for 2 minutes before serving.

HINT: Good as is or served between a hamburger bun.

Each serving equals:

HE: 2 Protein • ¼ Slider

---

116 Calories • 4 gm Fat • 16 gm Protein •
4 gm Carbohydrate • 112 mg Sodium •
36 mg Calcium • 0 gm Fiber

DIABETIC EXCHANGES: 2 Meat

Heartland Meat Loaf

What gives a particular meat loaf its unique texture? Everything from the meat or meats you use to the veggie or grain "mix-ins." In honor of my Iowa home, I decided to use cornflakes in this mixture, and I really liked what they did for the yummy result!

● Serves 6

⅔ cup Carnation Nonfat Dry
    Milk Powder
½ cup water
1¼ cups crushed cornflakes
½ cup finely chopped onion
¼ cup finely chopped green
    bell pepper

16 ounces extra-lean ground
    sirloin beef or turkey
    breast
¼ cup reduced-sodium ketchup
1 teaspoon dried parsley flakes
⅛ teaspoon black pepper

Preheat convection oven to 350 degrees. Spray a 9-by-5-inch loaf pan with butter-flavored cooking spray. In a large bowl, combine dry milk powder and water. Stir in cornflakes, onion, and green pepper. Add meat, ketchup, parsley flakes, and black pepper. Mix well to combine. Pat mixture into prepared pan. Bake in convection oven for 40 to 45 minutes or until meat loaf is cooked through. Place pan on a wire rack and let set for 5 minutes. Divide into 6 servings.

Each serving equals:

HE: 2 Protein • ⅓ Fat Free Milk • ⅓ Bread •
¼ Vegetable • 10 Optional Calories

---

155 Calories • 3 gm Fat • 18 gm Protein •
14 gm Carbohydrate • 155 mg Sodium •
106 mg Calcium • 1 gm Fiber

DIABETIC EXCHANGES: 2 Meat • ½ Starch/Carbohydrate

Basic Meat Loaf

I got a letter from a woman who said, "I love my convection oven, and I want to make EVERYTHING in it. Do you have a good recipe for a marvelous meat loaf?" Yes, I do—it's simple, it's satisfying, and it comes out great every time. ☾ Serves 6

> 16 ounces extra-lean ground sirloin beef or turkey breast
> 15 Ritz Reduced Fat Crackers, made into crumbs
> ½ cup reduced-sodium ketchup ☆
> ¼ cup water
> 1 teaspoon dried onion flakes
> ⅛ teaspoon black pepper

Preheat convection oven to 350 degrees. Spray a 9-by-5-inch loaf pan with butter-flavored cooking spray. In a large bowl, combine meat, cracker crumbs, ¼ cup ketchup, water, onion flakes, and black pepper. Pat mixture into prepared pan. Bake in convection oven for 30 minutes. Drizzle remaining ¼ cup ketchup over top of partially baked meat loaf. Continue baking for 10 minutes or until meat loaf is cooked through. Place pan on a wire rack and let set for 5 minutes. Cut into 6 servings.

HINT: A self-seal sandwich bag works great for crushing crackers.

Each serving equals:

HE: 2 Protein • ½ Bread • ¼ Slider •
1 Optional Calorie

140 Calories • 4 gm Fat • 15 gm Protein •
11 gm Carbohydrate • 115 mg Sodium •
12 mg Calcium • 0 gm Fiber

DIABETIC EXCHANGES: 2 Meat • ½ Starch

Oven Hamburger Stroganoff

I've tried this dish over all kinds of starches, and I have to admit, I don't have a favorite. So I am leaving that decision up to you. With all of the different kinds of noodles on the grocery shelf, you could make this every week for a couple of months to try and discover which you love best. ● Serves 6 (¾ cup)

½ cup chopped onion
16 ounces extra-lean ground
    sirloin beef or turkey
    breast
1 (10¾-ounce) can Healthy
    Request Cream of
    Mushroom Soup
1 (4-ounce) can sliced
    mushrooms, drained

¾ cup Land O Lakes no-fat
    sour cream
1 tablespoon all-purpose flour
¼ teaspoon dried minced
    garlic
⅛ teaspoon black pepper
2 tablespoons chopped fresh
    parsley

Preheat convection oven to 325 degrees. Spray an 8-by-8-inch cake pan with butter-flavored cooking spray. Arrange onion in prepared pan. Bake in convection oven for 10 minutes. Crumble meat over partially cooked onion. Continue baking for 15 to 20 minutes or until meat is no longer pink, stirring after 10 minutes. Add soup, mushrooms, sour cream, flour, garlic, and black pepper. Mix well to combine. Continue baking for 5 minutes or just until mixture is soft. Mix well before serving. When serving, sprinkle 1 teaspoon parsley over each serving.

HINT: Good over hot rice, pasta, or potatoes.

Each serving equals:

HE: 2 Protein • ½ Vegetable • ¾ Slider •
3 Optional Calories

---

161 Calories • 5 gm Fat • 17 gm Protein •
12 gm Carbohydrate • 345 mg Sodium •
86 mg Calcium • 1 gm Fiber

DIABETIC EXCHANGES: 2 Meat • 1 Other Carbohydrate

Cabbage "Roll" Bake

It seems like just tons of work to make stuffed cabbage, so I thought I'd deliver the goodies without the "roll!" This warm and soothing supper dish contains all the flavors you love but in a much easier version. ☻ Serves 6

> 16 ounces extra-lean ground sirloin beef or turkey breast
> 1 cup chopped onion
> 3 cups shredded cabbage
> 1 (10¾-ounce) can Healthy Request Tomato Soup
> 1 (15-ounce) can diced tomatoes, undrained
> 1½ cups cooked rice
> 1 teaspoon dried parsley flakes
> 2 teaspoons Worcestershire sauce
> 1 teaspoon prepared yellow mustard
> ⅛ teaspoon black pepper

Preheat convection oven to 350 degrees. Spray an 8-by-8-inch cake pan with butter-flavored cooking spray. In a large skillet sprayed with butter-flavored cooking spray, brown meat and onion. Stir in cabbage. Continue cooking for 5 minutes. Add tomato soup, undrained tomatoes, rice, parsley flakes, Worcestershire sauce, mustard, and black pepper. Mix well to combine. Spread mixture evenly in prepared pan. Bake in convection oven for 25 to 30 minutes or until mixture is hot and bubbly. Place pan on a wire rack and let set for 5 minutes. Divide into 6 servings.

HINT: Usually 1 cup uncooked instant rice or ¾ cup uncooked regular rice cooks to about 1½ cups.

Each serving equals:

HE: 2 Protein • 1½ Vegetable • ½ Bread • ¼ Slider •
17 Optional Calories

204 Calories • 4 gm Fat • 17 gm Protein •
25 gm Carbohydrate • 359 mg Sodium •
45 mg Calcium • 3 gm Fiber

DIABETIC EXCHANGES: 2 Meat • 1½ Vegetable •
1 Starch/Carbohydrate

Corn Bread Tamale Pie

In most recipes the crust goes on the bottom, but for this zesty, Mexican-inspired entree pie, I'm putting it on top! My taste-testers found the cheesy corn bread topping, coupled with the tangy meat mixture, a marriage made in kitchen heaven.　❤　Serves 6

> 16 ounces extra-lean ground sirloin beef or turkey breast
> 1 cup chopped onion
> 1 (10¾-ounce) can Healthy Request Tomato Soup
> 1 (8-ounce) can whole-kernel corn, rinsed and drained
> ½ cup chopped green bell pepper
> ½ cup water
> 1½ teaspoons chili seasoning
> ¾ cup yellow cornmeal
> 1 tablespoon all-purpose flour
> 1 tablespoon Splenda Granular
> 1½ teaspoons baking powder
> ¼ teaspoon baking soda
> ⅓ cup fat-free milk
> 1 egg, beaten, or equivalent in egg substitute
> 1 tablespoon vegetable oil
> 6 tablespoons shredded Kraft reduced-fat Cheddar cheese

Preheat convection oven to 375 degrees. Spray an 8-inch round cake pan with butter-flavored cooking spray. In a large skillet sprayed with butter-flavored cooking spray, brown meat and onion. Stir in tomato soup, corn, green pepper, water, and chili seasoning. Continue cooking for 3 minutes, stirring often. Spread meat mixture into prepared pan. Bake in convection oven for 15 minutes. In a medium bowl, combine cornmeal, flour, Splenda, baking powder, and baking soda. Add milk, egg, and vegetable oil. Mix well to combine. Stir in Cheddar cheese. Carefully spread corn bread mixture over top of meat mixture. Continue baking for 10 to 15 minutes or until top is golden brown. Place pan on a wire rack and let set for 5 minutes. Divide into 6 servings.

Each serving equals:

HE: 2½ Protein • 1⅓ Bread • ½ Fat • ½ Vegetable • 6 Optional Calories

---

285 Calories • 9 gm Fat • 21 gm Protein • 30 gm Carbohydrate • 502 mg Sodium • 138 mg Calcium • 3 gm Fiber

---

DIABETIC EXCHANGES: 2½ Meat • 1½ Starch/Carbohydrate • ½ Fat

South Seas Baked Pork Tenderloins

True, when it comes to Hawaiian luaus, the centerpiece is usually a crispy pig on a spit, but you don't have to set one up in your backyard to savor sweet 'n' tangy pork! There's no question that cleanup will definitely be easier my way.   ☻   Serves 4

> 4 (4-ounce) lean pork tenderloins or cutlets
> ½ cup chopped onion
> ½ cup chopped green bell pepper
> 1 (8-ounce) can pineapple chunks, packed in fruit juice,
>   drained and ¼ cup liquid reserved
> 1 tablespoon white distilled vinegar
> ⅓ cup reduced-sodium ketchup
> 1 tablespoon Splenda Granular

Preheat convection oven to 350 degrees. Spray an 8-by-8-inch cake pan with butter-flavored cooking spray. Evenly arrange pork tenderloins in prepared pan. Layer onion and green pepper over meat. Arrange pineapple chunks over vegetables. In a small bowl, combine vinegar, ketchup, Splenda, and reserved pineapple liquid. Evenly pour sauce mixture over top. Bake in convection oven for 30 to 35 minutes or until pork is cooked through and tender. Place pan on a wire rack and let set for 5 minutes. Divide into 4 servings.

Each serving equals:

HE: 3 Protein • ½ Vegetable • ¼ Fruit • ¼ Slider •
2 Optional Calories

---

217 Calories • 5 gm Fat • 25 gm Protein •
18 gm Carbohydrate • 58 mg Sodium •
23 mg Calcium • 1 gm Fiber

DIABETIC EXCHANGES: 3 Meat • ½ Vegetable •
½ Starch

Barbecued Pork Tenders

Instead of firing up the family grill, you can get that irresistible taste of barbecued pork in your convection oven! There are many "schools" of barbecue sauce, but Cliff and I both thought this one was terrifically tangy and ideal for pork. ☻ Serves 4

> 1 cup finely chopped onion
> 1/2 cup water
> 1/4 cup white distilled vinegar
> 2 tablespoons Splenda Granular
> 1 1/2 teaspoons prepared yellow mustard
> 1/2 cup reduced-sodium ketchup
> 2 tablespoons Worcestershire sauce
> 1/8 teaspoon black pepper
> 4 (4-ounce) lean pork tenderloins or cutlets

Preheat convection oven to 350 degrees. Spray an 8-by-8-inch cake pan with butter-flavored cooking spray. In a medium saucepan sprayed with butter-flavored cooking spray, sauté onion for 5 minutes. Stir in water, vinegar, and Splenda. Add mustard, ketchup, Worcestershire sauce, and black pepper. Mix well to combine. Continue cooking over medium heat for 5 minutes, stirring often. Evenly arrange pork tenderloins in prepared pan. Drizzle hot sauce over top. Bake in convection oven for 30 to 35 minutes or until pork is cooked through and tender. Place pan on a wire rack and let set for 5 minutes. When serving, evenly spoon sauce over top of tenderloins.

Each serving equals:

HE: 3 Protein • 1/2 Vegetable • 1/4 Slider •
14 Optional Calories

---

188 Calories • 4 gm Fat • 23 gm Protein •
15 gm Carbohydrate • 156 mg Sodium •
30 mg Calcium • 1 gm Fiber

DIABETIC EXCHANGES: 3 Meat • 1/2 Vegetable

Cheese and Ham Strata

This is my idea of a savory "bread pudding" of sorts, where a spicy-creamy blend is poured over the bread and other ingredients. The eggs make it puff up just enough to look bountiful and appetizing.

● Serves 4

> 8 slices reduced-calorie white bread
>
> ¾ cup shredded Kraft reduced-fat Cheddar cheese
>
> 1 full cup diced Dubuque 97% fat-free ham or any
> extra-lean ham
>
> ½ cup finely chopped onion
>
> 1 (12-fluid-ounce) can Carnation Evaporated Fat Free Milk
>
> 3 eggs, beaten, or equivalent in egg substitute
>
> 1 teaspoon prepared yellow mustard
>
> 1 teaspoon dried onion flakes
>
> 1 teaspoon dried parsley flakes
>
> ⅛ teaspoon black pepper

Preheat convection oven to 375 degrees. Spray an 8-by-8-inch cake pan with butter-flavored cooking spray. Evenly arrange 4 slices of bread in prepared pan. Sprinkle Cheddar cheese, ham, and onion over bread. Arrange remaining 4 slices of bread in pan. In a medium bowl, combine evaporated milk, eggs, mustard, onion flakes, parsley flakes, and black pepper. Pour milk mixture evenly over top. Bake in convection oven for 30 to 35 minutes or until top is lightly browned. Place pan on a wire rack and let set for 5 minutes. Divide into 4 servings.

HINT: May be prepared the night before and refrigerated until ready to bake. If so, let set on counter while oven is preheating.

Each serving equals:

HE: 2¾ Protein • 1 Bread • ¾ Fat Free Milk

---

305 Calories • 9 gm Fat • 28 gm Protein •
28 gm Carbohydrate • 830 mg Sodium •
442 mg Calcium • 1 gm Fiber

DIABETIC EXCHANGES: 2½ Meat • 1 Starch •
1 Fat Free Milk

Ham and Vegetable Medley

I make you this promise: You can walk in the door and get this hearty supper dish into the oven in only a few minutes! (Of course, it helps if you have a good knife for dicing up the ham . . .) There was a time when I might have made a recipe like this with just the creamy soup, but oh, how delightfully richer it is with a little half & half.   ☻   Serves 4

> 1 (10-ounce) package frozen mixed vegetables,
>   thawed
> 1 cup uncooked Minute rice
> 2 full cups diced Dubuque 97% fat-free ham or any
>   extra-lean ham
> 1 (10¾-ounce) can Healthy Request Cream of Celery or
>   Mushroom Soup
> ⅓ cup Land O Lakes Fat Free Half & Half
> ⅓ cup water

Preheat convection oven to 350 degrees. Spray an 8-by-8-inch cake pan with butter-flavored cooking spray. In a large bowl, combine mixed vegetables, uncooked instant rice, and ham. Add celery soup, half & half, and water. Mix well to combine. Spread mixture into prepared pan. Cover with foil and bake in convection oven for 45 minutes. Uncover and continue baking for 15 minutes or until rice is tender. Place pan on a wire rack and let set for 5 minutes. Divide into 4 servings.

HINT: Thaw mixed vegetables by placing in a colander and rinsing under hot water for 1 minute.

Each serving equals:

HE: 2¼ Protein • 1 Bread • ½ Vegetable • ½ Slider •
12 Optional Calories

224 Calories • 4 gm Fat • 19 gm Protein •
28 gm Carbohydrate • 906 mg Sodium •
126 mg Calcium • 3 gm Fiber

DIABETIC EXCHANGES: 2 Meat •
1½ Starch/Carbohydrate • ½ Vegetable

Bavarian Pork Bake

You'll see that I like to brown the pork first for this recipe before putting it in to bake with the potatoes and other ingredients. Searing meat is a great way to hold the juices in, and it also makes the finished dish taste even better.   ♥   Serves 4

4 (4-ounce) lean pork tenderloins or cutlets
2 full cups peeled and chopped cooked potatoes
1 (14½-ounce) can Frank's Bavarian Style sauerkraut, drained
1 (10¾-ounce) can Healthy Request Tomato Soup
½ cup finely chopped onion
1 teaspoon dried parsley flakes

Preheat convection oven to 350 degrees. Spray an 8-by-8-inch cake pan with butter-flavored cooking spray. Evenly arrange pork tenderloins in prepared pan. Layer potatoes evenly over meat. In a medium bowl, combine sauerkraut, tomato soup, onion, and parsley flakes. Spoon mixture evenly over potatoes. Bake in convection oven for 30 to 35 minutes or until pork is cooked through and tender. Place pan on a wire rack and let set for 5 minutes. Divide into 4 servings.

HINT: If you can't find Bavarian sauerkraut, use regular sauerkraut, ½ teaspoon caraway seeds, and 1 teaspoon Brown Sugar Twin.

Each serving equals:

HE: 3 Protein • 1¼ Vegetable • ¾ Bread • ½ Slider •
5 Optional Calories

265 Calories • 5 gm Fat • 25 gm Protein •
30 gm Carbohydrate • 908 mg Sodium •
10 mg Calcium • 2 gm Fiber

DIABETIC EXCHANGES: 3 Meat, • 1 Vegetable •
1 Starch/Carbohydrate

Canadian Bacon–Pineapple Supper Bake

If you've ever ordered a ham and pineapple pizza from your favorite pizza joint, you'll likely love this cheesy-meaty-creamy combo that comes steaming from your oven. There's nobody to tip, and only one dish to wash—now, that's what I call an easy night for the cook!　❍　Serves 6

> ³⁄₄ cup Bisquick Reduced Fat Baking Mix
>
> 6 tablespoons purchased graham cracker crumbs
>
> 1 (8-ounce) can crushed pineapple, packed in fruit juice, drained and 2 tablespoons liquid reserved
>
> 1 tablespoon Land O Lakes Fat Free Half & Half
>
> 1 tablespoon Land O Lakes no-fat sour cream
>
> 1 (3.5-ounce) package Hormel Canadian Bacon, chopped
>
> ³⁄₄ cup shredded Kraft reduced-fat mozzarella cheese
>
> 1 teaspoon dried parsley flakes

Preheat convection oven to 375 degrees. Spray an 8-by-8-inch cake dish with butter-flavored cooking spray. In a large bowl, combine baking mix, graham cracker crumbs, pineapple, reserved pineapple liquid, half & half, and sour cream. Add Canadian bacon, mozzarella cheese, and parsley flakes. Mix well to combine. Evenly spread batter into prepared pan. Bake in convection oven for 15 to 20 minutes or until top springs back when lightly touched. Place baking dish on a wire rack and let set for 5 minutes. Divide into 6 servings.

Each serving equals:

> HE: 1¹⁄₄ Protein • 1 Bread • ¹⁄₃ Fruit • 6 Optional Calories
>
> ---
>
> 169 Calories • 5 gm Fat • 9 gm Protein • 22 gm Carbohydrate • 478 mg Sodium • 123 mg Calcium • 1 gm Fiber
>
> ---
>
> DIABETIC EXCHANGES: 1¹⁄₂ Starch • 1 Meat

Deviled Corned Beef Hash

I leave the choice of mustard up to you in many of my recipes, because everyone's tastes differ, and that's what makes cooking a unique pleasure. If you love a fiery flavor, opt for the spiciest mustard on your shelf, but if you're like me, you might choose some good, old-fashioned, made-in-America yellow mustard instead.

⚫ Serves 4

> 2 (2.5-ounce) packages Carl Buddig lean corned beef, shredded
> 2½ cups finely chopped cooked potatoes
> 1 cup finely chopped onion
> ¼ cup fat-free milk
> ½ cup Kraft fat-free mayonnaise
> 1 tablespoon prepared yellow mustard
> 1 teaspoon dried parsley flakes

Preheat convection oven to 350 degrees. Spray an 8-by-8-inch cake pan with butter-flavored cooking spray. In a large skillet sprayed with butter-flavored cooking spray, combine corned beef, potatoes, and onion. Cook over medium heat for 5 to 6 minutes, stirring often. Add milk. Mix well to combine. Continue cooking for 2 to 3 minutes, stirring often. Stir in mayonnaise, mustard, and parsley flakes. Evenly spread mixture into prepared pan. Bake in convection oven for 18 to 22 minutes. Place pan on a wire rack and let set for 5 minutes. Divide into 4 servings.

Each serving equals:

> HE: 1¼ Protein • ¾ Bread • ½ Vegetable •
> ¼ Slider • 6 Optional Calories
>
> ---
>
> 201 Calories • 5 gm Fat • 13 gm Protein •
> 26 gm Carbohydrate • 984 mg Sodium •
> 34 mg Calcium • 3 gm Fiber
>
> ---
>
> DIABETIC EXCHANGES: 1 Meat • 1 Starch, ½ Vegetable

Becky's Banana Muffins

My daughter Becky thinks muffins are the best possible way to start the day, and so she's always been an interested taste-tester when she's in town and I'm making muffins. She gave these two thumbs-up!

● Serves 6

   ¼ *cup I Can't Believe It's Not Butter! Light Margarine*
   ½ *cup Splenda Granular*
   ⅔ *cup (2 medium) mashed ripe bananas*
   1 cup + 2 tablespoons all-purpose flour
   1½ teaspoons baking powder
   ½ *teaspoon table salt*

Preheat convection oven to 350 degrees. Spray 6 wells of a muffin pan with butter-flavored cooking spray or line with paper liners. In a large bowl, cream margarine and Splenda together. Stir in mashed bananas. Add flour, baking powder, and salt. Mix well to combine. Evenly spoon batter into prepared muffin wells. Bake in convection oven for 20 to 25 minutes or until muffins feel firm when lightly touched in center. Place pan on a wire rack and let set for 5 minutes. Remove muffins from pan and continue cooling on wire rack.

HINT: Fill unused muffin wells with water. It protects the muffin tin and ensures even baking.

Each serving equals:

HE: 1 Bread • 1 Fat • ⅔ Fruit • 8 Optional Calories

148 Calories • 4 gm Fat • 3 gm Protein •
25 gm Carbohydrate • 385 mg Sodium •
66 mg Calcium • 1 gm Fiber

DIABETIC EXCHANGES: 1 Starch • 1 Fat • ½ Fruit

Cranberry Banana-Nut Muffins

Muffins tipped with bits of bright red just seem to send out a message: "Eat me!" These combine a tart berry with a moist, sweet fruit like bananas, and the friendship is likely to be long-lasting.

Serves 6

> 1 cup + 2 tablespoons Bisquick Reduced Fat Baking Mix
> 1/2 cup Splenda Granular
> 1 teaspoon baking powder
> 1/4 teaspoon ground cinnamon
> 1/3 cup (1 medium) mashed ripe banana
> 1 egg or equivalent in egg substitute
> 1/2 cup Land O Lakes Fat Free Half & Half
> 2 tablespoons + 2 teaspoons I Can't Believe It's Not Butter! Light
>   Margarine
> 1 cup fresh cranberries
> 1/4 cup chopped walnuts

Preheat convection oven to 375 degrees. Spray 6 wells of a muffin pan with butter-flavored cooking spray or line with paper liners. In a large bowl, combine baking mix, Splenda, baking powder, and cinnamon. In a small bowl, combine mashed banana, egg, half & half, and margarine. Add banana mixture to baking mix mixture. Mix gently just to combine. Stir in cranberries and walnuts. Evenly spoon batter into prepared muffin wells. Bake in convection oven for 20 to 25 minutes or until muffins feel firm when lightly touched in center. Place pan on a wire rack and let set for 5 minutes. Remove muffins from pan and continue cooling on wire rack.

HINT: Fill unused muffin wells with water. It protects the muffin tin and ensures even baking.

Each serving equals:

HE: 1 Bread • 1 Fat • ½ Fruit • ⅓ Protein • 19 Optional Calories

188 Calories • 8 gm Fat • 4 gm Protein • 25 gm Carbohydrate • 444 mg Sodium • 100 mg Calcium • 2 gm Fiber

DIABETIC EXCHANGES: 1 Starch • 1 Fat • ½ Fruit • ½ Meat

Raspberry Chocolate Chip Muffins

What a pretty color these muffins turn, thanks to the raspberries! Chocolate and raspberry make a terrific team, and you can freeze the ones you aren't planning to eat right away.   ☻   Serves 6

> 1 cup + 2 tablespoons Bisquick Reduced Fat Baking Mix
> ½ cup Splenda Granular
> 1 teaspoon baking powder
> 1 egg or equivalent in egg substitute
> 2 tablespoons Land O Lakes no-fat sour cream
> ¼ cup Land O Lakes Fat Free Half & Half
> ¼ cup mini chocolate chips
> ¼ cup chopped walnuts
> 1½ cups fresh or frozen unsweetened raspberries

Preheat convection oven to 350 degrees. Spray 6 wells of a muffin pan with butter-flavored cooking spray or line with paper liners. In a large bowl, combine baking mix, Splenda, and baking powder. Add egg, sour cream, and half & half. Mix gently just to combine. Stir in chocolate chips and walnuts. Gently fold in raspberries. Evenly spoon batter into prepared muffin wells. Bake in convection oven for 25 to 30 minutes or until muffins feel firm when lightly touched in center. Place pan on a wire rack and let set for 5 minutes. Remove muffins from pan and continue cooling on wire rack.

HINT: Fill unused muffin wells with water. It protects the muffin tin and ensures even baking.

Each serving equals:

HE: 1 Bread • ⅓ Protein • ⅓ Fruit • ⅓ Fat •
½ Slider • 1 Optional Calorie

187 Calories • 7 gm Fat • 4 gm Protein •
27 gm Carbohydrate • 361 mg Sodium •
97 mg Calcium • 3 gm Fiber

DIABETIC EXCHANGES: 1½ Starch/Carbohydrate • 1 Fat

Cranberry Walnut Scones

Something a little different to serve with your tea? How British, right? But scones are a lovely change from your usual, whether it's bagels or toast. You'll be intrigued to see how much flavor a little butter-flavored spray adds. ☻ Serves 8

> 1½ cups Bisquick Reduced Fat Baking Mix
> ¼ cup Splenda Granular
> ½ teaspoon ground cinnamon
> ¼ cup fat-free milk
> ¼ cup Land O Lakes Fat Free Half & Half
> 2 tablespoons + 2 teaspoons I Can't Believe It's Not Butter! Light Margarine
> 1 teaspoon vanilla extract
> ½ cup dried cranberries or craisins
> ½ cup chopped walnuts

Preheat convection oven to 350 degrees. In a large bowl, combine baking mix, Splenda, and cinnamon. Add milk, half & half, margarine, and vanilla extract. Mix well to combine. Stir in cranberries and walnuts. Using a scant ¼ cup measuring cup as a guide, drop dough onto an ungreased baking sheet to form 8 scones. Bake in convection oven for 12 to 16 minutes. Lightly spray tops with butter-flavored cooking spray. Place baking sheet on a wire rack and let set for 5 minutes. Remove scones from baking sheet and continue cooling on wire rack.

Each serving equals:

HE: 1 Bread • 1 Fat • ½ Fruit • ¼ Protein • 10 Optional Calories

184 Calories • 8 gm Fat • 3 gm Protein • 25 gm Carbohydrate • 321 mg Sodium • 48 mg Calcium • 2 gm Fiber

DIABETIC EXCHANGES: 1½ Starch • 1 Fat • ½ Fruit

Raisin-Cinnamon Rolls

Instead of nibbling guiltily on one of those giant, super-sweet, very-high-fat mall-purchased cinnamon rolls, why not eat one of these tasty treats slowly and with complete pleasure? You'll save money and calories, and you'll feel good outside and in.   ☻   Serves 8

> 1 tablespoon all-purpose flour
> 1 (11-ounce) can Pillsbury refrigerated French loaf
> ¼ cup Splenda Granular
> 1 teaspoon cinnamon
> ¼ cup seedless raisins
> 2 teaspoons water

Preheat convection oven to 425 degrees. Spray an 8-inch round cake pan with butter-flavored cooking spray. Sprinkle flour on work surface on counter. Unroll French loaf and pat into a 15-by-10-inch rectangle. Lightly spray top of dough with butter-flavored cooking spray. In a small bowl, combine Splenda and cinnamon. Evenly sprinkle cinnamon mixture over dough. Sprinkle raisins evenly over top. Starting on the short end, roll up, jelly-roll style. Wet far edge of dough with water to seal roll. Cut into 8 (1½-inch) slices. Evenly arrange rolls in prepared cake pan. Lightly spray tops with butter-flavored cooking spray. Bake in convection oven for 9 to 11 minutes or until tops are lightly browned. Lightly spray tops with butter-flavored cooking spray. Place pan on a wire rack and let set for 5 minutes.

HINT: Leftovers reheat beautifully in microwave.

Each serving equals:

HE: 1 Bread • ¼ Fruit • 6 Optional Calories

---

109 Calories • 1 gm Fat • 3 gm Protein •
22 gm Carbohydrate • 245 mg Sodium •
5 mg Calcium • 1 gm Fiber

DIABETIC EXCHANGES: 1½ Starch/Carbohydrate

Heavenly Lemon Bars

Dreamy—that's the only word for these luscious lemon treats good enough to serve to your favorite angels! I've made the lemon peel optional, but if you're using fresh lemons anyway, you'll be amazed by how much extra lemon flavor it adds.

◑ Serves 8 (2 each)

> ⅓ cup I Can't Believe It's Not Butter! Light Margarine
> 1¼ cups Splenda Granular ☆
> ¾ cup + 2 tablespoons cake flour ☆
> 2 eggs or equivalent in egg substitute
> ¼ cup lemon juice
> 1 tablespoon grated lemon peel, optional
> 3 tablespoons Diet Mountain Dew
> ½ teaspoon baking powder
> ¼ teaspoon table salt

Preheat convection oven to 350 degrees. Spray an 8-by-8-inch cake pan with butter-flavored cooking spray. In a large bowl, combine margarine and ¼ cup Splenda. Add ¾ cup flour. Mix with a pastry blender until mixture is crumbly. Press mixture into prepared pan. Bake in convection oven for 12 minutes or until lightly browned. Meanwhile, in same bowl, combine remaining 1 cup Splenda, eggs, lemon juice, lemon peel, Diet Mountain Dew, remaining 2 tablespoons flour, baking powder, and salt. Mix well using a wire whisk until well blended and foamy. Carefully pour mixture over crust. Continue baking for 14 to 16 minutes or until golden brown. Place pan on a wire rack and allow to cool completely. Cut into 16 bars.

Each serving equals:

HE: 1 Fat • ½ Bread • ¼ Protein • ¼ Slider •
2 Optional Calories

113 Calories • 5 gm Fat • 3 gm Protein •
14 gm Carbohydrate • 207 mg Sodium •
27 mg Calcium • 0 gm Fiber

DIABETIC EXCHANGES: 1 Fat • 1 Starch

Blonde Brownies

Do blondes have more fun? That question, asked for the first time many years ago by a hair color company, annoyed a lot of brunettes! But can both blondes and brunettes, not to mention all you redheads, have more fun eating blonde brownies? What a question— of course! ☕ Serves 8 (2 each)

> 1 cup Splenda Granular
> 1/3 cup I Can't Believe It's Not Butter! Light Margarine
> 2 tablespoons Land O Lakes no-fat sour cream
> 1 egg, slightly beaten, or equivalent in egg substitute
> 1/4 cup Land O Lakes Fat Free Half & Half
> 1 teaspoon vanilla extract
> 1 cup all-purpose flour
> 1/2 teaspoon baking powder
> 1/4 teaspoon table salt
> 1/2 cup mini chocolate chips

Preheat convection oven to 350 degrees. Spray a 7-by-11-inch biscuit pan with butter-flavored cooking spray. In a large bowl, combine Splenda and margarine. Stir in sour cream, egg, half & half, and vanilla extract. Add flour, baking powder, and salt. Mix well just to combine. Fold in chocolate chips. Carefully spread batter into prepared pan. Bake in convection oven for 15 to 20 minutes or until lightly browned. Place pan on a wire rack and let set for 15 minutes. Cut into 16 bars.

Each serving equals:

HE: 1 Fat • 2/3 Bread • 1/2 Slider • 19 Optional Calories

---

146 Calories • 6 gm Fat • 3 gm Protein •
20 gm Carbohydrate • 185 mg Sodium •
28 mg Calcium • 1 gm Fiber

DIABETIC EXCHANGES: 1 Fat • 1 Starch/Carbohydrate

Raspberry Preserve Bars

Need a winning recipe to prepare for the school bake sale or a mayoral fund-raiser? I think you'll discover that these will sell like "hotcakes" and win lots of votes! Just make sure you save some for you and your family. ◒ Serves 8 (2 each)

1 cup + 2 tablespoons Bisquick Reduced Fat Baking Mix
2 tablespoons I Can't Believe It's Not Butter! Light Margarine
1 egg or equivalent in egg substitute
1 teaspoon coconut extract
¾ cup Splenda Granular
¾ cup raspberry spreadable fruit
2 tablespoons flaked coconut
¼ cup sliced almonds

Preheat convection oven to 350 degrees. Spray an 8-by-8-inch cake pan with butter-flavored cooking spray. In a small bowl, reserve 2 tablespoons baking mix. In a large bowl, combine margarine, egg, and coconut extract. Add Splenda and remaining 1 cup baking mix. Mix just until mixture is crumbly. Remove 2 tablespoons crumb mixture and add to reserved baking mix. Pat remaining crumb mixture into prepared pan. In a small bowl, stir spreadable fruit with a spoon until softened. Evenly spoon spreadable fruit over "crust" in pan. Stir coconut and almonds into reserved crumb mixture. Evenly sprinkle crumb mixture over top. Bake in convection oven for 18 to 22 minutes or until golden brown. Place pan on a wire rack and let set for 10 minutes. Cut into 16 bars. Allow to cool completely before serving.

Each serving equals:

HE: 1 Fruit • ¾ Bread • ⅔ Fat • ¼ Protein • 13 Optional Calories

155 Calories • 3 gm Fat • 2 gm Protein • 30 gm Carbohydrate • 230 mg Sodium • 20 mg Calcium • 1 gm Fiber

DIABETIC EXCHANGES: 1 Fruit • 1 Starch • 1 Fat

A+ Apple Crisp

This is one of those desserts that truly is perfect when served all year round. In the chilly winter months, it's a cozy-warm reminder of old-fashioned cooking; in the summer, perhaps served with a scoop of sugar- and fat-free ice cream, it's a celebration of the glories of the harvest.　　●　Serves 6

4½ cups (9 small) cored, peeled, and sliced cooking apples
1 tablespoon lemon juice
2 tablespoons Land O Lakes Fat Free Half & Half
½ cup Quaker Quick Oats
6 tablespoons all-purpose flour
½ cup Splenda Granular
1½ teaspoons apple pie spice
¼ cup I Can't Believe It's Not Butter! Light Margarine

Preheat convection oven to 375 degrees. Spray an 8-by-8-inch cake pan with butter-flavored cooking spray. Evenly arrange apple slices in prepared pan. Drizzle lemon juice and half & half evenly over top. In a large bowl, combine oats, flour, Splenda, and apple pie spice. Add margarine. Mix well using a pastry cutter or fork until mixture is crumbly. Evenly sprinkle crumb mixture over top. Bake in convection oven for 18 to 24 minutes or until apples are tender. Place pan on a wire rack and let set for at least 10 minutes. Divide into 6 servings.

HINT: Good served warm with Wells' Blue Bunny sugar- and fat-free vanilla ice cream or cold with Cool Whip Lite. If using, don't forget to count the additional calories.

Each serving equals:

HE: 1½ Fruit • 1 Fat • ⅔ Bread •
11 Optional Calories

144 Calories • 4 gm Fat • 2 gm Protein •
25 gm Carbohydrate • 99 mg Sodium •
21 mg Calcium • 3 gm Fiber

DIABETIC EXCHANGES: 1½ Fruit • 1 Fat • 1 Starch

Coconut Cherry Cobbler

Do you sometimes look at a married couple and think, "I don't get it—they seem so different, yet so happy together!"? You might feel that way about coconut and cherry, but only at first. This gorgeous cobbler looks downright irresistible, and it tastes even better than it looks. ☻ Serves 6

> 2 (20-ounce) cans Lucky Leaf No Sugar Added Cherry Pie Filling
> 1 teaspoon coconut extract
> 1 cup + 3 tablespoons all-purpose flour ☆
> ¼ cup Splenda Granular ☆
> 2 teaspoons baking powder
> ¼ teaspoon table salt
> ¼ cup I Can't Believe It's Not Butter! Light Margarine ☆
> ¼ cup fat-free milk
> 1 egg, beaten, or equivalent in egg substitute
> 3 tablespoons flaked coconut

Preheat convection oven to 375 degrees. Spray an 8-inch round cake pan with butter-flavored cooking spray. In a medium bowl, combine cherry pie filling and coconut extract. Spread pie filling mixture into prepared pan. Bake in convection oven for 10 minutes. Meanwhile, in a large bowl, combine 1 cup flour, 2 tablespoons Splenda, baking powder, and salt. Add 3 tablespoons margarine. Mix well using a pastry blender until mixture is crumbly. Stir in milk and egg using a sturdy spoon. Drop by tablespoonful onto hot cherry filling to form 6 biscuits. In a small bowl, combine remaining 3 tablespoons flour, remaining 2 tablespoons Splenda, and remaining 1 tablespoon margarine. Mix well with pastry blender or fork until mixture is crumbly. Stir in coconut. Sprinkle crumb mixture evenly over top. Continue baking for 20 to 25 minutes or until golden brown. Place pan on a wire rack and let set for at least 10 minutes. Divide into 6 servings.

Each serving equals:

HE: 1¼ Fruit • 1 Bread • 1 Fat • ¼ Slider •
9 Optional Calories

213 Calories • 5 gm Fat • 4 gm Protein •
38 gm Carbohydrate • 348 mg Sodium •
101 mg Calcium • 3 gm Fiber

DIABETIC EXCHANGES: 1½ Fruit • 1 Starch • 1 Fat

Fruit Cocktail Crunch Dessert

Baking canned fruit cocktail into a cake is a Midwestern cafeteria standby. It's sweet, tastes like Mom used to make, and reminds us of how good it was to be a kid. ☺ Serves 8

1¾ cups all-purpose flour ☆
1½ cups Splenda Granular ☆
1½ teaspoons baking soda
1 teaspoon table salt
1 (15-ounce) can fruit cocktail, packed in fruit juice, undrained
1 egg or equivalent in egg substitute
1 tablespoon vegetable oil
1 teaspoon vanilla extract
2 tablespoons I Can't Believe It's Not Butter! Light Margarine
¼ cup chopped walnuts

Preheat convection oven to 350 degrees. Spray an 8-by-8-inch cake pan with butter-flavored cooking spray. In a large bowl, combine 1½ cups flour, 1 cup Splenda, baking soda, and salt. Add undrained fruit cocktail, egg, vegetable oil, and vanilla extract. Mix well to combine. Spread batter into prepared pan. In a medium bowl, combine remaining ¼ cup flour, remaining ½ cup Splenda, and margarine. Mix well using a pastry blender or fork until mixture is crumbly. Stir in walnuts. Sprinkle crumb mixture evenly over top. Bake in convection oven for 20 to 25 minutes or until top springs back when lightly touched. Place pan on a wire rack and let set for at least 10 minutes. Cut into 8 servings.

HINT: Good served with warm with Wells' Blue Bunny sugar- and fat-free ice cream or cold with Cool Whip Lite. If using, don't forget to count the additional calories.

Each serving equals:

HE: 1 Bread • ¾ Fat • ½ Fruit • ¼ Protein •
¼ Slider • 13 Optional Calories

207 Calories • 7 gm Fat • 4 gm Protein •
32 gm Carbohydrate • 572 mg Sodium •
16 mg Calcium • 2 gm Fiber

DIABETIC EXCHANGES: 1½ Starch/Carbohydrate •
1 Fat • ½ Fruit

Baked Lemon Pudding Dessert

Homemade pudding from JoAnna, queen of three-minute pies made with instant? Well, I refuse to get stuck in a rut when it comes to creating recipes to win your heart, and so I went back to basics with this scrumptious dish that takes a little extra effort but is well worth it! ☻ Serves 6

> *3 eggs, separated*
> *1 (12-fluid-ounce) can Carnation Evaporated Fat Free Milk*
> *¼ cup lemon juice*
> *1 tablespoon grated lemon peel, optional*
> *1 cup + 2 tablespoons all-purpose flour*
> *1 cup Splenda Granular*
> *⅛ teaspoon table salt*

Preheat convection oven to 325 degrees. Spray an 8-by-8-inch cake pan with butter-flavored cooking spray. In a large bowl, beat egg whites with an electric mixer on HIGH until stiff. Set aside. In another large bowl, combine egg yolks, evaporated milk, lemon juice, and lemon peel. Add flour, Splenda, and salt. Mix well to combine. Fold in egg whites. Spread mixture into prepared pan. Bake in convection oven for 25 to 30 minutes or until top springs back when lightly touched. Place pan on a wire rack and let set for at least 15 minutes. Divide into 6 servings.

HINT: Good served with Cool Whip Lite. If using, don't forget to count the additional calories.

Each serving equals:

HE: 1 Bread • ½ Fat Free Milk • ½ Protein • 16 Optional Calories

---

187 Calories • 3 gm Fat • 10 gm Protein • 30 gm Carbohydrate • 166 mg Sodium • 179 mg Calcium • 1 gm Fiber

---

DIABETIC EXCHANGES: 1 Starch • ½ Fat Free Milk • ½ Meat

Cherry Cheesecake Pie

I've specialized over the years in "no-bake" cheesecakes, but I was thrilled at the delectable result I got with this oven-prepared filling. It's sweet and fruity, creamy and rich—a great birthday treat for a best friend!   ❤   Serves 8

> 1 Pillsbury refrigerated unbaked 9-inch pie crust
> 1 (20-ounce) can Lucky Leaf No Sugar Added Cherry Pie Filling
> 1 (8-ounce) package Philadelphia fat-free cream cheese
> ½ cup Splenda Granular
> 2 eggs or equivalent in egg substitute
> 2 tablespoons Land O Lakes Fat Free Half & Half

Preheat convection oven to 375 degrees. Place pie crust in an 8-inch metal pie plate. Flute edges. Evenly spoon cherry pie filling into prepared pie crust. In a large bowl, stir cream cheese with a sturdy spoon until soft. Add Splenda, eggs, and half & half. Mix well to combine. Carefully spread mixture evenly over pie filling. Bake in convection oven for 35 to 40 minutes or until top is golden brown. Place pie plate on a wire rack and let set for 30 minutes. Refrigerate for at least 1 hour. Cut into 8 servings.

Each serving equals:

HE: 1 Bread • ¾ Protein • ½ Fruit • ½ Fat •
8 Optional Calories

---

192 Calories • 8 gm Fat • 6 gm Protein •
24 gm Carbohydrate • 271 mg Sodium •
90 mg Calcium • 2 gm Fiber

DIABETIC EXCHANGES: 1 Starch/Carbohydrate •
1 Meat • 1 Fat • ½ Fruit

Yellow Cake with Cherry Topping

Just as deejays take requests for favorite songs to play on the air, you'll likely get lots of requests for this recipe as the ideal birthday, anniversary, or graduation finale! It's downright delicious from top to bottom. ☻ Serves 8

> 1½ cups Bisquick Reduced Fat Baking Mix
> ¾ cup Splenda Granular
> ½ cup fat-free milk
> 2 eggs or equivalent in egg substitute
> 2 tablespoons + 2 teaspoons I Can't Believe It's Not Butter! Light Margarine
> 1½ teaspoons vanilla extract
> 1 (20-ounce) can Lucky Leaf No Sugar Added Cherry Pie Filling
> ¾ cup Cool Whip Lite

Preheat convection oven to 350 degrees. Spray a 7-by-11-inch biscuit pan with butter-flavored cooking spray. In a large bowl, combine baking mix and Splenda. Add milk, eggs, margarine, and vanilla extract. Mix gently just to combine. Spread batter evenly into prepared pan. Bake in convection oven for 14 to 18 minutes or until top springs back when lightly touched. Place pan on a wire rack and allow to cool completely. Evenly spread cherry pie filling over cooled cake. Cut into 8 servings. When serving, top each with 1 tablespoon Cool Whip Lite.

Each serving equals:

HE: 1 Bread • ½ Fruit • ½ Fat • ¼ Protein • ¼ Slider • 5 Optional Calories

165 Calories • 5 gm Fat • 4 gm Protein • 26 gm Carbohydrate • 339 mg Sodium • 49 mg Calcium • 1 gm Fiber

DIABETIC EXCHANGES: 1½ Starch • ½ Fruit • ½ Fat

Pleasing Pumpkin Pie

Pumpkin pies have traditionally appeared on the menu between November and January, but there's no reason not to enjoy this rich and aromatic dessert all year long! Be sure to let it cool at least an hour, or it's likely to collapse when it's cut.

◐ Serves 8

1 Pillsbury refrigerated unbaked 9-inch pie crust	2 eggs or equivalent in egg substitute
⅔ cup Carnation Nonfat Dry Milk Powder	1 (15-ounce) can Libby's solid-pack pumpkin
¾ cup water	¾ cup Splenda Granular
¼ cup Land O Lakes Fat Free Half & Half	2 teaspoons pumpkin pie spice
	1 cup Cool Whip Lite

Preheat convection oven to 375 degrees. Place pie crust in an 8-inch metal pie plate. Flute edges. In a large bowl, combine dry milk powder and water. Stir in half & half and eggs. Add pumpkin, Splenda, and pumpkin pie spice. Mix well to combine. Evenly spread mixture into prepared pie crust. Bake in convection oven for 45 to 55 minutes or until a knife inserted near center comes out clean. Place pie plate on a wire rack and let set for 30 minutes. Refrigerate for at least 1 hour. Cut into 8 servings. When serving, top each with 2 tablespoons Cool Whip Lite.

Each serving equals:

HE: 1 Bread • ½ Fat • ½ Vegetable • ¼ Fat Free Milk • ¼ Protein • ¼ Slider • 13 Optional Calories

---

210 Calories • 10 gm Fat • 5 gm Protein • 25 gm Carbohydrate • 162 mg Sodium • 101 mg Calcium • 2 gm Fiber

---

DIABETIC EXCHANGES: 1½ Starch/Carbohydrate • 1½ Fat

Moist Raisin-Nut Snack Cake

If you didn't grow up baking with Bisquick, it's a great time to start! Here, it makes cake preparation easier than you may have expected, and with the addition of a surprise ingredient like mayonnaise, you will get mouthwatering results. ☻ Serves 8

1 cup hot water
1 cup seedless raisins
1 cup Splenda Granular
¾ cup Kraft fat-free mayonnaise
1 teaspoon vanilla extract
1½ cups Bisquick Reduced Fat Baking Mix
½ teaspoon baking powder
½ teaspoon ground cinnamon
¼ cup chopped walnuts

Preheat convection oven to 350 degrees. Spray an 8-by-8-inch cake pan with butter-flavored cooking spray. In a large bowl, combine hot water and raisins. Let set for 10 minutes. Stir in Splenda, mayonnaise, and vanilla extract. Add baking mix, baking powder, and cinnamon. Mix gently just to combine. Fold in walnuts. Spread batter evenly into prepared pan. Bake in convection oven for 22 to 28 minutes or until cake springs back when lightly touched in center. Place pan on a wire rack and let set for at least 15 minutes. Cut into 8 servings.

HINTS: 1. Batter is somewhat thin.
2. Good served with Cool Whip Lite. If using, don't forget to count the additional calories.

Each serving equals:

HE: 1 Bread • 1 Fruit • ¼ Fat • ¼ Slider •
9 Optional Calories

192 Calories • 4 gm Fat • 3 gm Protein •
36 gm Carbohydrate 473 mg Sodium •
57 mg Calcium • 2 gm Fiber

DIABETIC EXCHANGES: 1½ Starch/Carbohydrate •
1 Fruit • ½ Fat

Double Chocolate Pudding Cake

Remember how much you begged to lick the bowl when Mom made chocolate pudding, especially the kind you cooked on the stovetop so it was warm on the spoon? Well, double your pleasure and double your fun, with this doubly chocolate-y delight!

☻ Serves 6

> 1 cup + 2 tablespoons cake flour
> 1¾ cups Splenda Granular ☆
> 6 tablespoons unsweetened cocoa powder ☆
> 2 teaspoons baking powder
> ½ teaspoon table salt
> ½ cup + 1 tablespoon fat-free milk
> 1 teaspoon vanilla extract
> 2 tablespoons vegetable oil
> ¼ cup mini chocolate chips
> 1¾ cups boiling water

Preheat convection oven to 350 degrees. Spray an 8-by-8-inch cake pan with butter-flavored cooking spray. In a large bowl, combine flour, ¾ cup Splenda, 2 tablespoons cocoa powder, baking powder, and salt. Add milk, vanilla extract, and vegetable oil. Mix well just to combine. Stir in chocolate chips. Spread batter into prepared pan. In a small bowl, combine remaining 1 cup Splenda, remaining ¼ cup cocoa powder, and boiling water. Pour mixture evenly over batter. Bake in convection oven for 25 to 35 minutes or until cake feels firm when lightly touched in center. Place pan on a wire rack and let set for at least 10 minutes. Divide into 6 servings.

HINTS: 1. Good served warm with Wells' Blue Bunny sugar- and fat-free vanilla or chocolate ice cream or cold with Cool Whip Lite. If using, don't forget to count the additional calories.

2. This is supposed to be very moist and gooey!

Each serving equals:

HE: 1 Bread • 1 Fat • ¾ Slider • 10 Optional Calories

191 Calories • 7 gm Fat • 3 gm Protein •
29 gm Carbohydrate • 338 mg Sodium •
120 mg Calcium • 2 gm Fiber

DIABETIC EXCHANGES: 2 Starch/Carbohydrate • 1 Fat

Chocolate Fudge Cake

Every chef needs one "out-of-this-world" chocolate cake in his or her repertoire, something he or she can make when the occasion is special, the family is gathered, or somebody needs a chocolate fix! This one is especially luscious and perfect for any celebration.

● Serves 8

> 1 cup + 2 tablespoons cake flour
>
> 1 cup Splenda Granular
>
> 1/4 cup unsweetened cocoa powder
>
> 1 teaspoon baking powder
>
> 1/2 teaspoon table salt
>
> 1/2 teaspoon baking soda
>
> 1/2 cup Land O Lakes no-fat sour cream
>
> 1/4 cup water
>
> 1/4 cup I Can't Believe It's Not Butter! Light Margarine
>
> 2 eggs or equivalent in egg substitute
>
> 1 teaspoon vanilla extract
>
> 1/2 cup Hersheys Lite Chocolate Syrup

Preheat convection oven to 350 degrees. Spray a 7-by-11-inch biscuit pan with butter-flavored cooking spray. In a large bowl, combine flour, Splenda, cocoa, baking powder, salt, and baking soda. Add sour cream, water, margarine, eggs, vanilla extract, and chocolate syrup. Mix just until combined. Spread batter evenly into prepared pan. Bake in convection oven for 25 to 30 minutes or until top springs back when lightly touched. Place pan on a wire rack and allow to cool for at least 10 minutes. Cut into 8 servings.

HINT: Good served warm with Wells' Blue Bunny sugar- and fat-free vanilla ice cream or cold with Cool Whip Lite. If using, don't forget to count the additional calories.

Each serving equals:

HE: ¾ Bread • ¾ Fat • ¼ Protein • ½ Slider •
6 Optional Calories

---

149 Calories • 5 gm Fat • 4 gm Protein •
22 gm Carbohydrate • 398 mg Sodium •
65 mg Calcium • 1 gm Fiber

DIABETIC EXCHANGES: 1½ Starch/Carbohydrate • ¾ Fat

Colossal Carrot Cake

There's big, and there's really big, and then there's colossal. For me to name a dessert using that "gigantic" word, I'd have to feel that it delivers a huge amount of tummy-pleasing joy—and I do! Bet you'll agree. ☻ Serves 8

> 1½ cups cake flour
> 1 cup Splenda Granular
> 1 teaspoon baking powder
> 1 teaspoon baking soda
> 1½ teaspoons ground cinnamon
> 2 eggs or equivalent in egg substitute
> ¼ cup I Can't Believe It's Not Butter! Light Margarine
> ½ cup unsweetened applesauce
> 2 tablespoons Diet Mountain Dew
> 2 cups finely shredded carrots
> ½ cup + 2 tablespoons seedless raisins
> ¼ cup chopped walnuts

Preheat convection oven to 350 degrees. Spray a 7-by-11-inch biscuit pan with butter-flavored cooking spray. In a large bowl, combine flour, Splenda, baking powder, baking soda, and cinnamon. Add eggs, margarine, applesauce, and Diet Mountain Dew. Mix well just to combine. Fold in carrots, raisins, and walnuts. Spread batter evenly into prepared pan. Bake in convection oven for 20 to 25 minutes or until top springs back when lightly touched. Place pan on a wire rack and allow to cool completely. Cut into 8 servings.

HINT: Good served with Cool Whip Lite. If using, don't forget to count the additional calories.

Each serving equals:

HE: 1 Bread • 1 Fat • ¾ Fruit • ½ Protein •
½ Vegetable • 12 Optional Calories

207 Calories • 7 gm Fat • 4 gm Protein •
32 gm Carbohydrate • 314 mg Sodium •
63 mg Calcium • 2 gm Fiber

DIABETIC EXCHANGES: 1½ Starch • 1 Fat • 1 Fruit •
½ Meat

Chocolate Mint Angel Food Loaf Cake

When it's dessert time in heaven, I like to think that this festive loaf might be an angel's chosen treat! If you've always felt that angel food cakes are a bit plain, you'll be delighted by the transformation just a bit of peppermint and chocolate bring to the party.

☻ Serves 8

> ¾ cup cake flour
>
> 2¼ cups Splenda Granular ☆
>
> 9 egg whites
>
> ¾ teaspoon peppermint extract
>
> ¼ teaspoon table salt
>
> 5 to 7 drops green food coloring
>
> ¼ cup mini chocolate chips
>
> 1 tablespoon + 1 teaspoon I Can't Believe It's Not Butter! Light Margarine
>
> 1 (1-ounce) square unsweetened chocolate
>
> 2 tablespoons Land O Lakes no-fat sour cream
>
> 1 teaspoon vanilla extract

Preheat convection oven to 350 degrees. In a small bowl, combine cake flour and ½ cup Splenda. Mix well using a wire whisk. Place egg whites in a large glass mixing bowl. Beat egg whites with an electric mixer on HIGH until foamy. Add peppermint extract and salt. Continue beating until stiff enough to form soft peaks. Add another ½ cup Splenda, 2 tablespoons at a time, while continuing to beat egg whites until stiff peaks form. Add the flour mixture, ¼ cup at a time, folding in with spatula or wire whisk. Fold in green food coloring. Add chocolate chips. Mix gently just to combine. Spread batter into an ungreased 7-by-11-inch metal biscuit pan. Run a knife through batter to remove air bubbles. Bake in convection oven for 9 to 11 minutes or until tops spring back when lightly touched. Do not overbake. Place pan on a wire rack and allow to cool. Meanwhile, in a medium saucepan, melt margarine and unsweetened chocolate. Remove from heat. Stir in sour cream. Add remaining 1¼ cups Splenda and vanilla extract. Mix well to combine. Carefully spread chocolate glaze evenly over top of cooled cake. Let set for at least 5 minutes. Cut into 8 servings.

HINTS: 1. Egg whites beat best at room temperature.

2. The margarine and unsweetened chocolate can be melted by placing in a 4-cup glass measuring cup and microwaved on HIGH (100% power) for 60 seconds, stirring after every 20 seconds.

Each serving equals:

HE: ½ Bread • ⅓ Protein • ¼ Fat • ¾ Slider •
5 Optional Calories

132 Calories • 4 gm Fat • 5 gm Protein •
19 gm Carbohydrate • 164 mg Sodium •
14 mg Calcium • 1 gm Fiber

DIABETIC EXCHANGES: 1½ Starch/Carbohydrate • ½ Fat

Festive Microwave Menus Everyone Will Love

A "Night to Remember" Anniversary Dinner

Wilted Tossed Salad
Cheesy Scalloped Potatoes
Sunday Best Chicken
Chocolate Fudge Cake

An "April Showers" Indoor Picnic

Hot Potato and Romaine Salad
Sunshine Carrots
Juicy Baked Burgers
Majestic Sour Cream Raisin Pie

"The Family That Cooks Together" Soup-and-More Buffet

Zach's Chili Classic
Cliff's Clam Chowder
Mom's Creamed Green Beans
Tom's Nacho Cups
Grandma's Macaroni and Cheese
Becky's Banana Muffins

An "I Love NASCAR" At-Home Tailgate Party

Hot Dog and Corn Chowder
Hot Cabbage Slaw
Chili Burger Casserole
A+ Apple Crisp

A "Pizza and Parcheesi" Family Game Night Supper

Bacon and Tomato Pizza Bites
Italian Baked Potatoes and Onions
Pronto Pizza Steaks
Coconut Cherry Cobbler

A "Deck-the-Halls" Tree-Trimming Brunch

Cinnamon Biscuits
Breakfast Burrito
Alfredo Ham and Broccoli Dish
Pleasing Pumpkin Pie

Making Healthy Exchanges Work for You

You're ready now to begin a wonderful journey to better health. In the preceding pages, you've discovered the remarkable variety of good food available to you when you begin eating the Healthy Exchanges way. You've stocked your pantry and learned many of my food preparation "secrets" that will point you on the way to delicious success.

But before I let you go, I'd like to share a few tips that I've learned while traveling toward healthier eating habits. It took me a long time to learn how to eat *smarter*. In fact, I'm still working on it. But I am getting better. For years, I could *inhale* a five-course meal in five minutes flat—and still make room for a second helping of dessert!

Now I follow certain signposts on the road that help me stay on the right path. I hope these ideas will help point you in the right direction as well.

1. **Eat slowly** so your brain has time to catch up with your tummy. Cut and chew each bite slowly. Try putting your fork down between bites. Stop eating as soon as you feel full. Crumple your napkin and throw it on top of your plate so you don't continue to eat when you are no longer hungry.

2. **Smaller plates** may help you feel more satisfied by your food portions *and* limit the amount you can put on the plate.

3. **Watch portion size.** If you are *truly* hungry, you can always add more food to your plate once you've finished your initial serving. But remember to count the additional food accordingly.

4. **Always eat at your dining-room or kitchen table.** You deserve better than nibbling from an open refrigerator or over the sink. Make an attractive place setting, even if you're eating alone. Feed your eyes as well as your stomach. By always eating at a table, you will become much more aware of your true food intake. For some reason, many of us conveniently "forget" the food we swallow while standing over the stove or munching in the car or on the run.

5. **Avoid doing anything else while you are eating.** If you read the paper or watch television while you eat, it's easy to consume too much food without realizing it, because you are concentrating on something else besides what you're eating. Then, when you look down at your plate and see that it's empty, you wonder where all the food went and why you still feel hungry.

Day by day, as you travel the path to good health, it will become easier to make the right choices, to eat *smarter*. But don't ever fool yourself into thinking that you'll be able to put your eating habits on cruise control and forget about them. Making a commitment to eat good, healthy food and sticking to it takes some effort. But with all the good-tasting recipes in this Healthy Exchanges cookbook, just think how well you're going to eat—and enjoy it—from now on!

Healthy Lean Bon Appétit!

Index

I want to hear from you . . .

Besides my family, the love of my life is creating "common folk" healthy recipes and solving everyday cooking questions in *The Healthy Exchanges Way*. Everyone who uses my recipes is considered part of the Healthy Exchanges Family, so please write to me if you have any questions, comments, or suggestions. I will do my best to answer. With your support, I'll continue to stir up even more recipes and cooking tips for the Family in the years to come.

Write to: JoAnna M. Lund
c/o Healthy Exchanges, Inc.
P.O. Box 80
DeWitt, IA 52742-0080

If you prefer, you can fax me at 1-563-659-2126 or contact me via e-mail by writing to HealthyJo@aol.com. Or visit my Healthy Exchanges Internet web site at: http://www.healthyexchanges.com.

Now That You've Seen
Cooking Healthy with a Microwave Oven,
Why Not Order *The Healthy Exchanges Food Newsletter?*

If you enjoyed the recipes in this cookbook and would like to cook up even more of my "common folk" healthy dishes, you may want to subscribe to *The Healthy Exchanges Food Newsletter.*

This monthly 12-page newsletter contains 30-plus new recipes *every month* in such columns as:

- Reader Exchange
- Reader Requests
- Recipe Makeover
- Micro Corner
- Dinner for Two
- Plug It In
- Meatless Main Dishes
- Rise & Shine
- Our Small World
- Brown Bagging It
- Snack Attack
- Side Dishes
- Main Dishes
- Desserts

In addition to all the recipes, other regular features include:

- The Editor's Motivational Corner
- Dining Out Question & Answer
- Cooking Question & Answer
- New Product Alert
- Success Profiles of Winners in the Losing Game
- Exercise Advice from a Cardiac Rehab Specialist
- Nutrition Advice from a Registered Dietitian
- Positive Thought for the Month

The cost for a one-year (12-issue) subscription is $25. To order, call our toll-free number and pay with any major credit card, or send a check to the address on page 371 of this book.

1-800-766-8961 for Customer Orders
1-563-659-8234 for Customer Service

Thank you for your order, and for choosing to become a part of the Healthy Exchanges Family!